IRREPLACEABLE

A journey through love, loss and healing

LOUISE MOIR

THISTLE
PUBLISHING

First published in 2016 by:

Thistle Publishing
36 Great Smith Street
London
SW1P 3BU

www.thistlepublishing.co.uk

For Them
Your Dad was a good man and he loved you all immeasurably. In his 'well mind', he would not have left you for anything in the world. This is what happened.

'We find a place for what we lose. Although we know that after such a loss the acute stage of mourning will subside, we also know that we shall remain inconsolable and will never find a substitute. No matter what may fill the gap, even if it be filled completely, it nevertheless remains something else.'

Sigmund Freud – Mourning and Melancholia, 1917.

INTRODUCTION

When I began writing what has become this book, my intention was simply to write down all that I could remember about the time I shared with Daniel so that my sons and their sisters would know more about the man who would now always be their elusive father. I wanted to be able to give them an honest account and explanation of the illness that changed and ultimately killed him. And I wanted them to understand how much Daniel loved each of them. More than they will ever know.

Suicide is a word that carries a huge stigma and the bereavement process for anyone who has lost a loved one in this way is extremely complex. I don't want Daniel's children to have to grapple with the extra burden of dealing with the social taboo and cultural unease associated with their father's death, or to feel ashamed of the way he died. I want them to know that their dad was a unique and amazing man with wonderful strengths and talents and an incredibly bright and sharp mind. His memory should not be defined by his death.

The sense of shame and self-blame that historically and culturally accompanies suicide not only adds to the pain of the bereaved but also prevents people who are feeling suicidal from accessing help. I believe that the only way to tackle the taboo of suicide is to talk about it openly. We need to dispel the fears and myths that surround this topic and it is this strong belief that has led me to publish my story.

As a therapist, I am used to being a blank screen, never disclosing anything personal, and I am aware that making my story public may compromise that role. However, I believe that acknowledging that therapists are human too, experiencing their own vulnerabilities and struggles in life, is ultimately healing and does not make them any less professional.

Daniel was a self-confessed rebel and he used to rib me about my straight-laced, goody, goody lifestyle. He was a non-conformer in every sense and would say to me, 'you have to rebel at least once in your life'. Releasing this story is my way of not conforming to the silence and shame that surrounds suicide. This book is my way of rebelling, in Daniel's honour.

While everything in this book is true, some names have been changed in order to protect the privacy of those individuals.

CHAPTER ONE

We were in the sea. We'd been shipwrecked in the middle of a storm and we were all struggling to keep our heads above water. The waves were fierce, rain was lashing down and thunder crashed overhead. I was holding both the boys, one under each arm. I could see Daniel a few feet away, grappling for something to hold onto and I knew that he was battling to survive. In the distance there was an island. I felt quite confident that I could swim there and get the boys to safety. I kept looking at Daniel, wanting to take him too but I knew that we would all go under if I tried to support all three of them. Daniel could see that too and he was shouting at me to get the boys to the island. But I hesitated.

That was the point where I woke, frozen with panic.

I had been having the nightmare over and over again, for weeks.

It was early on Friday afternoon when I put Milo in his car seat in the back of the car, hugged Daniel and said 'see you on Sunday'.

I knew he was very low. The previous day I had tried once again to persuade him to go into hospital. I'd taken the softly, softly approach and got nowhere, so that morning I tried a different tack. He was still in bed and I went in and told him that enough was enough, he needed to go into hospital to get help and he couldn't expect everyone else's help if he wasn't going to help himself. I told him if he'd broken his leg he'd get it treated and this was no different.

He began to barter with me. He said he would consider it in a week's time because he needed to be at home to sell some items he'd put on eBay. Of course he was fobbing me off, but he wasn't going to give in so I backed down and took Milo out to the park.

I got home at lunchtime and Daniel had got up and vacuumed the house. He felt guilty and was trying to please me; he said that he didn't want me to be angry with him. I hugged him and cried and begged him again to go into hospital.

He'd been detached and had barely reciprocated the hug. Daniel used to give wonderful, warm, enveloping bear-hugs. But this time he'd put limp arms round me before turning back to the computer. He told me he was looking for work. I hoped that was a good thing.

I was about to set off for my parents' home, a couple of hours away, but I felt torn. My instinct was telling me to stay with Daniel but I needed to be with Mum at her hospital appointment the next morning. And then there was Theo. I'd been away from him for two nights, long enough for a four year-old.

I'd lost one of Milo's shoes and was searching all over the house. I found it behind a box in the utility room along with about ten other items that had gone missing, including a spare set of car keys. Milo was going through a phase where he loved 'posting' objects into small spaces. He'd found a little opening between two stacked boxes and pushed anything that would fit through the gap.

Daniel overheard me talking to Milo about what I'd found and he came to see. He chuckled affectionately at the thought of our 19 month-old going into the utility room to hide all his treasures. It was good to see him smile. His eyes were so often blank these days, but when he smiled they lit up, just for a moment, with the old sparkle. I reassured myself that he wasn't as low as I thought.

I loaded the car and got Milo strapped in. Daniel always helped me to the car and waved me off for long journeys, but today he was still at his computer. I went back to the front door and called him and he came to the door. I asked him to promise me that he would look after himself and not do anything stupid. For a split second his eyes darted away from mine, before he looked at me and said 'I promise'. I hugged him and said, 'remember there are a lot of people who love you'.

'I know,' he said, 'but I can't love myself'. There were tears in his eyes.

As I drove away I phoned his younger brother Adam, who lived a few miles away. I told him I would be away for the weekend and that I was worried about Daniel. 'Mum's here,' Adam told me. 'We'll call Daniel, get him to come over.'

I was relieved to think that Daniel wouldn't be alone. He was due to visit the local day hospital that afternoon and then he could go over to see Adam and his mum the next day. The estate agent would be coming in at two o clock to show people round the house, but Daniel didn't have to be back for that, the agent had a key. Five years after we'd bought it, we were selling our dream home; we could no longer pay the mortgage.

I didn't mind about that. What did it matter, really, where we lived, as long as Daniel got better? I longed to see him back to his old self, striding across the road to the beach to kite surf, swinging a shrieking Theo onto his shoulders, sweeping Milo into his arms, serenading me loudly with a love song. He was so full of passion and ideas, so unstoppable. And he loved us, his family; me, the boys and his two beautiful girls, Ella and Hannah, more than anything. Looking after all of us was what made his world turn.

Daniel would get better; he just needed the right help. I'd be back on Sunday, and then perhaps he would agree to go into hospital, just for a few weeks, just until they could stabilise his moods. He'd been in hospital a few months earlier and the break from responsibilities, with the regular, monitored medication really did help. But he saw going back as an admission of failure.

As I drove up the motorway I couldn't shake my nagging sense of dread. What was it that made me feel so afraid? He'd been low for a few weeks now, after plunging from the high of the previous months into a bleak state of depression. He'd been horrified by the trail of emotional and financial destruction he'd wrought when he was high, it had left him ashamed and embarrassed. Now he spent his days in bed and his evenings in front of the television, only very occasionally rallying to help me with the boys or the house.

An hour later I stopped at Reading services. Milo had a biscuit, I had a coffee and when we got back into the car I phoned Daniel. He said he was cycling back from the day hospital. They had offered him an art class but there was nothing else suitable. He was making an effort to sound upbeat, but I could hear the disappointment.

I told him that I was at the services and it was full of families. I said that I missed us being a family and wanted us to get back to the way we were. I wanted to give him hope. 'We can do it Daniel, I know we can.' But he seemed in a hurry. As he hung up I said, 'I'll call you tonight'.

When I arrived at my parents' house in Wiltshire, I scooped an excited Theo into my arms. It was so good to see him. Theo needed me, he'd been having a hard time understanding why the daddy who had been his hero, always ready for an adventure, was suddenly distant and withdrawn. Theo had lost so much; I didn't want him to feel he was losing me too.

Mum put the kettle on. She and Dad had been absolute rocks over the past year. They loved Daniel and they felt desperately sad about what had happened to us. Even after Mum's diagnosis two months earlier, she'd continued to look after the boys and help out as much as she could. They'd found an aneurysm in her brain, a swelling in an artery that was a ticking bomb. The only symptoms she had were an increasing squint in her right eye, double vision and headaches, but if it ruptured it could be fatal.

After dinner I put the boys to bed. They were a boisterous pair, up at five in the morning and running around all day, so bedtime at seven was set in stone and I looked forward to a bit of peace afterwards. I wanted to ring Daniel once the boys were asleep; I always rang him at seven if I was away so he'd be expecting my call, but that evening Milo wouldn't settle. Perhaps he was picking up on my anxiety, but it took me an hour to get him to sleep, so it was eight when I phoned Daniel. There was no answer from his mobile or the landline. I felt alarmed, that was so unlike him. I rang Adam and Daniel's mum, Maggie, answered. She reassured me that she had spoken to him at seven and he had agreed to go over for lunch the next day. That eased my worry, I told myself that after being up all day he had probably just gone to bed early. I would call first thing.

That night I managed to get to sleep but Theo woke me in the early hours, crying and complaining of growing pains. He often had night pains and tummy aches; he was such a sensitive little barometer of all the worry and distress in our family. I got into bed with him and rubbed his legs. He seemed frightened, he kept saying, 'it's not alright Mummy'. I tried to soothe him. 'Everything's going to be OK' I whispered, but I felt unable to believe my own words. I had a sudden, fleeting feeling of panic and impending doom, but I rationalised it with thoughts of phoning Daniel in the morning.

I finally managed to snatch a couple of hours sleep, wedged alongside Theo in his single bed, but I woke exhausted and strained, my eyes red and stinging. I rushed about getting the children fed and ready. We had to leave at eight for the drive to the hospital in Oxford. Dad had agreed to look after the boys, but I was concerned about leaving him to cope with them for too long, so we'd agreed that he would drive us all there and take the boys to a cafe for brunch while Mum and I went to her appointment. The consultant was going to explain the surgery options. Mum got nervous at these meetings and found it hard to take the information in, so whenever possible I went with her.

It was a beautiful, sunny, blue-sky morning, the first real day of spring. As we were setting off, I called Daniel. No answer, but I wasn't surprised, he was usually asleep at that time. I called again just before nine; again no answer. I called Adam and spoke to Maggie again. She seemed sure he would come for lunch, but I felt increasingly anxious.

I put thoughts of Daniel aside for the meeting with the consultant. He was a kind and thoughtful man, but he had bad news; a scan had revealed a second aneurysm. He suggested monitoring it, while he carried out surgery for the first, bigger one. Thankfully the surgery sounded less invasive and risky than we had expected. He would operate as soon as possible, he said.

When we came out of the meeting I phoned Daniel again; still no answer on either phone.

My mind started racing. His depression was always worse in the morning. Had he got up early and gone to Beachy Head? He'd more than once threatened to throw himself off, was he actually going to do it this time?

After trying his phone every twenty minutes on the way home, I phoned his mum again. She told me she had rung Daniel's psychiatric nurse, Nathan, the day before after I told her I was worried. Nathan had alerted the crisis team and a member of the team had visited him in our home at six the previous evening.

I hadn't known this until now. I phoned and spoke to one of the crisis team and said I was worried about Daniel and thought he might have gone to Beachy Head. She reassured me that the team member who saw Daniel felt that, although he was low, he had fixed plans for the weekend and did not have suicidal intent. She repeated it a couple of times.

It was now almost midday. She suggested we wait until one, when Daniel was due at Adam's. If he didn't show up, they would act. Everyone seemed calm, they weren't worried; to them it was just another day of managing Daniel. Yet I felt so sure something was wrong. Had I lost all perspective? Was I just being dramatic?

There was nothing to do but wait. I was beginning to feel panicky, but for the boys' sake I did my best to appear calm. Mum and I decided to go to the park to meet my brother Sam, and his girlfriend Katie. They were in the middle of moving house and were glad of an excuse to take a break.

The park was full of families. I wanted to be part of that, to enjoy the warmth of the sun on my back, to feel carefree and play with my boys, but I was consumed by the feeling that something terrible had happened. We waited for Sam and Katie at a table outside the kiosk. The boys had ice-creams and I had coffee in an attempt to ward off my tiredness. When Sam arrived I told him I was worried. He put his arm round me and said he was sure Daniel would be fine.

We all walked down to the play area where Sam helped Theo on the zip wire and Katie followed Milo, who walked up to a little girl of about the same age, lifted up her skirt, took a good look at what was underneath and then casually strolled off. It was impossible not to laugh. How could I be laughing at my toddler's antics while imagining my husband lying dead at the bottom of a cliff? It felt completely surreal.

As I paced around the edge of the play area I thought about the last couple of days. The night before I left, Daniel and I had spent the evening watching TV together on the sofa. We'd both felt hungry, so I made us peanut butter on toast. We shared a plate and watched Grand Designs. Daniel was very quiet, but it had felt nice to have that time together.

On the Friday morning he'd actually done more than he did most days. But there was something about him; the half hug, the averted eyes that bothered me. Had he given up? Was that it? I knew him so well, sensed his mood changes. Something had shifted.

My phone rang, making me jump. It was the estate agent, calling to let me know there had been an offer on the house from someone who had viewed it a couple of days earlier. I should have been pleased, but I just wanted to get her off the line. After the call I couldn't even remember how much had been offered.

At one o clock I phoned Daniel's mum. He hadn't arrived. She said he might still be in bed. I spoke to Adam and asked him to go round to our house and check on Daniel. He said he thought Daniel might have gone out and forgotten the lunch. He wanted to give it a bit longer. They seemed so calm and reasonable, but I needed to know where Daniel was. I phoned the crisis team who agreed to call the police and go round to the house. They asked if anybody could open the door, otherwise they would have to break in. I phoned Adam back and he said he would go over and meet them.

I didn't think Daniel would be there, I was afraid that he was already lying at the bottom of the cliff at Beachy Head. I felt very shaky. I phoned the estate agent to cancel the afternoon viewings.

As we were loading the boys into the car my phone rang. It was Adam. Daniel had been found at the house. He had taken an overdose. He was babbling and angry that he had been found, but he had walked to the ambulance.

I burst into tears of relief. He was alive.

I'd walked away from the car to talk to Adam. I walked back, wiping away my tears, and told Mum and Sam what had happened. Sam offered to take the boys and let me go straight to see Daniel. But Mum suggested she and the boys come back home with me, so that she could look after them while I went to the hospital over the next few days. It seemed like the best plan, I didn't want to leave the boys; I'd had to do that too much lately. So we drove back to my parents' house and while Mum and Dad fed Theo and Milo, Adam gave me the number for the doctor treating Daniel.

The doctor told me he was stable and comfortable. He said they were awaiting blood results and planning dialysis to clean out his kidneys. I asked if Daniel's life was in danger. The doctor sounded reassuring. 'No, he'll need dialysis tonight and we expect him to be with us in intensive care for a few days.'

I wanted to sit on the floor and weep. Everything would be alright. It had all been so hard, so painful, so lonely, but at least now Daniel would get the help he desperately needed.

I packed our things and with the boys in the back of the car, Mum and I set off back to Sussex.

Half an hour into the journey my phone pinged. It was a text from Imogen, Adam's wife. Mum read it. 'Daniel had twice the toxic level in his blood.' I didn't really understand what that meant but it didn't sound good, I worried that the dialysis would be painful for him.

Fifteen minutes later Adam rang. He asked if I was driving. I told him I had my hands-free set on. He hesitated. 'Louise, Daniel has passed away. I'm sorry.'

I couldn't stop and I couldn't speak, I felt paralysed. Mum asked me what was wrong and I shook my head. I managed to pull off at the next exit. Mum was ashen. We both tried to sound normal for the boys, strapped into their seats chattering in the back, unaware that their world had just changed forever.

I got out of the car, walked a few yards away and phoned Adam. He told me that Daniel's heart had stopped when they started the dialysis. They'd tried for ten minutes to resuscitate him. I slumped to the pavement, shaking uncontrollably. How could this have happened? He had walked to the ambulance. They had said he would be alright.

He was the love of my life.

He couldn't be dead.

This wasn't how it was meant to be.

CHAPTER TWO

I spotted him the moment I walked into the bar.

Wearing a khaki surfer shirt and jeans, he was stocky, with broad, powerful shoulders and shaved dark hair, sprinkled with grey. Nothing like the type I normally went for.

Oh well, I told myself. I've only come for an hour. Then I can slip off home and curl up on the sofa with the telly and a cup of tea. Chalk this date up to experience. I took a deep breath and headed over.

'Hi, I'm Louise, you must be Daniel.'

His smile was warm and endearing.

'Nice to meet you.'

I sat down while he ordered drinks. He might not be my type, but there was something about him that I liked, his easy-going confidence and charm were infectious.

Five minutes in and I'd forgotten all about leaving after an hour.

I'm a cautious person; thoughtful and fairly serious. I'm slightly wary of first impressions; I like to get to know someone well before I let them get close and I tend to observe people before opening up. But that evening with Daniel I felt drawn to him in a way that took me by surprise. He talked non-stop, but he was never boring. He asked me all about myself and he was intelligent, insightful, amusing, opinionated without being pompous, and often extremely funny.

He appeared to be a man of many aspects. He had a senior managerial job in IT, yet he said he loved to skateboard, sail and kite-surf. He was crazy about the sea and he was doing up a camper van that he'd named Betty. He also loved to cook, sing opera and play the saxophone.

As we stepped out into the cool night air at the end of the evening, he turned to me. 'Would you like to meet Betty?' he said. 'I'll walk you to your car, she's on our way.' A few minutes later he opened a garage door to reveal Betty in all her shabby, lilac-painted glory. He beamed like a proud dad, and I couldn't help smiling too. I'd always wanted a VW camper van.

Back at my car, I thanked him for a lovely evening. It really had been. He kissed me on the cheek and I drove home to my flat.

As I got ready for bed, I thought about him. I'd enjoyed his company and decided I would be open to another date. That night, I dreamt that he was in my bed. It wasn't a sexual dream, he was simply sleeping beside me, and I felt comfortable with him there. When I woke I felt surprised that he had, metaphorically, got into bed with me after one date. He'd obviously made a bigger impression than I realised.

I went to work with a spring in my step. I worked as an art therapist, two days a week in a child and adolescent mental health unit and three days in a medium secure forensic unit for adults who had committed crimes and needed psychiatric treatment. It was a career that I loved; absorbing, demanding and fascinating.

When I was working there was little time to think about anything else, so it wasn't until my lunch break that I checked my phone and found a text from Daniel:

I really enjoyed meeting you and it would fascinate me to spend more time with you. I have often looked enviably at some couples

*who seem to have an amazing chemistry that has led them to build
a beautiful relationship with longevity. I always thought that was
unattainable for me but meeting you has made me feel it is possible.
I would really like to see you again very soon xx*

I could have dismissed it as cheesy or too forward, but
I actually found it refreshingly open and straightforward.
I wasn't interested in playing games or in fragile egos and
clearly neither was he. I sent a text back to say I'd be happy
to see him again, and we arranged to meet in a seafood
restaurant later that week.

'How was your date?' asked Tania as I passed her in the
corridor a few minutes later.

'Oh, you know nothing special, not really my type.'

She raised an eyebrow. 'So what's that grin about then?
I'm coming over tonight, eight o'clock, no arguing. I want
details.'

I smiled, Tania and I were absolute opposites; she
was as outspoken and disorganised as I was reserved and
ordered, but she was an amazing friend. We'd met at work
and it was Tania who had persuaded me to join the online
dating agency in the first place. I'd never have done it on
my own, but she helped me with the profile, took a terrible
photo of me and, despite my reluctance and protestations
that this wasn't the kind of thing I felt comfortable doing,
generated so much enthusiasm that some of it actually did
rub off on me.

Despite the dismal photo I received hundreds of
responses. Too many to sift through, so in the end I decided
to keep my profile hidden and to browse through the men
on the site and choose who to contact.

The first person I emailed was James. We met and I
liked him enormously, but there was no spark of attraction.
James was easy going, empathetic and a good runner and

he quickly became my good friend and running partner. I had been marathon running for a few years, so we'd meet for long runs almost daily, and talk about anything and everything as we pounded the streets.

James filled a gap in my life, but a platonic male friend, lovely as that was, wasn't what I was after. I was almost 33 and although I had a nice life, with a beautiful flat that my Dad and I had lovingly renovated, a good job and great friends, my biological clock was ticking; I was broody and I wanted to meet someone, settle down and start a family.

It was early in 2005 when I joined the dating agency. A year earlier I had finally freed myself from a relationship that was going nowhere, with a man who just didn't want to commit. He wanted me in his life, and made it difficult for me to leave him, but he didn't share my vision of long term commitment and children. After it ended I felt almost ashamed that I'd wasted so much time and emotional energy on him.

In the months that followed the break-up I sorted myself out, went travelling to all kinds of wonderful and exotic places with Tania, who brought out the thirst for adventure in me, and reached a point where I felt content with myself and my life. I'd worked hard to achieve a career in art therapy and I was earning enough money to pay for my flat, my travels and clothes and shoes in abundance.

As I trawled through the profiles again, something drew me to Daniel's photo. It wasn't really flattering, but I was drawn to his warm eyes. I contacted him, he emailed back and for a month we swapped news, chat and bits of information. Daniel told me that he was 35, Irish, worked in IT and was divorced with two young daughters. I hadn't imagined getting involved with someone who already had children, but I enjoyed our emails and decided to keep an open mind.

After these online exchanges we agreed to talk over the phone. His voice was rich, deep and confident, with an accent that I couldn't place but which turned out to be Irish tinged with American – he'd spent a lot of time in the States. He told me he was about to fly to New York on business and that he'd ring me when he got back the following week so that we could arrange to meet.

I took it all very lightly; I wasn't expecting anything to come of it. But a week later, true to his word, he called. He said he was in London with his daughters; they had been to see his father, who was an actor, in a play. We arranged to meet a couple of days later on the late May bank holiday.

I was having a busy weekend too. It was the Brighton Festival and I'd been immersed in the buzz of it, meeting up with friends and going to dance performances, art shows and concerts. On the Sunday I went out with a group of friends to the firework display marking the festival's finale, before deciding it was time to head home. But when I got to the car park I couldn't find my car. It took a while for it to dawn on me that it was gone – my little silver convertible MX5, my pride and joy, with my belongings inside it, had been stolen.

I was shocked. I'd had such a lovely, friendly night out, the whole of Brighton seemed to be celebrating, but my happy bubble had well and truly popped. And, quite apart from my sense of loss, how was I going to manage without a car? Both my work venues were hard to reach using public transport.

I hardly slept that night, but the next morning I went out for my usual run with James and he offered to lend me his car for a week, insisting he wouldn't need it as he commuted to work in London by train. I was truly grateful.

I was still feeling a bit low and a bit tired when Stevie popped round to commiserate. Prone to emotional outbursts and drama, Stevie was also utterly endearing and impossible to dislike. He made me laugh until my sides hurt and listened patiently to my woes. He was the kind of friend every single girl needs.

I told him I was feeling a bit half-hearted about my blind date that night, after losing my car. Stevie insisted I show him Daniel's profile on the website. 'He's hot, you have to go,' he said. I was glad I'd taken his advice. As the week passed I found myself looking forward to seeing Daniel again.

After a very busy day at work I made my way to the restaurant Daniel had chosen, an upmarket seafood place where he insisted on ordering a whole lobster. I had never actually eaten lobster before, but I agreed to share it with him and as we tucked in, the conversation flowed. As before, I felt he was something of a paradox; he had strong opinions on serious matters, but he could be hilariously flippant and witty, he was bold and brash and at the same time extremely sensitive.

After our meal, we moved on to a bar and settled into an alcove. Here, the discussion became a bit more serious as I grilled Daniel about his failed marriage. I wanted to know what had gone wrong. Daniel later referred to this as 'the interrogation', but he didn't object and he was open and honest. He told me that his relationship with his ex-wife was acrimonious and gave me details about his marriage that set off my inner alarm bells, so my guard remained firmly up. He was refreshingly honest about the fact that he had not been a great husband and while I didn't like what I was hearing, I was impressed by his insight and ability to own his mistakes. And I was moved by the way he spoke about his daughters, he was deeply troubled and full of regret about the way his marriage breakup had affected them. I could see that they were his world.

When Daniel asked me about my relationship history and future hopes I was equally honest. I told him that I wanted to settle down with somebody special and that I wanted a family, although marriage itself was never really high on my agenda. In response to this Daniel dropped a bombshell by telling me that he'd had a vasectomy.

I was lost for words. He took my hand and told me that he regretted having it now that his circumstances had changed, that a vasectomy was reversible and that he would love to have more children with the right person. The evening ended abruptly after that and I drove back to my flat feeling deflated. This man had too many complications in his life that I didn't want to be a part of. I felt disappointed, I was drawn to him but he was not the right man for me.

I didn't plan to see him again – but Daniel had other ideas. Over the next few days, he sent texts, asking to meet again and I was unable to shut the door on him. In truth, I didn't want to, so I told him that I was open to a platonic friendship, but nothing more. Daniel said that was fine, so we continued to meet a couple of times a week.

I felt very at ease with him, I really enjoyed his company and, despite the platonic boundary that I had set, Daniel didn't hold back in expressing his feelings for me. He let me know that he thought that I was the best thing since sliced bread, without putting any pressure on me to reciprocate his feelings.

Meanwhile, a work colleague had been doing a bit of matchmaking and she sent me on a date with an osteopath friend who she had decided was a catch for me. We went on a few dates and he was a thoroughly nice chap, but I was a little bored in his company and I found myself thinking about Daniel.

Over the next few weeks, I realised that my heart really wasn't in the courtship with the osteopath and I spent more time with Daniel. We went to restaurants, walked on the beach together, went on spur-of-the-moment outings in Betty and he cycled alongside me on my runs. The more time I spent with him, the more I liked him, but I remained wary because of his vasectomy and his acrimonious relationship with his ex-wife and my guard remained firmly in place until life intervened.

My mum had slipped a disc in her spine. After years of caring for her family she had been able to put her skills to good use once we had all flown the nest, as a carer for elderly and disabled people in their homes. She loved the job, but it involved a lot of lifting and inevitably that led to injury. She had been in discomfort for a good month before her doctor suggested that she try an epidural in her spine to reduce the pain. Dad had set up health insurance for them both some years earlier so she booked into a private hospital for the procedure. She expected to be out within a few hours.

I was at work when I got the call from Dad to say that something had gone wrong. Mum had had an adverse reaction to the epidural, she was very sick and the numbness in her lower body had not worn off. He sounded extremely worried.

I left work early and it was Daniel I phoned. I had decided to drive to Wiltshire to see mum that evening. I knew I would have to drive back for work the next day, which meant a five to six hour round trip, so when Daniel offered to do the driving I accepted gratefully. We set off in my new black MX5, bought the previous week to replace my stolen silver one, and arrived at the hospital at about 10pm. Daniel stayed in the waiting area and met Dad for the first time while I went in to Mum.

I could see that she was very ill, she couldn't stop vomiting and she looked dreadful. I stayed for about an hour and then we had to leave again. I felt awful, I kept telling Daniel I should have stayed, but we both needed to be at work the next day and I thought that Mum was in good hands. But the next morning, before leaving for work, I rang Dad who told me that she had suffered three massive seizures during the night and was in a bad way. She was being transferred from the small, private hospital to a larger general hospital and Dad was on his way there.

I phoned work to tell them I wouldn't be in, packed a small bag and got straight back on the motorway. I felt really afraid that I was going to lose her. To add to my turmoil, an accident detour meant that I had to take an unfamiliar route and I was in such a daze that I drove 50 miles out of my way. When I eventually arrived it was early afternoon and Mum was in the intensive care unit. Dad and my brothers, Tom and Sam, were sitting next to her with ashen faces. Mum didn't know who I was; she thought I was a nurse. She was barely able to talk as she had bitten her tongue during a seizure and she was being prepared for a lumbar puncture. As she was rolled onto her side she yelped in pain and Dad told me that her shoulder had been broken during a seizure. An X-ray later confirmed that her shoulder bone had completely shattered. It was harrowing for us to see her like that, she had gone into hospital for what we thought was a routine procedure and was now terribly ill and injured.

She spent three weeks in intensive care and never really made a full recovery. I took those three weeks off work and, with Dad and my two brothers took shifts to ensure that she had one of us with her day and night. It was a horrible time.

I turned to Daniel for support and he was an absolute rock. He phoned me regularly throughout the day, researched her condition, offered to pay for alternative treatments and travelled down to see me at weekends. He would drive down in rusty old Betty, pick me up from the hospital, take me out and then drop me back at Mum's bedside a few hours later. He provided me with much-needed respite during that dreadful time, his kindness won me over and my reservations about him began to disappear.

By the time Mum was moved from intensive care and I returned to Brighton, my relationship with Daniel was on a different footing. We were a couple, and despite my earlier doubts, I knew I was falling for him.

CHAPTER THREE

Our courtship was never conventional. Although we did sometimes go for drinks or meals out, dates with Daniel were often a little more alternative.

One warm, still summer evening he arrived outside my flat in Betty and announced that we were going onto the Downs. He drove to a secluded spot and unloaded sleeping bags and torches, a flask of Horlicks and some biscuits. We lay there for hours looking at the stars and talked about everything and anything.

Sometimes I'd hear the sound of wheels bumping down the road and look out of the window to see him on his skateboard, wearing a suit and a baseball cap and holding an enormous bunch of flowers. It made me laugh; he was eccentric and full of contradictions and that made him interesting. I'd never met anybody like him before. Given his creativity and love of drama and music, IT seemed a strange choice of career. When I asked him about it he agreed that he'd got into it almost by accident. His degree had been in drama and English literature and he'd planned to travel. But he met his first wife, Beth, at a party and soon afterwards they conceived Ella. Without any formal training he taught himself IT because he needed a way to support his new family. He was good at it and he worked his way up the ladder and became used to earning a high salary which was hard to give up, especially once he had two children. When I met him, he was employed by an American IT company with a British base in Brighton. All the more senior people were in the States so he was pretty much in charge of the Brighton branch and this gave him a lot of flexibility.

Daniel worked to live. His job didn't stretch him or use his creative talents, but it suited him, and his real passions in life were outside work; his children, his music, the sea, and his gardening. He could leave the office and be on the beach in 15 minutes.

Over that first summer I met most of his family. I first met his younger brother Adam one evening in a Brighton bar and liked him immediately. Six years younger than Daniel, he was warm and easy to talk to; he had a calm manner and was deep and interesting. He lived in London with his girlfriend Imogen, but he and Daniel were very close and saw a lot of one another.

Adam turned 30 at the beginning of that summer and Imogen had arranged a big celebration at her parents' house, which was only half an hour from where my parents lived. The party coincided with the day Mum was discharged from hospital and Daniel drove me and his younger half-sister, Lottie, to the party, stopping to see Mum on the way. Daniel's parents, who were both Irish actors, had split when he was seven and his father had remarried, so Lottie was more than a decade younger. Daniel was very affectionate with her and they shared a constant stream of banter. I met Imogen for the first time at the party; she had heard all about me and couldn't have been more welcoming.

Daniel's mother Maggie lived in Dorset but she visited him and the girls every few weeks. I met her for the first time at Daniel's flat and she was friendly and warm. His father and stepmother lived in London and I met them at a theatre after Daniel's father had appeared in a play. A few weeks later we were invited to their flat in London for Lottie's birthday. It was a small family celebration but it involved lots of singing and raucous laughter and although I felt like a fish out of water, I was drawn in by their energy and enthusiasm.

Daniel had been keen for me to meet his daughters but I'd been holding off, wanting to be certain that we were serious and committed first. I didn't want them to be hurt or confused. By late August, when we'd known each other for four months I felt sure of my feelings about him and ready to meet his girls.

Daniel cherished his time with Ella and Hannah, he had them to stay on alternate weekends and sometimes he would ring me late at night to say that he'd only just got them to bed. He liked to make the most of every minute they spent with him. I didn't like the depth of his anger and bitterness towards his ex-wife and her new husband and I insisted that he tell Beth about the plan for me to meet the girls so that she could prepare them. I wanted to do things properly and I certainly didn't want to get embroiled in the bad feeling between them. Daniel was reluctant, but he agreed and we arranged for me to meet Ella and Hannah one Sunday afternoon on Brighton seafront.

It was a beautiful, sunny afternoon. I cycled from my flat to the spot on the beach where I knew Daniel would be and found him sitting on the rocks, with the girls running around the beach. I met seven year-old Ella first; she greeted me with open arms and was warm and welcoming; just as Daniel had predicted she would be. I could see that she had inherited his openness and sociability; she wasn't at all shy and behaved as if she had known me for years. Daniel had said that Hannah would probably be more wary and take a while to warm to me, so I was a little nervous about meeting her. Strange to fear rejection from a three year old, but I wanted it all to go well. Daniel brought her over and she was clearly reluctant to meet this strange woman. She was clutching a plastic Snow White doll and I asked her if she knew the story of Snow White. She brightened immediately. She told me all about Snow White, the seven dwarfs and the evil queen and, in that brief exchange, I was accepted and we bonded. She was a girly girl, wanting to know all about my nail varnish and was very disappointed that I didn't have any make up in my handbag.

I wasn't really used to being around young children and I was struck by how small both girls were. But being with them was so much easier than I had anticipated; they were very easy to fall in love with. Daniel suggested that we all go to the pier and Hannah skipped along holding my hand singing 'ten currant buns in the baker's shop' while Ella told me all about their recent holiday in Sardinia for their mum and stepdad's honeymoon. Hannah asked if Daniel and I would be having a honeymoon – awkward for me but Daniel grinned and gave me a devilish wink.

The girls dragged us on all the rides and Daniel took photos of us on the trampolines, the ghost train and one of Ella and me getting drenched on the water coaster. He phoned me later that evening to tell me that I had won the girls approval. I think he was more relieved than I was. I told him they were gorgeous little girls and I'd loved being with them, I was touched by how warm and accepting they were.

After this first meeting it became usual for me to spend some time with the three of them at weekends, but I was careful to ensure that the girls also got time alone with Daniel and we waited a while before I stayed the night. Ella and Hannah were never resentful towards me, if anything, as their mum had someone new, they wanted their dad to have someone too.

Sitting at the kitchen table with Ella one evening, making birthday cards, she drew a picture of her mum, stepdad Pete, Daniel and me with her and Hannah in the middle. She told me that her mum was the queen, her dad the king, Pete and I were the prince and princess and she and Hannah were the flower fairies. She said she loved her mum and dad the most, Hannah second and Pete and I last. She looked at me apologetically, worried that I would be hurt by her rankings of love but in fact I felt extremely touched that she had said that she loved me after knowing me for such a short time. I told her that, it was right that she loved her mummy and daddy the most and that they loved her and Hannah more than anything in the world too. She looked extremely relieved that I understood her attempts to make sense of her new family dynamics and gave me a hug.

Throughout that summer my relationship with Daniel seemed to be gathering momentum, and as autumn beckoned, we decided to have a week's break in Egypt. Daniel had been many times before because it's a kite-surfer's haven, but I'd never been.

I felt excited and a little nervous. Although, Daniel and I had been spending a lot of time together, we still had our own homes and separate lives. A holiday would mean an entire week together. Would we still feel the same at the end of it?

We stayed in a basic hotel, a bus ride from the beach. We arrived to find rose petals on our bed and champagne on ice. Daniel had cheekily told the staff that we were honeymooners. It was a lovely start to a really special week.

Daniel was always taking the mickey out of my passion for running. He couldn't understand how anyone could enjoy something which, to him, was synonymous with torture. So he laughed when he saw I had packed my expensive high-tech trainers to run in the forty degree heat! Two days into the holiday, he put my trainers in the bin telling me that I was mad to consider running in Egypt. I ignored him and assumed that he would retrieve them, but the following day, as I prepared for an early morning run, we realised that the trainers were gone. Daniel felt terrible and darted around the hotel trying to retrieve them but it was too late. I was not happy, but it was a story we laughed about later.

In revenge – unintentional, of course – on the last day of our holiday I managed to drown Daniel's state of the art camera. We spent our days on the beach, where I was happy to laze and read in the sun while Daniel went into action with his kites. He soon made a wide circle of buddies, something he did wherever he went, and he'd disappear for hours kite-surfing with them. On our final day, he asked me if I would take some photos of him and his friends kite-surfing and suggested that I swim out to a small island and take the pictures from there. I am not a good swimmer but the island didn't look too far away so I agreed. Daniel's camera, in its waterproof case, was strapped around my waist as I swam.

I hated every minute of it. When I got out of my depth I imagined sharks, jellyfish and other gruesome sea creatures beneath me as I swam. I remember thinking, 'I can't believe I am doing this; I must really love this guy'. Once on the island I attempted to take some pictures as Daniel pranced about, jumping and twirling as he saw me with the camera poised. Afterwards I told him I wasn't sure I'd managed to get any shots so he took the camera, looked at it and then fell about laughing and said, 'you sure know how to get even'. I hadn't clasped the waterproof case properly and it had filled with water. His camera was ruined, as were most of our holiday shots.

One of the things I remember most about Egypt was falling in love with Daniel's feet. As bizarre as that sounds, I really did. As we stood together on the bus to the beach every day, my eyes would fall on his 'Havana' clad feet. They were enormous, almost as wide as they were long, but perfectly formed. His toes splayed out like the feet of children's cartoon characters and I couldn't help laughing at them and calling him 'monster feet'.

It was a blissful holiday and it cemented our relationship. Shortly after we returned from Egypt, we celebrated our six month anniversary. We went out for a meal and Daniel presented me with a pair of diamond earrings. That evening he asked me to move in with him. I was blissfully happy with Daniel but I knew that we were just getting to know each other and I was reluctant to give up the flat I loved and the independence it represented.

There was something else holding me back as well – the fertility issue. For me, this was crucial. I had fallen in love with Daniel but I didn't want to sacrifice my chances of motherhood. Soon after our Egyptian holiday we agreed to find out about getting his vasectomy reversed.

We visited three different consultants and the verdict was unanimous; Daniel's prognosis of a successful reversal was good. The sooner he had the operation, they all said, the higher the chance of a successful outcome.

Meanwhile, I was doing a lot of running in preparation for a challenge I had booked a year earlier; I was going to the Himalayas for three weeks, the culmination of which was to run and trek 100 miles in four days. It had seemed a good idea when I was single and had a gap in my life to fill, but after seven months with Daniel it had lost its appeal.

I could have cancelled it but, scared of losing my independence, I was determined to go ahead. I knew Daniel didn't want me to go but he was wise enough to support me, kitting me out with all the essential gear and cycled alongside me as I trained.

I flew to Delhi and after a couple of days we were taken to the Himalayan base camp. On day one of the run I was feeling fit and excited. Though I was missing Daniel, I was meeting interesting people and I was in awe of the breath taking scenery. We covered about 35 miles and it wasn't actually much of a run, more a vigorous walk, as we went up an unrelenting 3000 foot incline.

That evening I developed a bad headache and felt shaky, with an unquenchable thirst. I was sharing a tent with a doctor who was concerned that I was dehydrated. She went to fetch the trek doctor who agreed and put me on a drip.

The next day we were to cover a full marathon and, despite feeling shaky and tired, I was determined to carry on. A few others were suffering from the altitude and were being sick, but nobody pulled out; after all, this was an endurance challenge. I stayed with the slower group and just kept walking and drinking, determined to get to the end of the day. At one point, I found myself walking alone, between the two groups, when I saw what I thought was a large brown dog idly crossing my path about 200 feet ahead. I wondered what a dog was doing up there, until it dawned on me that it was more likely to be a wild bear. Suddenly scared, I just wanted to be at home with Daniel. I knew, in that moment, that I absolutely wanted to be with him forever, settled and safe.

We got to the finish line to cheers and hugs and after dinner we were summoned to a meeting to discuss the next day's route. I remember sitting listening to the instructor and I don't recall feeling faint, but that was my last memory for six days.

I woke to find myself in a hospital bed with tubes and drips inserted into my arms, hands and stomach. I couldn't remember anything and thought I'd been in a plane crash. When an interpreter arrived with Bob, the trip organiser from the UK, I was told that I'd had a seizure and had been carried for eight hours down the mountain by Bob and the Indian doctor.

I remained in hospital for another night before returning to the base camp in Darjeeling. The rest of the group had returned from the mountains triumphant and were preparing to travel back to Delhi for their flight home. I felt a bit of a failure for not completing the challenge and desperately wanted to get home.

I was greeted by Daniel, Ella and Hannah at the airport with a huge banner that the girls had made for me. My parents were there too. Everybody was very worried but, apart from feeling very tired, I was alright.

My GP examined all the medical notes from India and it seemed I had suffered from over hydration, not altitude sickness. The drip that I had been given that first night had saturated my system with water leading to dangerously low levels of sodium (hyponatremia) and an electrolyte imbalance. I'd had a close shave and I was extremely lucky to have got off so lightly. I could have died.

I hadn't forgotten the strong feeling, on the mountain, that I wanted to be with Daniel, and my lucky escape had cemented that. I was so glad to be back with him. And he had been busy while I was away. In a bid to persuade me to move in with him, he had been preparing his flat. Daniel was probably the most untidy person I had ever met; on a par with Tania whose propensity for collecting clutter took some beating. He was a man of spontaneity, living in the moment, so when the girls were with him, there were no set mealtimes or bedtimes. They just grabbed food when they were hungry and went to bed very late. It worked for Daniel but I found it a difficult way to live.

While I had been away, Daniel had laid lino on the bare bathroom floor and put up shelves in the living room ready for my vast collection of books. He'd started to paint the kitchen and had a massive clear out. I was very touched by all his efforts. In what I came to learn was typical of Daniel, none of these little projects were ever totally completed. He would start lots of ambitious projects and have a few on the go simultaneously. But his initial enthusiasm would wane or his mind would have raced onto his next venture. Often this would infuriate me but I learned to live with it.

Soon after my misadventure in India I agreed to move in with him. I was sad to leave my beloved flat and not particularly thrilled to be living in the home that Daniel had shared with his ex-wife, but I knew that it was the most sensible next step for us. We weren't yet ready to sell our homes and his place was a lot bigger than mine so it made sense for me to move there.

Daniel had been pulling out all the stops to demonstrate his commitment and his investment in 'us' and I felt ready to do the same. I rented my flat to my friend James, who was looking for somewhere to live with his girlfriend, and put all my furniture and most of my belongings in storage. I took only my clothes and everyday essentials to Daniel's; I knew it was only a stepping stone for us. And while the flat wasn't my ideal home, I was happy to be with him and excited about our future.

CHAPTER FOUR

In the New Year, Daniel and I prepared ourselves for his imminent vasectomy reversal. We were both a little nervous but also hopeful. The procedure was to be done in a private hospital, it would be a three hour operation but he would be home the same night.

Daniel was courageous and cheerful about it, cracking jokes with the medical team until the moment he was wheeled away and when he came round, we were told that the operation had gone well. He walked like John Wayne for a week afterwards.

We decided it was time to look for a house to buy. If we did have children together we would need more space and we both wanted somewhere that was neither his nor mine but ours, together. Daniel threw himself into house-hunting with enthusiasm and tenacity. We were both used to living centrally in the city but accepted that we would get a lot more for our money if we moved further out and we were excited about the prospect of a garden.

It wasn't even a year since we'd met and I was very aware of how fast things were moving, but I was happy and I allowed myself to be swept along in Daniel's enthusiasm. I wanted all that we were moving towards; a home, children, a life together. But my life was changing so rapidly that at times I felt I was somebody else, living an unfamiliar life. It was during those first few months of living together that I first saw glimmers of a darker side to the man I had fallen in love with. The first time I heard alarm bells ringing Daniel and I had gone up to London for a day trip. We planned to go to the Tate Modern and then to visit Daniel's brother, Adam and his girlfriend, Imogen, in their flat. We had a lovely time at the Tate, bouncing our opinions and views on art back and forth. Daniel always had intelligent views and I loved these discussions. At Adam and Imogen's we had a meal and the conversation flowed. When Imogen went off to have a bath, Adam and Daniel began to debate the pros and cons of counselling and psychotherapy. As it was a subject that I had first-hand knowledge and experience of, I joined in, but I soon realised that Daniel had no interest in hearing my views; he was just trying to beat me down. It wasn't a debate; it was about Daniel winning. I thought he was talking utter rubbish about a subject that he knew nothing about, but I shut up because I could see that the conversation was pointless. Daniel seemed to feel triumphant, but I didn't like the way he'd behaved and was very quiet during our journey home.

I had also been a little alarmed by Daniel's attitude towards what had happened to me in India. Though he had made every effort to look after me physically when I got home he had chastised me over my decision to go in the first place. He felt that I had chosen to do something extreme that had resulted in a huge amount of worry for everyone, which was ironic, given his own attraction to extreme activities. It was almost as if he didn't like it when he saw those same qualities mirrored in me. He didn't really like my athletic trait, he saw it as a threat; he wanted to be the stronger one in every sense.

Daniel found a house online that was up for sale in a small coastal town a few miles outside Brighton. The house overlooked the beach; Daniel knew the area well and already had some water sports buddies there. He was full of excitement and persuaded me to go with him to view the house. We both loved the fact that our city flats boasted a sea view, albeit a tiny glimmer in Daniel's case, but this house was something else. From the upstairs front windows there was a stunning, unspoilt view of the beach and the sea. The décor was very dated; every room was decked out in bright, eighties-style flowery wallpaper complete with contrasting border. But the house had a spacious feel. It was by far the nicest house we had looked at and Daniel was sold – it was his dream house.

It was slightly over our budget and would stretch us. Daniel went home and did all the sums; he was sensible with finances and I trusted his view. He decided that we could afford it as long as we were prepared to sacrifice other things. We were both used to having a generous disposable income and this would change.

We discussed it from all angles and decided that the house itself would provide us with a new lifestyle. This would be the trade-off for expensive holidays and the house would be an investment. We would need to borrow a colossal amount of money but Daniel had a high, secure salary and I was earning a reasonable wage. This was boom time, house prices were at an all-time high and it was normal for people to borrow four times their annual income. I buried my doubts and we decided to go for it. Our offer was accepted and we quickly found a buyer for Daniel's flat. We had decided to keep my flat in the short term as a safety net. James' rent covered my mortgage and maintenance costs and it saved us the stress of selling two flats at once.

Six weeks after Daniel's vasectomy reversal, we went to a follow-up appointment at the hospital, where he underwent some routine tests. We had been told that it took an average of nine months for a man to become fertile again and the consultant told us that Daniel's sperm count was low and unlikely to result in a pregnancy for a while. However he was optimistic and asked us to return in six months when he predicted we would have a more positive result.

Meanwhile, I had thrown myself into training for the London marathon. I'd got an elite place, based on my time the previous year, so the pressure was on and I was into hard-core training. I ran the Brighton half-marathon in a good time but a few weeks later struggled a little in the Hastings half-marathon. I was only a few minutes slower than predicted but I just didn't feel my best. Mentally too, I'd lost a bit of the grit and determination that normally fuelled me. Instead of pushing my body through the tough bits I just felt, 'Oh well, so what if I'm a bit slow today'. This wasn't really like me.

A few days later, I began feeling a bit wiped out and very pre-menstrual and realised I was almost a week overdue. It suddenly dawned on me that there was a very slim possibility that I could be pregnant. I rushed out and bought a pregnancy test and was thrilled and amazed when a blue line appeared in the window. I went straight back to the chemist and bought two more. All three tests displayed a clear blue line. I was overwhelmed with excitement and joy.

I couldn't wait to tell Daniel when he got home from work, but to my dismay, he brought a 'friend of a friend' with him to fix our broken oven, so I waited patiently. The oven was soon repaired but Daniel, always so sociable, invited the bloke to stay for a beer. They spent the next hour sitting at our kitchen table putting the world to rights – full of blarney, as Tania put it – while I waited with mounting frustration.

Finally the man left and I dragged Daniel to the sofa and handed him the pregnancy testing sticks. He looked bemused for a few seconds and then leapt off the sofa and yelped for joy.

We were both a little shocked as we'd been told only days earlier that it would be extremely unlikely for me to fall pregnant. But we were wildly happy and, unable to contain our excitement; we phoned our families that night.

I pulled out of the London marathon and began to feel much more positive about the new house. I started thinking about how amazing it would be to raise children so close to the beach.

Our offer had been accepted but the whole process of buying the house was fraught with complications, but Daniel was tenacious. This was the first time I had really seen how determined he could be. When he wanted something he would put everything into making sure he got it. I wanted the house too but began to think that it wasn't meant to be, there seemed to be so many obstacles along the way. But Daniel continued to negotiate with both ends of the chain until we exchanged. He was elated and I felt relieved.

The following week we went to Paris for my birthday. I was about ten weeks pregnant and feeling constantly nauseous and tired. Daniel was stressed and tired too, after long hours at work and all his efforts to secure the house purchase so it could have fallen flat, but in fact we had a wonderful time.

We'd booked a cheap package deal, but we struck gold with the hotel. Though it was very modest, we were on the top floor and our room had a large window with the most amazing views of the city. We could see the Eiffel Tower and the Sacre-Coeur. Daniel was in awe and didn't tire of sitting on the little windowsill, gazing out. He was always so wowed by beauty in the world; he would never let a sparkling star, an unexpected sunset, an amazing view or the smell of spring blossom pass him by. Almost daily, he would force me to stop what I was doing and acknowledge something beautiful and I loved that about him.

We didn't cram in all the sights as I would normally be inclined to do, I was feeling sick and drained and that forced us to slow down. We enjoyed boat trips along the Seine, wandered around street markets and sat about in cafés. We were delighted one day when we found ourselves in the café where Daniel's favourite film, Amelie, had been filmed.

We ate every night in an Indian restaurant because I had developed a really strong craving for Bombay potatoes. On my birthday we decided to go for a walk before heading to the restaurant as usual. It was a mild spring evening and we found ourselves in the Jardin du Luxembourg, a stunning park full of sculptures and beautiful plants. In the centre was a large pond, filled with fountains and surrounded by statues of fish and cherubs. We sat for a while to soak up the beauty of it all and suddenly Daniel fell to one knee and started declaring his love for me. I thought he was joking, but when he pulled out a little box from his pocket I realised he was serious. He had chosen a beautiful, simple but elegant diamond ring and he asked me to marry him.

I was totally surprised. It's not that we hadn't talked about it; Daniel had told me that he'd asked my dad for his permission a few months before and he had said he would propose to me somewhere special. But we'd had so much going on, with the house sale and my unexpected pregnancy that I thought marriage wasn't on the agenda, at least until sometime in the future.

I didn't hesitate. I had been swept off my feet by Daniel many months before and was happy to be swept further along with him. I loved him, I knew that he loved me, we were expecting a baby and I had never been happier. I said yes, and Daniel literally threw me up in the air with delight.

When we returned from Paris we told our families who congratulated us, but our engagement was rather overshadowed by my pregnancy and our imminent house move, so there was no party or big announcement, although friends and work colleagues couldn't fail to notice the sparkling rock on my finger. I'm sure that some people felt that it was a response to my pregnancy; that we were going to 'do the right thing'. But it really wasn't like that. We had committed to one another before his vasectomy reversal and that was a far bigger deal to both of us than marriage.

On moving day, we had hired a man with a van to help. This turned out to be two distracted and unmotivated teenagers with a small transit van and Daniel ended up doing most of the loading himself. There was little I could do to help so I took a car full of belongings and drove to our new house with my parents who had travelled down to help. It was a pleasant spring day and we sat on the low wall by the beach in front of our house and waited. We were expecting to get the keys around midday, but the previous owner was still loading things into a skip on the drive, so Daniel got on the phone to the solicitor who said that our deposit had not been paid due to a clerical error and we couldn't move in until Monday. Daniel, tenacious as ever, drove the van full of our belongings to his solicitor's office. I don't know how he did it but somehow the money was paid and we got the keys to our new home at about 5.30pm.

Later that evening Daniel's mum, Maggie arrived from Dorset to help out too. There was a lovely atmosphere as we all scurried about cleaning and unpacking. The stress of the day evaporated and we all celebrated this new beginning.

Mum had organised a meal and Dad had brought champagne. As we were getting ready for bed Daniel called out to us all, insisting that we go out onto the balcony to see the spectacular full moon reflecting on the water below. At that moment, life couldn't have felt any better to me.

During the night, our sleep was interrupted by a very loud bang. The next morning we discovered that it had been the second bottle of champagne exploding; Daniel had put it into the freezer and forgotten it. Dad said what a waste it was but Maggie's view was that it was the house's way of toasting our arrival and a very good omen. We all chose to believe her.

The girls arrived later that day and were completely thrilled with the house and delighted that it was so close to the beach.

Daniel and I both took the following week off work to sort out the house and get to know our new neighbourhood. We made a trip to IKEA in Betty to buy some essentials. Daniel hated shopping, especially in IKEA, and to make it more enjoyable he'd made it a ritual to have a meal in the IKEA café both as we arrived and departed the store. He liked to count how many couples we could see arguing or 'having a domestic'. It made it entertaining and prevented us from arguing ourselves. We were never in agreement about home furnishings, our tastes and ideas were very different and we always spent more than we planned to, but somehow we always seemed united in there and I have fond memories of our IKEA excursions.

That first week in the house Daniel was busy trying to put furniture together and was very bad tempered. When he attempted to move a radiator in order to fit the new wardrobe into our bedroom, he managed to burst a pipe. Water spurted everywhere as he tried frantically to find an emergency plumber. He was overwhelmed by how much there was to do in the house and became snappy. I was worried that he was having regrets, but he didn't want to talk about it and I realised that it was best to back off and give him space. The following week when he went back to work, he reverted to his usual happy and loving self. He apologised for his black mood and we both put it down to stress and exhaustion.

At our twenty week scan we discovered that I was carrying a boy. Daniel was over the moon and so was I. I'd been secretly hoping for a boy, simply because Daniel already had two girls and I wanted us to be sharing a new experience together.

As the birth date came closer we had disagreements over the pace of the DIY. I wanted to get as much as we could done before the baby arrived and then put it all on hold to enjoy our son, but Daniel couldn't see the hurry. He wanted to do everything himself but had no sense of urgency about any of it. He was enjoying living in the house and getting to know the neighbours and didn't want to feel tied down by tasks. We had a lot of differences, we were both strong characters and there were always negotiations going on, but we were both willing to make sacrifices when we could see the other felt strongly about an issue.

Life seemed to be close to perfect until, seven months into my pregnancy, I was made redundant. It was a shock and I hadn't seen it coming. Less than a year before I had taken up the offer to increase my part time work for a private healthcare company to a full time post. I knew that the company had recently been sold to venture capitalists and that cuts would be made, but the company had hospitals nationwide and the one I worked in was making huge profits, so we had all been led to believe that our jobs were safe.

It was a worry for me and a horrible way to leave a job I'd loved but Daniel was very supportive and unfazed. He felt secure in his job and knew that we wouldn't feel it financially for another year, as I had maternity and redundancy pay. He insisted I shouldn't worry, so I decided to make the best of it and enjoy preparing for the arrival of our son.

CHAPTER FIVE

The birth was long and complicated. Fifty nerve-wracking hours of labour left me exhausted – but deliriously happy to have my baby boy in my arms.

Daniel had driven me to hospital soon after my waters broke. He said he knew where the hospital was, but in fact he'd never been there and, while I crouched in the foot well of the car enduring waves of nausea, he got lost.

Despite the regular contractions, the midwife who examined me found I was only 2cm dilated. I was sick throughout the night and I developed a high temperature. By morning my contractions had eased off and I was clearly very unwell. Thankfully, the baby was doing fine through all the drama; I was repeatedly told that he had a strong heartbeat which was reassuring when I felt so rough.

After a few hours on a hydration drip and some anti-sickness medication, I began to feel a bit better, though very weak and exhausted, but I was still only two centimetres dilated. I was offered the choice of staying in hospital or going home to rest. The midwife explained that nature seemed to have slowed down my labour in order for my body to deal with my illness which, they suspected, was food poisoning. I would have to be induced the following morning if things didn't progress. I opted to go home and rest, hoping the contractions would speed up naturally.

It was a relief to get home and Daniel immediately made me some mashed potato; his Irish cure for everything. While Daniel later slept soundly, I had another fitful night, kept awake by intense contractions every twenty minutes. The following morning, we arrived at the hospital at eight and by ten the decision was taken to induce. Within minutes the contractions were fast and furious. It was as if the volume in a disco had suddenly been cranked to the highest level. I paced the room and practiced my breathing techniques, determined to handle the pain.

A punishing twelve hours later I was still only six centimetres dilated. Long past the point of moving, I was now hooked up to a monitor and an antibiotic drip to treat my fever. I felt exhausted beyond comprehension and desperate. The only positive aspect of this relentless labour was the regular reassurance that my baby was alright.

At about ten in the evening I was offered an epidural. Daniel and I were both very fearful of epidurals after what happened to my mum, so I had been adamant that I wouldn't have one, but after holding out for another hour, I gave in. Up to this point Daniel, who was wearing his lucky 'liquorice allsorts man' t-shirt that he had worn to the births of his first two children, had been confident and relaxed. He wasn't at all squeamish because he was a third timer at the birthing business. But he was nervous at the idea of a needle going into my spine. He commented, rather unhelpfully, on how large the needle was, but by that stage I was too desperate to worry about what was happening and just welcomed the pain relief when it kicked in.

I managed to doze for a few hours as Daniel curled up on the floor beside my bed, but I was abruptly woken by the bleeping monitor and found two midwives looking worried beside me. What happened next is a blur. The room was suddenly swarming with medics and I was wheeled off to theatre. There was a sense of panic and I heard the words 'emergency caesarean' and 'baby's heartbeat crashing'. I felt very afraid for my baby. I didn't care what they did to me at that point; I just wanted him out safely.

Minutes later it was all over. He came out blue and silent and seemed very shocked but alert, with wide open eyes. I was allowed a brief cuddle with my baby before he was whisked away to be given intravenous antibiotics as the doctors felt he was at risk of infection because I'd been so ill and it had been 48 hours since my waters had broken. His poor little head was shaped like a cone from being stuck in my pelvis for so long and he had purple bruises all over his head and the side of his face. Poor little thing, he hadn't had an easy entrance into the world.

Daniel held our ten-minute old baby as he anticipated the inevitable wail. However, as the doctor put the needle into his tiny arm, a nurse dropped some sugar solution into his mouth and he frowned and then sucked on the sugar, licked his lips and cooed. There was no cry. Afterwards Daniel would recount this tale to any willing listener with sheer delight and declare that his son was a brave little soldier who would take on the world. How right he was.

Finding a name we both liked had seemed like mission impossible, we had such different tastes, but just as I was beginning to think we'd never agree, I came up with Theo. It seemed so right and to my amazement, Daniel liked it.

I was ill for a few days after the birth and Theo had to remain on antibiotics so we both stayed in hospital for a week. On the day that we took him home, I dressed him in a mint green baby grow and a white knitted cardigan and hat. I shuffled slowly behind Daniel as we made our way out; I felt like a very different woman to the one who had arrived a week earlier. As dramatic as it sounds, I felt butchered, I remember looking at my lovely boy and thinking, I love you so much but I never want to do this again.

As soon as I got home the misery was forgotten and I really started to enjoy my baby. I felt utterly blissed-out, euphoric and in love. It was a feeling that lasted throughout Theo's first year. It was the happiest time of my life. Daniel and I were still very much in the honeymoon phase of our relationship so we both worked hard to amend any differences.

We were still working on the house, and despite having a new baby, Daniel was still determined to do all the DIY himself. A few days after Theo's homecoming, he decided that, as winter was drawing in, we had to get a wood burner. He went and bought one, only to discover that in order to use it we needed a flue in our chimney. He was adamant that he could fit it himself and persuaded our next door neighbour Sean and his dad Derek to help. They arrived with their tools and quite a few cans of beer, so I took Theo upstairs for a nap and left them to it.

When I woke a couple of hours later there was a celebration going on downstairs. I was told by an excited Daniel that the mission had been a success but had not been straightforward. They had attempted to feed the flue down from the top of the chimney but it had got stuck halfway, so Daniel had decided to sort it out by getting into the chimney via the fireplace. As he recounted the story to me, all I could see were the whites of his sparkling eyes; he was covered from head to toe in black soot. He'd also left sooty handprints all over our new white curtains, but he looked so comical that I couldn't be angry.

Theo was a happy and contented baby. He was crawling by six months and walking at nine and once he was on his feet he wanted to be running or climbing all the time. I would be the mum running about after him in the playground while the other parents sat about chatting with their coffees, their children close by. Theo was a handful but he had a confidence and zest for life that was so like his father.

I made a new circle of friends through my antenatal group; six or seven mums who hung out together with our babies, took them to various groups and supported one another with the challenges that new motherhood brings. We were soon meeting up with our partners and the dads also formed strong friendships. Daniel enjoyed the dads group and he became very friendly with our neighbours and made new friends through his kite-surfing and sailing. He became well-known and well-liked in the area and a familiar figure on the local beach. It was a lovely time for us both.

Daniel was always honest about the fact that he didn't really like babies that much. He loved his own babies but he wanted them to grow up and do more. He couldn't wait for Theo to become a little boy. He was very involved though, applying what he called 'the tricks of the trade'. When I was struggling to settle Theo Daniel would swaddle him in a blanket and rock him to sleep, or sing his favourite opera song 'Caro Mio Ben'. He had sung it to my pregnant bump and when he heard it Theo would instantly become mesmerized and settle.

Daniel's sense of humour often came to the rescue if I was feeling tired or overwhelmed with it all; he would do impressions of Theo's funny little ways and nick-named him his 'Little Gnat'.

Ella and Hannah came every other weekend. They loved their little brother but he was too young to join in with their activities. Daniel would whisk the girls off to the beach or on some adventure and I would be left at home to look after Theo. On those weekends I felt very conscious of being a family in two halves.

When he was nine months old, Theo started going to a nursery a few mornings a week. I had picked up a couple of private art therapy clients and a small freelance contract with another private healthcare company. Being self-employed allowed me to collect Theo at lunchtimes and spend the rest of my time with him. He was a happy, confident and secure child.

Daniel was seldom home before Theo's bedtime in the evenings so we fell into a pattern where I did the night shifts and Daniel did the early mornings. This time he had with Theo in the mornings was precious; in the spring and summer they would go to the beach before breakfast and in the winter Daniel taught Theo the alphabet, numbers and colours. I would often come downstairs to find the pair of them dancing around the living room to Daniel's favourite music. I'll never forget taking Theo to a music group in our local library when he was two. At the end there was some time for singing nursery rhymes and the children were told to ask for the nursery rhyme they would like to sing. After we'd sung The Grand old Duke of York, Humpty Dumpty and several others, Theo put up his hand and requested 'Don't Funk with my Heart' by The Black Eyed Peas. Daniel was literally rolling about on the kitchen floor when I told him about it later that evening.

Theo and Daniel shared the same hunger for adventure, Theo would always be game to join in the fun whether it was swimming in the sea, sailing, sledging, or rolling down a big hill. He was his father's son and the bond between them was very strong.

Once when Theo was just over a year old Daniel was working from home so I seized the opportunity to nip out to do an exercise class, leaving Theo with him for an hour or so. The friend that usually came with me had phoned to say she couldn't come that day as she didn't have childcare for her toddler. I knew Daniel wouldn't mind having them both so off we went, leaving the two tearaways in Daniel's capable hands. It was a very cold January morning and we came home to find Daniel's 'Gone to the Beach' sign hanging from the door handle. We wandered over there to find Daniel running about pretending to be an aeroplane with the two toddlers waddling behind him like penguins. He had layered them up so tightly in Theo's warm clothing that they could barely move their limbs. He'd been unable to find any gloves so had put a couple or pairs of Theo's socks over each of their hands. What I remember most is their rosy little cheeks and beaming faces, they'd had such an adventure.

Daniel and I had always talked about having two children. Theo's conception had been so surprising and easy that I assumed we would have another one as soon as we wanted to. At thirty-four I was aware that my fertility would soon decline, so after Theo's birth, we had agreed not to use contraception and to see what happened. When Theo was ten months old, I noticed that my period was a couple of weeks late. A pregnancy test revealed a very definite blue line and I felt both excited and apprehensive. I think that my apprehension was rooted in my bond with Theo. I felt a little sad that he would have to share me so early; he would only be nineteen months old when the second baby arrived. I visualised double buggies and jostling around the supermarket with two babies, and the more I thought about it, the more excited I became.

When I told Daniel later that day, he seemed surprised and quite blasé about it. We agreed not to tell anyone this time. We felt more cautious and needed a little time to get used to the idea of another addition to our family. A few days later I took Theo to play with some friends. Some of the other mums were discussing the idea of a second child whilst I sat quietly, nursing my delightful secret. I felt deliriously happy about it and my mind went into overdrive as I imagined another baby in my arms, thought of names and looked forward to telling our families.

Eight days after the pregnancy test, I began to bleed. It was late afternoon on a Friday so I didn't visit the doctor immediately. I tried to cling to some hope that it would be alright, but the bleeding continued into Saturday morning. I had no choice but to put a brave face on things, it was a busy weekend; we had the girls with us and Daniel's mum, Maggie, had also come to visit. Daniel's attitude was 'what will be, will be' but I felt knotted inside; I knew that my baby was slipping away from me. Around six o'clock on Saturday evening I miscarried. I felt distraught but Daniel didn't share my grief. He felt that the timing wasn't right and accepted nature's intervention.

I channelled my sadness into a preoccupation with becoming pregnant again. I loved being a mum and desperately wanted a brother or sister for Theo. And although Daniel didn't share my yearning for a second child, he cheerfully went along with what rapidly became my obsessive quest to conceive. He took responsibility for calculating our optimal fertility time according to my menstrual cycle and he agreed to give up saunas and limit his cycling to maximise his own fertility.

Practically, we were united on the issue but emotionally we were on a different plane. Daniel had three children already and felt fulfilled. But as more of my new friends announced that they were pregnant for a second time, my yearning for a second child increased.

In January 2008, four months after my miscarriage, I discovered that I was pregnant again. I had been buying pregnancy tests every month and using them if my period was so much as a day late, so I was thrilled to see a very faint blue line on the test stick and told Daniel immediately. His response was a cautious, 'don't get too excited, baby'. But it was impossible for me not to get excited; I felt relief and elation.

Less than a week after taking the test, I miscarried again. I put a brave face on it, but felt desperate. And once again, Daniel did not share my grief. I didn't tell any friends about the miscarriages or my desperation to get pregnant again because I didn't want them to feel awkward around me as they celebrated their pregnancies, so I felt very isolated.

In the wake of this second miscarriage, Daniel suggested that we get married. We had been engaged for almost three years but had simply been too busy to think about a wedding before. It seemed like a good idea and I welcomed the distraction. It was the end of January and we set a date for the third of May, which only gave us three months to plan the wedding.

CHAPTER SIX

I set off on the trail for venues, flowers and dresses. A friend and her son came with me and with two high-wattage toddlers in tow; there was no time for indecision. I had to make snappy choices.

We started with the dress. Choosing it was not a relaxing business. With my friend chasing the two tearaways round a very upmarket shop, I struggled to get in and out of dresses while avoiding their sticky fingers. I was told that three months was the minimum time scale in which to order a dress, which meant I had until the end of the week.

I ended up ordering a dress that bore no resemblance to the image of a sleek, white strapless gown I'd had in mind. I knew that Daniel hated convention and wanted to see me in a more alternative frock; he'd actually suggested bright purple or shocking red, so the classic white bridal gown was definitely out. But while I was open to a variation on the traditional theme, I also felt that this would be my one and only experience of being a bride and I wanted to feel like one.

In the end, in an effort to make us both happy, I chose a satin, champagne-coloured Grecian style gown, subtly encrusted with gold and silver beading. It flattered my figure and I felt it was both sexy and classy. Despite the rushed choice I was happy with it.

Meanwhile Daniel designed and printed the invitations himself. He took a classic Michelangelo reproduction of a naked Adam and Eve and imposed our heads on it. It was quirky, funny and very Daniel. We booked a ceremony in a beautiful stately home and a reception in a local pub and Daniel chose an Irish band. The preparations united us again. He loved any kind of social occasion so was very excited about the idea of bringing together all our family and friends. We wrote our own wedding vows and recited them to each other every night so that we would know them by heart.

Five days before the wedding it was my birthday. Daniel had bought me a huge framed picture; a black and white print by graffiti artist Banksy of a couple embracing in diving masks. It was a classic Daniel gift; quirky and alternative and I loved it.

On the morning of our wedding, I felt surprisingly calm and relaxed. After a week of fierce winds and heavy rain, it was a gloriously sunny and mild spring day and everything was in place; all I had to do was get ready. Daniel had gone to stay with Adam the night before, while I stayed at our home with Theo and my parents.

I was woken at the crack of dawn by a beaming Theo. I was used to it; at that stage he slept through the night but woke, like clockwork, at 5.30 every morning. Bleary-eyed, I fed him, made coffee and began getting ready. By nine a steady stream of people had begun to arrive. The hairdresser and make- up artist were followed by Ella and Hannah, who were wild with excitement about being bridesmaids.

Mum seemed to be carrying all the nerves that morning. She was worried about everything and anything and I was so busy reassuring her that I didn't have time to feel nervous myself.

Theo was slightly under the weather with a cough and cold and wasn't his usual happy-go-lucky self. I think he was feeling confused and unsettled with all the excitement and commotion in the house and he was uncharacteristically grumpy all day. I wanted him to eat and have a nap before our two o' clock ceremony but he refused both and then protested tearfully about my hair being put up and tried to pull it down. He wanted normality back.

Just before I left the house, I opened the small gift that Daniel had left for me the day before. It was a tiny silver charm of a squirrel and a poem that he had written about me, titled 'The Enchanting Running Girl'. I laughed, remembering how he often called me his 'little squirrel' because I was always tidying all the mess and clutter that he left all over the house.

As Dad and I drove to the venue in a snazzy white Beetle convertible that I'd hired as a wedding day surprise for Daniel, he turned to me and said, 'you know you don't have to go through with this, don't you? It's not too late to back out. You must do what your heart says is right.' Dad was genuinely fond of Daniel, they'd formed a strong bond; he just wanted to make sure that I was sure. I was his only daughter and he wanted me to be happy. I knew Daniel well, I knew he was a challenge but I knew we loved each other and were committed to a future together. I turned to Dad and said, 'I'm sure'.

As I waited outside the wedding hall in the stately home, I peeped in through the doors and felt overwhelmed by the sight of all our close family and friends gathered there. I could sense their anticipation as they waited for my entrance. Tania turned around and caught a glimpse of me. 'You look amazing' she mouthed and I smiled, grateful for her support. With my natural reserve, I was never entirely comfortable with being the centre of attention.

I had to time my entrance carefully because Daniel had decided to serenade me as I walked up the aisle. He had chosen Nat King Cole's 'When I Fall in Love, It Will Be Forever' and we'd rehearsed it to perfection. I had to start slowly walking when he was midway through the song, so that I would arrive by his side just as he finished.

It was a truly wonderful moment; walking arm in arm with my dear dad towards Daniel, who was holding Theo in his arms as he sang lovingly to me, his voice full of passion and feeling as guests around us reached for their handkerchiefs. Beside him, in their powder blue dresses, stood Ella and Hannah, both of them glowing with excitement.

We said the vows we'd written and exchanged rings and then Maggie sang us an Irish blessing. At the end of the ceremony, Adam began strumming his guitar and singing 'Let There Be Love'. After the first verse, the entire wedding party were out of their seats singing and dancing. It was a glorious start to a marriage, full of love and hope.

Later, at the reception, Ella and Hannah, with Adam's help, also performed a very sweet and touching song for us and Daniel, his father and brother, showmen all, entertained the guests with their music and hilariously comic speeches.

The whole wedding was a whirlwind of love and laughter and my feet were never on the ground. But while I loved it, there was a hazy, dream-like quality to the day. I felt as though I was spinning and it was intoxicating.

That night, Daniel and I left the reception and got a taxi to a quaint little guest house in a nearby village. Exhausted and full of champagne, Daniel soon fell into a blissful slumber but even though I had only drunk one glass of wine I was wired and stayed awake for most of the night. As I watched him sleeping beside me I felt totally in love with him, wholeheartedly committed to this man and full of hope and excitement about our future.

When I look back now, after all that has happened, I wonder if the hazy feeling that I had all the way through my wedding day was masking something else. Deep down, I did have a slight sense of unease. It was just a tiny sprouting bud that was easy to ignore. If I'd stopped focusing on all that felt so good and hopeful to examine it, I would, perhaps, have realised that something was not quite as it should be. But how could I have known then what the future held for us both? Could anything have prevented what unfolded, or was it all inevitable?

After the wedding, and our short 'mini -moon', life returned to normal. The week before our wedding I had visited my doctor to arrange to have my fertility tested. A simple blood test confirmed that I was ovulating normally so, at my request, Daniel agreed to have his fertility checked by a specialist in a private clinic. The results showed that his sperm count was extremely low and of poor quality. It was unlikely that we would be able to have another child naturally. I think Daniel quietly hoped that I would accept that we would just have Theo, but my desperation for a second child persisted. I began to look into the possibilities of IVF, which would give us a much better chance of conceiving and reduce the risk of further miscarriages, which were probably caused by Daniel's poor sperm quality. But Daniel refused to consider the idea. He had more pressing issues on his mind as he had narrowly escaped redundancy at work. It was a shock to him, he had believed his job to be completely secure, but now he became increasingly worried about the financial stability of the company he worked for. At the same time, our two-year fixed mortgage came to an end. Interest rates had substantially increased and the best mortgage deal we could find left us with an extra three hundred pounds a month to pay.

I tended to focus on what directly affected me, but Daniel had a much more global perspective and he had been predicting a worldwide recession and a slump in the housing market for some time. The previous year, when the housing market was still buoyant and prices had peaked, Daniel had insisted that we sell my flat in Hove and put the money into our mortgage fund. He loved our house more than I did but he knew that buying it had been a risk and was now frightened by the idea of losing it. We drew up spreadsheets and budgeted sensibly, aware that our income needed to stretch further. In order to generate more income, Daniel decided that we could convert our huge double garage into a bedsit to rent out. Unwilling to pay for an architect, he taught himself how to draw up the plans and successfully gained planning permission.

He was becoming increasingly unhappy and unfulfilled at work. He felt he was being undermined and devalued. He often brought these worries home with him and I tried to help, offering him strategies to deal with work situations. He coped with stress by escaping; he would kite-surf, go on sailing or canoeing trips and socialise more in the evenings with friends or neighbours. These activities helped to relax Daniel but they didn't unite us as a couple and tensions were developing. We were on a different page in terms of our feelings about a second child and our financial situation. I knew that money was tight but while Daniel had a job and we were managing, I didn't really worry, I had my head buried in the sand. It was Daniel who was able to see the bigger picture at that stage, not me. And he was right; a few months after our wedding the world plummeted into global recession and the housing market crashed.

In the summer after our wedding, we went on a six-day visit to Ireland. One of Daniel's cousins, Annette, was getting married just outside Galway and Daniel was very excited about showing me the place where he'd been born and had spent much of his childhood. I had met most of Daniel's Irish relatives at our wedding but he wanted me to get to know them better. I was looking forward to the trip too. We hadn't had a holiday since we moved into the house and we both needed a break. It would also be twenty month-old Theo's first time on an aeroplane so he was full of excitement too.

Galway was as charming as Daniel had described. He took me for a walk around the town to see the house where he was born and the house that had belonged to his grandparents. We stayed in a guesthouse on the outskirts of Galway where our hosts couldn't have been more hospitable and the first few days in Ireland were blissful. Daniel's relatives were friendly and welcoming and I could see where his warmth and sense of fun had come from. Ireland is very child friendly and everybody made a huge fuss of Theo, which he loved.

I was secretly feeling very happy and hopeful about our future too because my period was a few days late. Daniel forbade me from doing a test while we were away. He told me to just relax about it until we got home and I agreed, while quietly convincing myself that I was pregnant.

Annette's wedding was in a hotel, with a reception in a country castle. Daniel and Theo wore the matching suits they had worn to our wedding a few months earlier and looked very dapper. The wedding was lovely, but the next morning my period arrived, ten days late and very heavy. I suspected that it may have been another early miscarriage and I felt completely deflated.

After the trip to Ireland, Daniel realised how unhappy I was about the miscarriages. He explained that he wasn't against the idea of having another child but was concerned about how much IVF would cost and that if it failed I would want to keep on trying and it would lead to huge debt. We talked about his money worries and I agreed to take in a lodger, while he agreed that we could try IVF if I would promise to stop once the money ran out. We planned to raise the money by selling our lovely Betty and I calculated that it would probably cover three cycles. I agreed to accept that, if that didn't result in a pregnancy, it wasn't meant to be.

CHAPTER SEVEN

We both had heavy hearts as we said goodbye to Betty, but she had been sitting in our garage, neglected and unused, for over two years. We still had an awful lot of work to be done on the house and we knew that this would always be prioritised over doing-up Betty. We sold her for ten thousand pounds, enough for three attempts at IVF.

I was thrilled to be taking action over my inability to conceive, and now that we'd agreed to take in a lodger, Daniel was feeling less stressed. He built a lovely double bunk bed for the girls to share in Ella's room and we prepared Hannah's single room to rent out. Although I hated the idea of sharing our home, we were really lucky to find Kenny, a twenty three year-old student from Macau. He spent most of his time in his room phoning his lovesick girlfriend back home, but he emerged for meals and always made a fuss of Theo and I grew fond of him.

IVF is invasive and unpleasant. Your body is pumped full of drugs and artificial hormones to put your ovaries into overdrive so that they'll release multiple eggs, and inevitably you feel hormonal and uncomfortable. I didn't mind because I felt all the procedures took me nearer to having the child I longed for, besides which after the horrendous labour and birth I had with Theo, anything else felt like a piece of cake. It was the emotional roller coaster that IVF puts you through that I found so hard; the anxiety of taking the right drug at the right time and of injecting myself with hormones at a specific time each day, the constant uncertainty and the terrible wait to discover if I was pregnant or not. It was draining.

Daniel had to go to New York for two and a half weeks during the middle part of my IVF cycle, which meant I was doing most of it on my own. I got used to injecting myself and found it wasn't as bad as I'd thought, and I was monitored closely by the clinic. Luckily it was near the gym that I used, which meant that I could leave Theo in the crèche for an hour while I nipped into the clinic for blood tests to check that the hormone levels were right and occasional scans to check on my ovaries.

I was very aware of how much we were investing in this process. Though we had drawn up plans and agreements concerning our finances I still felt sick every time I wrote out a cheque to the clinic, aware that it would be money lost if it failed.

I was glad that I had Theo to keep me occupied during the whole process; he prevented me from getting too obsessed or stressed about any of it. He was approaching his second birthday and the day after the penultimate injection he had an early joint party with some of his friends in a soft play centre. It was boisterous and exuberant and just what I needed to take my mind off the whole process and to avoid feeling too nervous about the following day's operation.

Daniel and I were instructed to be at the clinic at seven thirty in the morning. I would be put under anaesthetic for the eggs to be collected but would be home later that day. I felt excited and hopeful. My parents came to look after Theo and we set off, me with Theo's scan pictures tucked into my bag for luck and Daniel wearing the dreadful liquorice allsorts man t-shirt that he'd worn at all three of his children's births. I was so touched that he had thought to wear it, it seemed to symbolise that we were doing this together and that he really wanted it to work.

Daniel was very jovial about his contribution to the process. Towards the end of my operation he had to spend a few minutes in a room alone with some seedy pornographic magazines so that my eggs could be fertilized in the lab straight away. The operation was quick and painless and afterwards I was monitored for a couple of hours before going home. I felt a bit sluggish and spaced out for the rest of the day but was otherwise fine. It was now a wait to see if any of the eggs had been fertilized.

A few days later we were informed that we had six embryos – a really good outcome. We were then faced with the decision about how many we would implant back into my womb. We only wanted one baby, but the more we used the higher the chance we had of a pregnancy. Surprisingly, Daniel wanted to implant two. He was looking at the statistics and thinking facts, figures and finances. We had a much better chance of conceiving a baby if we used two embryos but there was also a small chance that we could have twins.

I didn't want twins, I knew that would stretch us too much on all levels, and it just didn't feel right to me to implant two embryos when one wasn't wanted. Of course I desperately wanted one to survive, but implanting two felt as if I was willing one to die. It was a difficult decision but I wanted one baby and my gut told me to use one embryo and hope and pray for the best.

The choice of which embryo to use was easy; the embryologist had been phoning us regularly to let us know how they were doing and right from the start one of them was developing at a faster rate than all the others and seemed stronger. Decision made.

Daniel took the day off work to come with me for the implantation and afterwards I was told to try to keep still for a few hours, and to take it easy for the next two weeks, with no exercise or heavy lifting. Tricky, given that Theo was still not quite two and dependent on me lifting him into his high chair, cot and car seat. We arranged for my mum to spend the first week with me, followed by Daniel's mum for the second.

We were due to find out whether I was pregnant on November 27, which happened to be Theo's birthday. I had bought three pregnancy testing kits and put them in the drawer next to my bed, intending to leave the test until the evening so that the day would be about Theo. I planned an outing to the zoo with my mum and a few other friends. I had made a giant teddy-bear chocolate cake and the night before his birthday I put all his presents on the living room floor and Daniel and I blew up balloons and hung banners around the house.

I was looking forward to seeing the excitement on Theo's face when he came down in the morning, but in the early hours he woke up crying inconsolably and then vomited all over me. I cleaned him up and Daniel and I took turns comforting him until morning. We managed a few small interludes of sleep, but woke feeling exhausted.

Theo was uncharacteristically subdued all day; he just sat in a sea of balloons looking dopey and miserable. He wasn't even interested in opening any presents. I was so concerned for him that I forgot about the pregnancy test until I went to the loo and realised I was bleeding heavily. I felt gutted.

Daniel felt worse for me than for himself. He went to work and I phoned to cancel the friends who were coming to celebrate Theo's birthday with us. The whole day had become miserable. I spent the morning with Theo on the sofa watching television, so it was early afternoon before I got round to phoning the clinic to let them know that the IVF cycle had failed. The specialist nurse suggested I do a test, just to be sure.

I did, though without any of the usual excited anticipation. After five minutes, I looked down at the stick and couldn't see a line. I sat on the edge of the bath for a few more minutes; just staring into space and feeling hollow. I kept telling myself how lucky I was to have Theo, and just to focus on him and on Ella and Hannah. We were already a family; that would be enough.

When I glanced back down at the stick, I could see a faint blue line. I held it closer, trying to work out if it really was a line or if I was imagining it. I rang the clinic and they told me to come in for a blood test. As I lay in bed that night I tried hard to not get my hopes up.

The following morning Theo was back to his cheeky, boisterous self so I didn't get much time to dwell on what was happening inside me. When I got to the clinic I sat in the waiting area for some time. All around me there were couples on the emotionally draining quest for a child and I felt a pang of guilt that I was feeling so bereft and desperate when I already had a healthy little boy at home.

The blood test confirmed that I had the pregnancy hormone in my blood. However it would be a further three weeks before they would be able to scan for a heartbeat and until then we wouldn't know if the bleeding was a sign of a miscarriage or not. In the meantime, I could have weekly blood tests and if the amount of pregnancy hormone in my blood increased, I could feel more hopeful. I was delighted to hear this news, but it was all so inconclusive and precarious that I didn't dare feel happy or hopeful about it all.

I wanted to wrap myself in cotton wool, but with Theo to look after there was no chance of that. I got on with our usual routines and as blood tests each week confirmed the pregnancy hormone was still present my hopes grew. When the three-week scan revealed an unmistakable heartbeat I felt a flood of euphoria. It was a wonderful moment. We left the clinic clutching a black and white photograph of what looked like a tiny grain of rice.

Christmas, just two weeks later, was gloriously happy. The only fly in the ointment was Daniel's underlying worry about the recession. The housing market had crashed, companies were going bust and Daniel was concerned about his future. I tried hard to reassure him that we would be OK; he still had a job and there were no imminent signs that he would lose it. And if the worst happened, he would find another one. He was a capable, intelligent and resourceful man who had never been unemployed in his life.

Daniel loved being part of a big family, but he wanted and needed to be the provider. It was a role that gave him confidence and a sense of worth. That Christmas he was beginning to feel fearful that his role, and our security, was in danger. I didn't want to see it, I was blinkered by my own happiness and preoccupied with motherhood and home-making, but his fears were uncannily accurate.

Once I reached the half-way point in my pregnancy, I came off all the artificial hormones and felt so much better on all levels. The headaches I'd been suffering from subsided and I got my energy back. The twenty week scan reassured me that there were no problems and we discovered that we were expecting another boy. I was just so delighted to be carrying a healthy baby that I didn't mind at all what gender it was. Another boy was wonderful.

During the second half of my pregnancy it felt as though all the strains in our marriage were behind us. Now that Theo was older, the weekends with the girls were much easier. Daniel would include him in whatever they were doing and we were one family unit.

A couple of months before the baby was due, my old friend Lisa and her children, Brooke and Arney, came to stay with us during half-term. The girls were also with us and Lisa's children were a similar age to Ella and Hannah, then ten and seven, so they were all getting on well. Daniel offered to look after the five children for a few hours so that Lisa and I could go out for lunch and a walk. When we returned, they greeted us with a performance that they had been working on all afternoon. Daniel had typically got them all singing, dancing and playing various instruments; they put on a wonderfully entertaining show and were all beaming with joy and enthusiasm.

With the pressures that infertility had created behind us, Daniel and I reconnected as a couple and our relationship felt very strong and special. But I was aware that he was still afraid of losing his job and weighed down by our mortgage. Daniel had incredible foresight and knew that the company he worked for was struggling and he feared that the UK branch would be closed down. He talked about moving to a smaller home, but I didn't want to think about that while I was heavily pregnant. Daniel still had a job and I wanted to believe that he was just thinking the worst. He started looking for other jobs, but we both knew that there were none locally that would match his seniority and salary. A new job would almost certainly mean dealing with a commute to London and neither of us wanted that.

Daniel was clearly troubled, we would talk late into the night about his work stresses and I would listen and advise him, but when I look back I feel overwhelming regret that I didn't do more to alleviate the pressure he was under. If only we had moved house. Would it have made a difference? I'll never know.

It is comforting for me to remember how happy and close we were. Daniel was bonding with my bump, singing 'Caro Mio Ben' to it every night and getting excited by the idea of another son. Theo and Daniel adored one another and they would spend hours on the beach together in all weathers. I would watch them walk across the pebbles, hand in hand.

Daniel's herb garden and vegetable patch was another of his passions. He would take Theo into the garden to pick rosemary for Sunday lunch or strawberries for breakfast and to collect wood for the fire from the beach. They'd go out to the woodshed that Daniel had built and Theo would carry logs of wood back into the living room. I complained about the mess as they came in with their muddy shoes, trailing sawdust through the house, but I didn't really mind. Theo delighted in helping his dad to scrunch up the newspaper and lay the logs for the fire. They were close companions.

The final weeks of my pregnancy were blissfully happy. I spent as much time as I could having fun with Theo, aware that our relationship would change with a new baby around, and I made plans for Daniel's fortieth birthday. It wasn't until early September, five or six weeks after the baby was due, but I knew I would be too busy to do much after he was born. I wanted to give Daniel something special so I planned a big surprise party. I invited over a hundred of our friends and family – swearing them all to secrecy – and booked a buffet.

Ten days before the baby's due date, Daniel and I decided to go away for the weekend. It was very last minute but we realised it might be our last opportunity to spend time together for a while. The plan was almost derailed when Theo knocked a vase off the windowsill and gave his big toe a hairline fracture, but we left him with my parents, who we knew would spoil him rotten. Daniel had booked a hotel in the Oxfordshire countryside and it was stunning. We stayed in a little apartment next to a stream; it was very private and absolutely perfect.

Daniel took me round all the sights he remembered that his father had shown him as a teenager when his dad had worked in the city. And of course he took me punting, looking masterful and singing at full volume as he swung the punt along. It was a blissful weekend and just what we both needed.

Our second son, Milo, arrived in late July. This time I opted for an elective caesarean and there were no complications. Everyone was very calm and relaxed, until Milo arrived and screamed his lungs out as if he was protesting at this abrupt entrance into the world. The consultant held him up over the screen, and Milo peed all over him. Daniel and I couldn't help laughing and Daniel, once again in his liquorice allsorts man t-shirt, declared that he was 'a feisty fella'.

For me it was pure love, the moment he was handed to me. He was perfect, with a little scrunched-up face and a lot of thick, black hair. At seven pounds eleven ounces he was a good weight, but his body was long and thin, with skinny legs so that he somehow looked like a very malnourished chicken, so unlike our chubby and dimply Theo.

I asked my parents to bring Theo in to meet his brother that day; I wanted him to be the first visitor that we had.

He came into the room quite cautiously and glanced at Milo nonchalantly as he slept in the Perspex cot beside me. He didn't say anything but he glared at me with a look of betrayal that said 'How could you?' I'll never forget it. My relationship with Theo altered in that moment and I knew it.

I was discharged after two nights because the maternity ward was bursting. It was good to get home, but I still felt very sore and I wasn't going to be able to pick Theo up for six weeks, which I knew would be terribly hard for both of us. Theo was boisterous and we were all protective of Milo, who seemed so fragile next to his big brother.

Theo was furious with me for a long time. I tried very hard to do special things with him while Milo slept and I made sure I put him to bed each night and read his story, but the damage to our bond was deep. He would look at Milo and say 'put him back in your tummy'.

Thankfully Theo and Daniel became even closer during this time. Daniel had two weeks paternity leave and he spent almost every afternoon with Theo. They would go off on Daniel's bike, Theo sitting happily in a little blue seat on the front. He was utterly spoilt with far too many ice creams but I knew they were having fun together and that Theo was feeling special.

During his paternity leave Daniel decided to paint the outside of our house. I took the boys out for the afternoon and as we arrived home he came out to the drive to greet me with the words, 'we've had some freak weather; it's been snowing in the garden'. It was August. I marched out to the back garden to see what he was talking about and sure enough, virtually our entire garden was a vision of glistening winter white; poor Daniel had dropped ten litres of pure white paint from the top of his ladder. We both decided to laugh rather than despair about it.

A few days later, Daniel was informed that he was being made redundant. He had been expecting it for a long time, but it was still a huge blow and the timing was brutal. He was given a month's notice. He felt humiliated even though his job was one of many lost and it was only a matter of time before the whole company folded. The pressure on him was enormous, but he managed to stay upbeat and positive and put all his energy into finding another job and shortly afterwards he was invited for an interview with a major finance company in London. I knew it would mean a big change for us as a family and that the boys and I would barely see him during the week. But it seemed selfish to think that way, especially as there wasn't really an alternative.

The interview went well and he was asked to go to three more with various members of the company. A week before his birthday he got the call offering him the job. He put the phone down, fell to his knees, his hands together in prayer and said 'Thank you, God'. We were both tearful with relief. We were going to be alright.

Daniel's surprise party was a huge success. There were so many people in on my plans; friends and family who had been sharing the secret for two months, and nobody had leaked a word. My next door neighbours had their fridges full of alcohol and everyone knew exactly when to arrive.

Daniel's mum was given the job of taking him out for a long walk and then arriving back at our house at the right moment. Once they'd left my parents and I rushed about preparing the house and I finished decorating the cake that had been hidden in our garage overnight. It was supposed to be shaped like a boat in full sail but didn't turn out quite as I'd imagined; it tasted delicious though and the thought was there!

Pete brought Ella and Hannah over, they had also been keeping the secret for many weeks, the buffet was delivered and over a hundred guests arrived and hid in the kitchen and garden. The girls had been given the job of watching out for Daniel's return and Maggie did a magnificent job of getting him back at precisely the right time. As the kitchen door opened, we all shouted, 'surprise'.

The genuine astonishment and delight on Daniel's face was something I will always treasure. I am very thankful that somebody recorded the moment and I have it to cherish and share with the boys. A few minutes later, without prompting, little Theo came in from the garden and sang Happy Birthday. It was a lovely moment and Daniel was deeply touched.

The party was a success; children were playing all over the house and Daniel was the happiest I'd ever seen him. Five week-old Milo slept as he was passed around all the guests for a cuddle and Theo, sociable as ever, loved the occasion. A lot of the guests with children left in the early evening, but for Daniel the party was still in full swing. His father had bought him a saxophone for his birthday, Adam had his guitar and the whole family put on a musical performance in the back garden while the remaining guests sang and danced. I put the boys to bed and joined the party, thrilled to see Daniel so happy.

The following day was Daniel's last in his Brighton job. He returned early with his possessions in boxes. It was hard for him but he had a new job on the horizon and we both felt hopeful about the future.

CHAPTER EIGHT

Daniel hated his new job from the start. It consumed his life; he had to leave home at six-forty five in the morning and was never home before eight-thirty in the evening.

When he worked locally he would commute to work on his bicycle, or kite-surf, if the wind conditions were right. He had time to spend with his family in the mornings and time to socialise in the evenings. He had his vegetable patch and herb garden; he could go canoeing, kite-surfing or sailing and he had time to work on the house. All these activities kept Daniel's life in balance. He even had the flexibility of working from home if he needed to. He had worked to live and, even though he put a brave face on it, he found the new routine oppressive.

The office he worked in had no natural daylight, which he found especially difficult. He told me that at lunchtime he would walk to a nearby park and hug a huge oak tree. He felt trapped and miserable.

At home, he became angry and irritable. He was exhausted by the long days and the demands of a young family. When we had Theo Daniel would get up in the night and help me get him settled after I'd fed him, but it was very different with Milo. I didn't expect Daniel to help during the night, but both children were wakeful, so I was barely functioning on a very small amount of broken sleep. I tried hard to stay up to greet Daniel when he arrived home from work but had to collapse soon after, so we were barely seeing each other during the week and Theo and Milo didn't see their father at all except for Milo's 10pm bottle feed, which Daniel liked to do. Theo had not yet regained his sense of security after Milo's arrival and he was now grappling with the change in his relationship with his father too. After having Daniel at home with us for six weeks, Theo was now sorely missing him and every morning would ask, 'is it Saturday?'

The weekends were fraught too. The dynamics between the four children had become very strained since Milo's arrival; they were all in need of their father's time and attention, they became rivals and Theo's behaviour started to reflect this. He became overly boisterous, hyperactive and generally chaotic at home. He developed anxieties around food, refusing to eat all but a small selection of familiar foods, and was rough to other children. He was also jealous of the girls when they were with Daniel, and they probably assumed that Theo got more attention than they did. Resentments and tensions were setting in and our marriage was feeling the strain.

Every other weekend, when the girls were not with us, Daniel tried to make up for all that he had sacrificed. He would go kite-surfing, cycling or socialising with friends, but the result was that he spent hardly any time with me and the boys. I was on my own for most of the time with a new born baby and a demanding toddler and my resentment was growing too.

At the end of November we celebrated Theo's third birthday with a big party for family and friends at home. I knew he was really struggling with the way his family life had changed so much and I tried hard to make it special for him. He was still very jealous of his little brother, showing no interest in him and asking me to send him back or 'lose him'. I could see that he felt rejected and displaced and his behaviour was becoming increasingly challenging.

Theo was obsessed with cement-mixers, so the day before his birthday I spent hours making him a red and yellow striped cement-mixer cake. Ella also had a birthday in November and that year she had celebrated her twelfth birthday with a party at her mum's. She was a very mature twelve and I thought cupcakes, iced with sugar flowers and set on a lovely cake stand would appeal to her.

Daniel returned from work at about nine that evening, stressed and agitated; he had clearly had a bad day. I took him through to the kitchen to show him the cakes, expecting him to be delighted with my efforts. He was a bit of a caveman in many ways and liked me to be domesticated. I've never enjoyed cooking, it was always tedious to me, but I did make a huge effort for all the children's birthdays and decorating their cakes gave me a chance to put my dormant creativity to use.

Daniel took one look at the cakes and flew into a rage because Theo's cake looked bigger and more magnificent than Ella's cupcakes. He thought this was blatant favouritism and that Ella would be upset. I was hurt and shocked by his reaction. I had put a lot of thought into Ella's cakes and believed, rightly, that she would be pleased with them. I couldn't understand his anger. I look back now and can see that he was under immense strain and incidents like this were the first hint of the coming breakdown.

By Christmas Daniel's dissatisfaction with his job had come to a head. We spent it at home with Ella, Hannah and Daniel's mum, as we always did on alternate years. Daniel cooked a spectacular lunch and the girls helped with the preparations.

Daniel had fallen out with his mother over some heavy-handed advice he'd given her about the man she was dating, and he was short-tempered and irritable with everyone. It was a tense day and Theo absorbed it all and then acted it out. The combination of Daniel's short temper and Theo's increasingly challenging behaviour was explosive; Theo would test Daniel to the limit and Daniel would respond with impatience and anger. And as he found it harder to cope with the demands of his sons, he turned to his daughters. We were a divided family. Daniel spent most of Christmas week taking Ella and Hannah off on outings and I was left to look after Theo and Milo. Resentments were growing on all fronts. My parents came to spend the day after Boxing Day with us and, despite my best efforts to be positive; they could see I was struggling and unhappy. I asked them to take Theo home with them for a couple of days. It seemed wrong to ship Theo out as if he was the problem, but I could see how much he was struggling with all the tensions at home and I didn't know what else to do.

Daniel, meanwhile, was applying for other jobs. In early January 2010 he was invited for an interview by a new and upcoming internet company. The director was impressed by Daniel and he was offered the job. The salary was substantially higher and Daniel seemed excited by a company in which most of the workers were young and creative.

He was days away from the end of his probationary period, but he went to his current manager and told him that he'd been offered another job. His manager, who Daniel had not really liked, immediately offered to match the new salary and allow him to work from home on Fridays. It was a huge confidence boost; Daniel now had the choice of two, very senior, well paid jobs. He clearly felt pulled towards the new, more exciting role, while I felt that his current job was a much safer bet. It was a big, very reputable finance company, while the other company was very young and unknown and he would have to do another three months on a temporary contract.

Daniel couldn't bear dilemmas of any kind. He would normally just decide immediately. But he went into work the next day still unsure. When his boss pressed him for a decision he asked for a couple of days to think it over. His boss said that if he needed to think about such a generous offer, he could stuff it. The decision was made.

I did feel a pang of fear and regret when Daniel told me, but I did my best to focus on the possible perks of the new job. Daniel was excited by it and we all needed him to feel happier.

He threw himself into it and this time he got on really well with his manager. He was also happier in his working environment, which was modern, airy and trendy, and he was working with young, creative colleagues who inspired him.

The downside, for me at least, was that Daniel immersed himself in the social aspect of the job. Most of his colleagues were unmarried and childless, so they would work late and then spill into city centre bars for the evening. Daniel joined them, at first only once or twice a week but more frequently as time went on. I had hoped that his new job would bring us closer, but it did the opposite. The more I pleaded with him to come home, the more resentful he became.

Daniel had always texted or phoned me once or twice during the day. Often his texts were wonderfully romantic and I'd text back, asking him what he would like for dinner or I'd tell him something amusing that Theo had done. We had always shared our days, but now that changed. Daniel felt nagged by my attempts to get him to come home after work and he stopped answering my texts and calls during the day. He left for work at about 6.45am and often didn't get home until 11 or 12 at night and he was out of contact during that time.

For the first time since I'd met him, I began to question his faithfulness. He denied an affair and argued that the social scene was all part of the job, while I felt that he had bailed out of family life and was doing all he could to avoid spending time with us. I was even more outraged when I discovered, from our bank statements, that he was funding a lot of these nights out. There were large payments to bars and restaurants, but when I asked him about them Daniel maintained that he had to reward his team for their hard work. Until that point I'd felt totally secure in his love and loyalty to me. Now, I felt that we were disconnected.

It is easy, in retrospect, to see that this was another step along Daniel's descent into mental illness. The irrational anger, the need to socialise, the wild spending; he was becoming high. I sensed I was losing him, and I was, but I didn't understand what was really going on.

By the following April there were glimmers of improvement in our family life. One weekend Daniel spent time with the boys and then we watched a film together once they were in bed. I felt closer to him than I had in several months and he must have felt it too, because for the first time since he'd started the job he was willing to discuss the enormous strain that we had both been under during the previous few months.

He told me that he was finding his current job very stressful. He had a very senior position with lots of responsibilities and was feeling out of his depth. He had a good relationship with his boss, he felt valued and liked by him, but he had been given a lot of projects to manage as well as a staff team of thirty and he felt the amount of work expected of him was unrealistic. He only had a few weeks of his probationary period left, so we agreed that it would be best if he carried on and then talked to his boss about it once he was on a permanent contract.

Talking eased some of the tension between us. We had talked about the possibility of him working one day a week from home; he felt that his boss might well approve that in the near future. I began to hope that we would get our relationship back on track and look back on this time as nothing more than a very stressful period in our marriage.

Daniel had responded to my pleas for more family time and taken a day off for my birthday, which fell on a Wednesday. It was a lovely spring day and we spent a happy few hours at a farm with the boys. Daniel seemed almost his old self again. He gave me a lovely painting by one of our neighbours who was a successful artist. He knew I liked her work and he chose a modern landscape that looked very much like the area where we lived. I loved it.

The following weekend was our second wedding anniversary. I bought Daniel a white cotton shirt with a pale grey floral design on it and he bought me some pale blue cotton underwear. We decided to go out to a country pub for Sunday lunch. Money had been tight and we had prioritised renovating our house over everything else, so this was a rare treat. Everything felt hopeful; Daniel's probationary period was due to end that week and then the pressures on him would ease.

Daniel left for work as dawn was breaking the next morning, ready for the much anticipated appraisal with his boss. He wasn't really worried, he'd been working ridiculously hard over the past three months and he'd had lots of indications from his boss that he'd been pleased with Daniel's contribution to the company.

He arrived home at 8.30pm with a bottle of champagne in his hand and a smile on his face. All had gone well. He insisted that we go over to the beach to celebrate and as Mum was staying for a few days and the boys were in bed, we did. I sat with him on the rocks looking out to the sea. We both felt optimistic; once his contract was drawn up he could start to relax in the job a little more and in a couple of months he would ask his boss if he could work from home on Fridays. This would make a huge difference to both of us. Four days in London with three days at home seemed a much better balance.

Three days later Daniel arrived home in good spirits. My parents were staying the night, on their way to a holiday in Cyprus, and Daniel asked to take Dad out to the pub. I waved him off, but asked that he just make it a quick one as I wanted to see him and talk to him about Milo who was unwell with an ear infection.

They arrived home after eleven. I'd gone to bed but had been unable to sleep and when Daniel got into bed it was obvious that he'd been drinking heavily. He was talking very fast, mainly about how wonderful my dad was, but he also told me that he'd had a disagreement with his boss earlier that day. He had tried to renegotiate his workload and he'd done it in a heavy-handed manner. He knew that he could be like a bull in a china shop at times, so I suggested he go in the next day and eat a bit of humble pie.

That Friday morning I said goodbye to my parents and felt a bit bereft. They would only be away for ten days, but I was used to speaking to Mum daily, it was often my only adult contact during the day. My feelings of dependence on my parents were really a sign of how wrong things were at home and how much I had been struggling on my own with Theo and Milo. I was very unhappy but had not dared admit it to anyone, including myself. I just held onto the hope that the pressure would ease now that Daniel was through his probation. I also knew that I was chronically sleep deprived, with a new baby waking me every night and Theo still very unsettled. I hoped that all these struggles were going to become easier and that this was just a tough patch for us all. I couldn't have predicted that our lives were, in fact, about to implode.

The following day, Saturday May 15, we pottered around the house in the morning and then Daniel took Theo swimming in the afternoon. In the evening, we had a takeaway and watched a film together. I was glad to have time with Daniel and he seemed calm and relaxed. We went to bed happy and united.

I was aware of Daniel going downstairs in the early hours and when I was woken at 5.30am by Milo I was concerned that Daniel hadn't come back to bed. I went downstairs to find him working on his laptop. I asked what he was doing and he replied, without looking at me, that he was sending emails to work colleagues, that it was really important and that he had to do it now. I asked if it was really necessary to be doing this in the early hours of a Sunday morning. Daniel became very angry and accused me of being unsupportive, so I closed the door and left him to it.

He stayed in the office for the next few hours while I got the boys through their breakfast and morning routine. I heard him phone Adam and tell him that he thought he might lose his job and that he didn't think his boss could work with him as their personalities clashed. Now I was very worried.

I'll never know what happened that Sunday morning but it seemed that something had erupted as a result of that email exchange. Daniel was extremely tense and irritable when he switched off his computer. He said he was going to go to church and he took Theo with him to attend the Sunday school. This was something Daniel had begun to do more often; he found church nourishing and comforting.

Daniel had arranged for Adam to come over for lunch with his one year-old daughter Ava so that he could give Imogen a chance to rest as she was pregnant and tired. We were spending a lot more time with them now that they had moved out of London to a new home a few miles away from us. I was cooking a roast so I put it all in the oven and rang Adam to find out what time he would be arriving. Imogen answered and I told her that I was worried about Daniel. She told me that Adam was concerned too.

Daniel arrived back in better spirits. He was very enthusiastic about the service and was talking very fast and not making a lot of sense. I was trying to cook the dinner with Milo under one arm and I wasn't really listening to him, I was just relieved that he was less angry.

In hindsight I can see that he was slipping into mania, but it didn't enter my head to think of that at the time. I had a lot of experience of working in mental health settings, but this was not a patient; it was my husband, who was having some problems at work. I was worried about him but I didn't think for a minute that he was losing his mind.

After lunch Adam spent some time talking to Daniel in the garden. Adam was Daniel's best friend, the only person, other than me and his mum who he confided in. To everyone else, he was ultra-confident, ultra-capable, ultra-funny, Daniel.

I wanted to get the boys out so we decided to walk into town for tea and cake. The only café open was very small and going in with two buggies and three very young children was not a good idea. We ended up squeezed around a small table, trying to keep the children still and quiet. Daniel was talking in a very animated way and he knocked over his camomile tea, which spilt onto Milo's hand. I grabbed a screaming Milo from Daniel and put his hand into a glass of water. Thankfully it wasn't scalded, he stopped crying and Daniel mouthed 'sorry' to me.

We got out of the café and, after a visit to the playground, decided to head home. Daniel ran off across the grass with Theo while Adam and I followed with the buggies. Beyond the grassy field was a busy road with a pelican crossing. I watched Daniel hurtling towards it with Theo running along beside him, trusting that he would stop before he got to the road. But he didn't slow down, he seemed unaware that Theo, aged three and with no sense of road safety, was with him.

I left the buggy and ran after him; screaming at him to stop Theo. Daniel did grab Theo and then, still holding him, lay down on the pavement beside the crossing. I grabbed Theo, too shaken to register how odd and inappropriate it was that Daniel was lying spread-eagled on the pavement. He was laughing, and completely oblivious to my panic.

After Adam and Ava left, I got the children bathed and into bed. Daniel's euphoria seemed to have worn off and he had reverted to irritability. He did tell me that he thought he might lose his job and I struggled to take this in as only days earlier he had sailed through his probationary period. Then he turned on me and said that I had been unsupportive, making too many demands on him to help with the children and nagging him about his after-work drinks. I was very, very upset and felt unfairly attacked. I knew there was no point in putting up a defence while Daniel was in such an angry state. We went to bed in separate rooms.

CHAPTER NINE

I hadn't slept well and I knew that Daniel had been up during the night. I went downstairs in the early hours to find him at the computer and urged him back to bed. He went, but I don't think he slept.

I was downstairs giving the children their breakfast when he came down. Ignoring us all, he rushed about gathering his things, grabbed some toast and literally sprinted across the kitchen and out of the back door shouting, 'Gotta go!'

I ran to Theo's nursery that morning, with the boys in the double buggy. Crazy, in a way, to be running on so little sleep, but fresh air and exercise had always been my way of managing stress.

After the events of the past few days and his verbal attack on me the night before, I felt deeply unhappy and terribly worried about Daniel, his job and our marriage. When I collected Theo from nursery at midday his teacher, Mrs Hodson, told me he had been unhappy that morning, crying and asking for me. This was unusual for Theo, he rarely cried or clung to me and I was sure he must have been affected by all the tension at home.

An hour later Daniel called and he said, 'baby the worst has happened – I've been fired'. He was on the train heading home and for a split second I felt relief. That bloody job, that commute and the socialising that came with it were destroying our marriage. I preferred to lose the job and the income than our marriage and I hoped that we could all have Daniel back now. My heart went out to him, I knew he would be mortified, but he was on his way home where he belonged and I would help him in any way I could.

The boys and I greeted him at the door. He looked totally deflated, his manic mood gone. He was a broken man. He told me that his boss had taken him out to a café to tell him that he was 'not the right fit' for the company and as Daniel had not yet received a written contract his boss was legally able to dismiss him on the spot.

I suggested that we all go out for the afternoon, but Daniel wanted to make a start on looking for jobs. He did admit that, for a split second, he also felt relief, but he was clearly very worried and he kept apologising to me. He had been out of his depth in that job, it was unsustainable and destroying our family and Daniel knew that. But he was also very aware of the current climate in the employment market and the fierce competition for high-salary jobs. Daniel had no formal qualifications in IT, he was self-taught and although he had a lot of experience he felt like a fraud when he came up against other candidates with degrees in IT.

I took the boys to the park and left him to it. I felt shell-shocked; everything suddenly felt very insecure and I was acutely aware that I shouldn't spend any money, even on a cup of tea in the cafe. That evening Daniel stayed at his computer while I bathed the boys and got them ready for bed. It was lovely to have him at home and when Theo asked him for a bedtime story he seemed happy to do it. I was busy getting Milo to bed when I heard Daniel trying to coax Theo, who had spilt his water over himself, into another pair of pyjamas. Theo wasn't cooperating and I tensed, expecting

Daniel to lose his temper. I desperately didn't want that to happen, Theo was so happy to have his daddy home at bedtime. But Daniel didn't get angry, instead he started begging and pleading with Theo to get changed and I could hear that he was close to tears. I'd never known Daniel to be like that. I left Milo and took over.

When I came downstairs, Daniel was sitting on the bench in the back garden with his head in his hands. We sat together for a while and talked. Although I was worried I had faith in him, he was tenacious and very capable and I trusted that he would be able to turn things around. I hoped that losing this job might even turn out to be a blessing and he would find one closer to home. But although he tried to sound positive he was in despair and I knew that he felt he'd failed us all.

That night we went peacefully to bed together and drifted off to sleep, but I was awoken abruptly in the early hours of the morning by loud music. I went down to find Daniel typing away at the computer, thumping dance music blaring beside him. What was he thinking? We were all trying to sleep and sleep was a precious commodity in our house. I turned off the stereo but he was annoyed and told me to stop stressing. When I asked what he was doing he said he was sending emails to his former work colleagues warning them about various hazards in the working environment.

Suddenly the penny dropped and I realised that he was manically high. I knew the symptoms; it's easy to recognise them in patients; paranoia, delusional thinking and talking intensely at high speed. The next stage, grandiosity, followed after we went back to bed. He started telling me that everything was going to be all right, that we were going to make millions from media interest after he had informed them about his unfair dismissal. He told me to prepare myself for reporters camping on our doorstep. I asked him why he thought they would be interested in him and he said, 'baby, I'm the guy who kite-surfs to work, everybody knows me'.

I lay beside him, rigid with shock. He had, quite literally, lost his mind overnight. The man I knew and loved had been replaced by a stranger. My Daniel was gone and I never really got him back. Losing him was gradual; it began a long time before his death.

He didn't stay in bed for long; he was unable to stay still and was downstairs 'being busy' an hour later when I tried to get the boys dressed and ready for the day. I felt wretched, shaky and tearful and was struggling to hide it. As I dressed Milo, music blared again and Daniel danced around the living room with Theo. I phoned Adam and told him that Daniel was having a breakdown. He didn't seem as surprised as I would have expected and, much to my relief, said he would take the day off work and come straight over. He also offered to research our benefit entitlements as he knew we would be in dire straits.

As I was getting Theo ready for nursery, Daniel got hold of Milo and threw him up in the air like a beach ball. This was always his party piece and I was never happy with how far he threw the children, we'd had many arguments about it. But this time he threw nine month-old Milo almost to the ceiling and I could see he was out of control. Terrified, I snatched a startled Milo from him and hurried out of the front door.

As soon as we got to the nursery Theo started crying and clinging to me. He had always been confident and sociable, wanting to go and play with his friends but today he was a different child. I could barely hide my distress and Mrs Hodson, seeing the look on my face, knew that something was very wrong and asked me in. It was a small, private nursery run from her home, and parents usually just dropped their children at the door. But she got a member of staff to prise Theo from me and ushered me and Milo into her living room. I told her that Daniel had lost his job and that things were very tense at home. I didn't tell her that he had also lost his mind, I just couldn't, it was too shocking a thing to say. She was very kind and told me it had happened to her son-in-law. She assured me that she would phone me if Theo didn't settle after I left.

I got home with Milo just as Adam was arriving. I was enormously relieved to see him. We spoke briefly and I asked him not to allow Daniel to hold Milo. Adam looked alarmed, he probably thought I was over-reacting. We both knew that Daniel would never normally do anything to harm his children, but it was a different Daniel I had seen throwing Milo recklessly up to the ceiling an hour earlier.

Daniel greeted us with euphoria. He had been up in the loft digging out his memorabilia and had a large briefcase full of old photos and mementoes that he wanted to show us. He didn't question Adam's presence at our home at 9am on a Tuesday morning; he was in a different reality.

Adam obliged him and they went out into the garden together to look through the photos, but I could not indulge Daniel. I was feeling confused, angry and scared. How could he be so happy when we were in such a crisis? Where was the Daniel who had been so low and distressed by the loss of his job the previous day?

I knew Daniel was ill and urgently needed help. I also knew that he couldn't access any mental health services without a GP referral so I phoned the surgery, explaining that the appointment was for my husband whom I suspected was having a psychotic breakdown. The receptionist gave me an appointment for later that day and said she would ask a doctor to phone me beforehand for some information. The GP who rang was Dr Shank, a kind, gentle and patient doctor whom I had seen a few days earlier about Milo's ear infection. I told him that I thought Daniel was hyper-manic. He asked me about any previous history of mental illness and I told him the only thing I knew; Daniel had once told me that he'd had a brief drug-induced psychotic episode when he was 20.

To my relief, Daniel agreed to go with me to see the doctor. In the waiting room he was talkative and lively, cheerfully engaging anyone he could in conversation. I was embarrassed, and grateful to get into the doctor's office. Milo sat on my knee while Dr Shank asked Daniel questions. Daniel spoke very quickly, leaping randomly from subject to subject and asking the doctor about his personal life. He laughed a lot but became tearful when he was asked about losing his job. He was utterly devastated by this; it was the reality his mind could not face.

Dr Shank said he would refer Daniel to a community mental health service that would assess him in the next couple of days. He asked Daniel how he would feel about going into hospital and Daniel turned to me and asked if I could cope without him for a few days. Thinking about this now saddens me, Daniel always thought about his family first and he still felt useful and needed. He had lost his job but not, at that point, his complete sense of worth.

I got a call from the mental health team later that evening and managed to get an appointment for the following day. Their offices were a short walk from our house, in a building that we had probably walked passed most days, but had never noticed. We were ushered into a small waiting room and as we sat there I began to shake. I had been in places like this many times before, as one of the professionals. Now I was here with my husband, the man I'd always seen as so strong and together and who, up until two days earlier, had been in senior professional employment. It was hard to take in the reality of what was happening.

We were seen by a man who introduced himself as Carl and explained that he was an occupational therapist but that his role included initial assessments. He was a similar age to Daniel and had a very warm and friendly manner. He instantly put us at ease. He ushered us into a small room where we were asked a lot of questions about our lives together and what had happened in the last few days. We answered honestly and as we talked I realised how much stress we had been dealing with in the past few months. When I was asked to give an account of how our lives had been since Milo was born I became tearful, but Daniel was angered by my tears and began to tell Carl that I was an emotionally weak person and he thought I was cracking up. He said he had left his job in London because I hadn't been able to cope with the long hours and had pressured him to. He went on to rant about what a dangerous driver I was. I sat and listened and felt very, very alarmed by how distorted his world had become.

After talking to us together Carl saw us separately. He asked me about the safety of the children and Daniel's anger levels. I told him that Daniel had never been physically violent but that, as he had just witnessed, he could be verbally attacking and intimidating. I also told him that I was concerned about his reckless behaviour around the children. He said he would arrange for a member of the team dealing with family welfare to visit me.

Next we were invited to see Dr Anton, a consultant psychiatrist. He was a middle aged man with a gentle

demeanour, very personable and clear in his recommendations. He explained that he thought Daniel was suffering from an adverse reaction to acute stress. Daniel was
unhappy about the idea of taking any kind of medication
but he didn't put up as much resistance as I thought he
might. He was prescribed a mood stabilizer and Dr Anton
said it might make him drowsy in the mornings and would
probably take four to six weeks to take effect. That felt like
an age; how on earth were the children and I going to live
with Daniel in his current state for four to six weeks? In the
meantime he would have regular appointments with Carl.
None of it felt enough to deal with the immediate crisis,
but I did feel more hopeful that Daniel was having a stress
related breakdown and, with treatment and rest, would get
well again soon.

Later that day, I started looking into which benefits we
might be entitled to. We were both hard working professionals and it felt humiliating to be requesting claim forms over
the phone. I phoned my mum in Cyprus and told her what
was going on and she sent texts to my brothers, who both
phoned later that day and offered to help in any way they
could. They both lived close to my parent's in Wiltshire. I
knew that my older brother Tom, who was a single parent,
would be busy with his seven year old son Oscar so I took
up my younger brother Sam's offer to take a few days off
work to come and help. Sam worked for the local council
as a sports development manager, often putting in far more
hours than he was paid for, which meant he was occasionally able to take some time off at short notice.

I was desperately worried about Theo, he was clearly
absorbing all the stress and knew that something was terribly wrong with his father. I had told him that Daddy wasn't
well but this had angered Daniel, who told him that Mummy

was lying. Poor little boy, he must have been so confused and frightened.

The shock of the last few days hit me, I couldn't stop shaking and was unable to eat; my stomach was in knots. I was relieved that Sam was coming; I needed help shielding the boys from what was happening. He arrived later that evening and Daniel greeted him with the words, 'I'm not cracking up, you know', before disappearing for a bike ride.

The following few days seemed a little easier. Daniel wasn't spending very much time at home with us, he would get up and go out in the morning and I didn't know where he was most of the time. He wandered around Brighton, buying clothes, CD's and books, visiting churches or going for cycle rides. He would usually come home around five. He didn't look for jobs when he was high. He was in another reality, where he wasn't worried about unemployment or financial matters. He was still very grandiose and insisting that he would make money through his creativity. It was hard to not feel resentful about his happy-go-lucky mind-set. I was worried sick about our finances and acutely aware that we would lose the home into which we had both put our hearts and souls.

In the evenings, Daniel would wander out and find a neighbour's door to knock on. He would come home in good spirits and tell me about our wonderfully hospitable neighbours. I felt embarrassed, wondering if they could tell that he was unwell, or if he was giving them the story that I was the one having a breakdown.

It was exhausting and alarming to be around him. He was losing things on a daily basis; his keys, wallet, bag, CD's and so on and he would get very anxious about the lost item and then very angry with me, convinced that I had thrown out whatever he was looking for.

One afternoon I left him with Theo while I made a phone call. I returned to find Theo jumping up and down on the table on the balcony, a few inches from the railing and a two-storey drop. Daniel was encouraging him and laughing. Heart pounding, I threw my arms round Theo. After that I didn't dare leave Daniel alone with either of the boys.

Sam stayed for a couple of days and did much to shield Theo and Milo from the enormous tension pervading their home. Theo spent the afternoons with Sam which freed me up to fill in benefit applications and I managed to arrange a mortgage break. When Sam left he told me to call if I needed him. I was worried about the weekend ahead but my parents were due back the following Monday evening and Adam had offered to come and stay on Saturday night.

It turned out to be a gloriously hot weekend. Daniel didn't go out wandering, he attempted to spend time with us but it really was impossible. He had become very authoritarian, criticising every little thing that I did. That Saturday it was the way I hung the washing on the line that didn't please him. He began to show me the correct way of pegging it out, which was infuriating since he was not doing anything at all to help me around the house. I didn't react because I knew how angry he could become and I didn't want the children to witness it and in any case, there was no reasoning with Daniel.

I was relieved when Adam arrived at about midday. He was the closest person to Daniel and had a very calming influence on him. He had lunch with us, and then he and Daniel went for a walk while I stayed in the garden with the boys. When they came back Daniel wanted us all to go to the beach so that he could take his canoe out. We did go, but it quickly became unbearable. Daniel became very bossy and angry, shouting at Theo and calling him a pain in the arse. I reminded him tersely that Theo was three years old which simply ignited his anger further. I put the boys in the buggy and left. Adam helped me to get the buggy back up to the road and said, kindly, 'Don't worry about how Daniel is treating Theo, Louise, it won't last and children are resilient'. I snapped, 'Children are not resilient Adam, they are easily damaged' and walked down the road with tears streaming down my face.

When we got home, I got on with getting the boys fed and Adam bathed them, while Daniel played loud music and announced that he wanted to go and watch a band playing in a local pub. He was trying to persuade Adam to go with him. Once the boys were settled, Adam rustled up a stir-fry. It was lovely for me to be cooked for, I'd been struggling to eat all week, but the wait to go out was making Daniel agitated.

During the cooking the frying-pan handle broke which enraged an already agitated Daniel and he became angry with his brother. As we ate Adam and I both tried to reason with him but he just became more and more irrational. He clearly saw us as enemies conspiring against him. It didn't matter how calmly we explained that we loved and cared for him; to him we were persecutors. Adam and I exchanged a look of mutual despair and worry. We could both see how unwell Daniel was. He was intent on going out so Adam reluctantly went with him. I stayed at home, crying. In desperation I phoned Sam and told him how dreadful the day had been and he said that he and his girlfriend Katie would come the next day.

In the morning Daniel was full of joy, grinning like a Cheshire cat. He had been looking forward to Sunday all week as he was planning to go to church, which had become vitally important to him in recent weeks. He said he had ambivalent beliefs about God and religion but he enjoyed singing in the choir and the sense of community he felt there.

After breakfast I took the boys with me to the shops where Theo had an almighty meltdown. He wanted to choose the milk himself and picked up a full fat bottle, while I was try-ing to put semi-skimmed in our basket. He became both angry and heartbroken at the same time, there was no paci-fying or comforting him, his distress just had to come out. I was aware that other people in the shop were observing his uncontrollable tantrum, but all I could see was how dis-turbed he was. I felt helpless. Thankfully when we got home Sam and Katie had arrived and the atmosphere lifted. Theo was thrilled to see Uncle Sam and rushed to him with open arms. It was the start of Sam's role as the antidote to the boys' crumbling relationship with their father. His warm and loving relationship with them distracted from their pain and confusion and gave them some of the things that they were losing. Katie, a PE teacher, had met Sam through their work and was already very much a part of our family, she was also warm and loving and an enormous support, as was Adam, who was the only person who was able to calm Daniel.

Daniel and Adam went off to church and Sam and Katie played in the garden with the boys while I made spaghetti Bolognese for lunch. We ate in the garden and had some much needed respite from all the tension. Sam and Katie had to leave in the early evening and I was grateful to them for keeping both the boys shielded and happy.

My parents arrived back the following day, shocked by what had been happening to us. In the ten days that they had been away our lives had been turned upside down. They agreed to stay for a few days, to give me some rest and to offer what support they could to Daniel. They were deeply fond of him and couldn't comprehend how enormous the change in him was. But Daniel, still manically high, was oblivious to the distress and concern of everyone around him.

CHAPTER TEN

D aniel's high lasted for about six weeks after which, as his medication began to take effect, he appeared to gradually re-enter reality. For about a week to ten days it seemed almost as if he was back, before his mood plummeted into a deep, relentless depression.

At that point Daniel became very distressed about his unemployment and our financial prospects. He started obsessively applying for jobs, spending up to ten hours a day on his computer. In his mind, the problem was all about unemployment; if he could just land a job, everything would be fine again.

Nobody could have tried harder to gain employment in a very harsh climate. Daniel would get excited about each job he applied for, imagining that he already had it and he did have interviews for some very good jobs, but he was not offered any of them. This was new territory for Daniel. He had a natural charm and confidence that had always swung him the job in the past. But that had been when he was well. Now he was going to interviews severely depressed, desperate and faking confidence, and it showed. It was always a terrible knock when he wasn't successful, pushing him even deeper into his depression.

Within a few weeks his anxiety became crippling. He was worried about all the things that were wrong with the house and convinced that we would never be able to sell it. He was worried about food being out of date, about the sea being polluted and of course, about money. Outside it was worse; he would get anxious about driving, about the boys getting dirty and about being in crowds of people or around loud noises. Mostly he avoided going out, leaving home only to attend his mental health meetings or interviews.

Throughout this time Daniel saw Dr Anton and Carl every couple of weeks. Daniel had a good relationship with Carl and was very disappointed when he left the team and was replaced by Nathan, a community psychiatric nurse.

When Dr Anton told Daniel he was suffering from bipolar disorder I wasn't surprised. I was aware of the main diagnostic criteria for bipolar; an extreme high mood followed by an extreme low mood or vice versa. It didn't seem hugely important to me what label they gave his condition, I just wanted him to get better. But Daniel was shocked and upset. It challenged his whole identity, he couldn't accept it and he hung onto the idea that if he could just get a job, everything would be alright.

In July it was Milo's first birthday. I've always felt that first birthdays are special, as babies develop so phenomenally in a year. Milo had grown from a new born 'blob' as Daniel put it, to being a little person, running around and full of character. For months I had been hoping that by his birthday Daniel would be back at work. I still thought that the nightmare we were living through would be a blip, a build-up of stress that we would look back on as a terribly tough time. I clung to the hope that Daniel would soon be back to his old self and happy in a job closer to home, even if it meant him earning less and us moving house.

In reality he was very low on Milo's birthday. I had organised a picnic at a local farm for friends and family, but I didn't know if Daniel would be coming or not. In the morning he decided that he did want to come and I admired his courage, knowing that he was feeling ashamed and humiliated in front of our friends, who knew that he had lost his job and was having a breakdown. When I asked if he was sure he could manage it he said, 'What kind of a bastard doesn't go to their son's first birthday party?' It was an ordeal for him but he wanted to be there for Milo.

It was good to get out of the house and the children enjoyed the day immensely. Daniel paired off with Roger, the only other dad to come along. He made a huge effort and seemed to cope well with the day and I hoped that getting out might have lifted his spirits, but on the way home he started getting anxious about missing time from his job search and as soon as we got in he retreated into himself.

The day after Milo's birthday Adam and Imogen had a baby boy, Oliver. Daniel was delighted for his brother but with two children under eighteen months, it meant that Adam would now have far less time to spend with Daniel. And he was seeing less of the girls too. Ella and Hannah were still coming every other weekend, but just for an afternoon rather than the whole two days. Daniel wasn't well enough to do much at all and I couldn't cope with looking after all four of them and him on my own. The dynamics between the children had become very difficult; they were constantly bickering and vying for attention. Theo was still intensely jealous of his new brother whose arrival probably seemed like the cause of all that had gone wrong in our family. The girls probably thought that Theo and Milo were getting much more of Daniel than they were, but in fact he was barely getting out of bed all week and was too unwell to engage with any of us. From Theo's point of view the girls got the best deal because when they visited, Daddy got up and tried to join in.

I was so worried about Theo's increasingly chaotic and challenging behaviour that I contacted Ann, a play thera-pist who had been recommended by a work colleague. I knew Theo was struggling emotionally and needed help and we started seeing Ann fortnightly, as I couldn't afford to take him weekly. Ann worked privately from a little ter-raced house. I warmed to her immediately and knew that she was going to be a rock. She had a warm and generous spirit and she was clearly experienced and confident in her work. I stayed for most of the sessions and the four of us, Theo, Milo, Ann and I would be on our knees playing with every kind of toy possible in a small but cosy playroom. Sometimes she would spend time alone with Theo and I would enjoy some respite with Milo in a café down the road.

We all loved our visits to Ann. It was often utter chaos but she was always able to make sense of the chaos and she helped me to feel that the difficulties the boys and I were facing were perfectly normal, given the context of what was happening at home.

A few days after each session, Ann would set aside a time for a phone call in which she would offer me insights and advice on managing the boys. She did all this at low cost knowing that we were in financial crisis. I felt that she com-pletely understood all the turmoil that I was experiencing in addition to helping both the boys. She really was a life-line at a time when I was at risk of cracking myself.

Daniel was like an empty shell, physically present, but barely communicating. One day, aware that a house move was now inevitable he said he was going to start clearing out the loft, which was full of clutter. I took the boys to the park and left him to it, but when we got home, Daniel was on his hands and knees checking the carpet for shreds of glass. He had been dropping items down the loft hatch and something had hit the Banksy picture he had given me for my birthday, just before our wedding. The glass frame had smashed into what seemed like a million pieces and Daniel was desperately upset and worried that he would miss a shred of glass and the boys would get hurt when they tumbled about on the carpet. This incident reinforced his sense of uselessness and I felt that it was a terrible omen, symbolic of our hopes and dreams, our relationship and our happy future literally shattering before us.

All the children were very disturbed to see their father so unwell. Theo, the loudest and most challenging, bore the brunt of Daniel's intolerance and would spend most of the time on the naughty step. I worried that he was becoming the family scapegoat, but the truth was that all the children suffered. None of them were getting what they needed and I was stretched to my limit.

Despite this, because our finances were becoming increasingly tight, I took a part-time job contract with a previous employer, working in a medium secure unit for people with severe mental health problems. Of course it was too close to home, but it was the field I had been working in for ten years, and it was nice to be in the role of a professional for a short while each week and to have a distraction from my despair.

Mum came to stay with us for two days a week to look after the children, so she saw first-hand the tensions and strains in our household. Despite her own health problems, she was a fantastic support – I don't think I could have got through those months without her and the rest of my family and as Daniel had always been close to them he was happy to have them around.

On Daniel's birthday, in September, he was extremely low. The previous year he'd had such a happy time at his surprise party. Now he was 41, and our lives had changed beyond recognition. He wanted to stay in front of the computer, but I insisted that we go out and try and escape all the misery for a day. I packed a picnic and persuaded him to come out with the boys and me to a farm for a few hours. He got into the car reluctantly and sat silent, as I drove with the boys chattering excitedly in the back. Five minutes into the journey, we stopped at traffic lights and he leaped out of the car saying, 'I can't do this'. I was very concerned and disappointed, but I carried on with the outing for the boy's sake. Daniel didn't return home until that evening and all he would say was that he had been, 'out wandering' and needed some space.

The following day he continued with the feverish job hunt which had been going on all summer. It was as if there was no other meaning or purpose to his life. He was a desperate man, but while we all needed him to get a job, everyone but Daniel could see that he needed to get well first. Day after day he would spend up to ten hours in front of the computer. And he did get some positive responses; agents called and he managed to sound confident and professional when he was talking to them.

In late September a job came up that looked perfect for him. It ticked all the boxes; not too far away, the right salary and a role he'd been in before. When he was given an interview he became very excited. He poured all his energy into preparing for it and when he was invited back for a second interview he was buoyant, his depression suspended. He talked as if the job was his; he had even planned his train route to work.

The more excited he became, the more I worried. I wanted to share his optimism but I was scared about what would happen if he didn't get it. His second interview was on a Friday and by the following Thursday morning there was still no news. I was due to take the boys to my parents' for the weekend, as Dad and Sam both had birthdays around that time, but I didn't want to leave Daniel alone when we hadn't heard about the job.

I phoned Nathan to tell him of my concerns about Daniel's vulnerable state of mind and what would happen if he didn't get the job. Nathan was dismissive and told me not to worry. But later that day Daniel heard that he hadn't got the job and I could see that he was totally crushed. He wouldn't talk about it at all, but I saw him in the bedroom writing in his journal.

I asked him to come with us for the weekend but he refused, insisting he would be alright. I felt uneasy about leaving him, but Mum had to get home after she had been with us providing childcare whilst I worked. The boys were in their pyjamas ready to snuggle down in the back of the car for the drive and the bags were in the boot when I went upstairs to get my handbag and saw the journal Daniel had been writing earlier that day. Something made me look inside. The entry for that day was a suicide note written to his brother asking him to look after me and the boys after his death.

Shakily, I called Mum and showed her what I had found. I knew I couldn't possibly leave, so I told Daniel that we weren't going after all because I had a headache and felt too ill to drive. We arranged for Dad to come and collect Theo and Mum and when they'd left I told Daniel that I had seen the journal and he admitted that he had planned to jump from Beachy Head the following day. He also confessed that when he jumped out of the car on his birthday he had gone to Beachy Head, to check it out. He had been contemplating suicide there ever since.

I stayed up all night, scared that if I slept he would sneak out, and in the morning I phoned Nathan, who asked us to come in straight away. We took Milo with us and the four of us sat in an interview room while Daniel insisted that he felt differently now and had no intention of taking his life. I hadn't warmed to Nathan over the phone and in person I found him detached, inefficient and unhelpful. He seemed very blasé about the suicide note and unwilling to take any action. He appeared to accept Daniel's assurances and was happy to let him go. I was flabbergasted. I had expected them to hospitalise him, and if they weren't going to, I wanted some help.

I had heard about a crisis team that offered an alternative to hospital. I asked Nathan about it and he said that Daniel 'didn't meet the criteria'; he wasn't sick enough for them to take him on. I reminded him that if I hadn't found the note he might well be at the bottom of Beachy Head by now, but he insisted that Daniel no longer had suicidal intent.

I was furious. I told Nathan that I wouldn't leave until he got us a referral to the crisis team. Faced with the prospect of me and a baby in the building all day he agreed to phone them and to my relief they said they would visit us at home the following day.

In the morning two women from the crisis team arrived. They were informal and friendly and they sat with us on the sofa and chatted. It all felt surreal; the women cooed over Milo and Daniel was as hospitable as always, yet here we all were discussing, over tea and biscuits, his plan to kill himself. He admitted that if I hadn't found his journal entry he would now be dead. It was too frightening to take in.

The two women went out to their car to talk and came back soon afterwards to present us with a 'care package'. A member of their team would visit Daniel at home daily and he would be referred to a psychologist for an assessment and fast-tracked for counselling. We both felt there was just a glimmer of hope that he would now get the right help.

The crisis team's visits helped, but they lasted for a week and were then decreased to every few days and he was discharged soon after. They felt that Daniel was less vulnerable, but I knew that his mood was still extremely low. He was still totally immersed in job-hunting and every rejection was devastating for him. He was rapidly losing confidence in himself and began to say that his whole career had been fraudulent, based purely on luck and deceit. Every time his phone rang, he would sprint to it and my heart would sink when I heard his dejected voice.

The psychologist visited and said that she felt Daniel needed to take the emphasis off job-hunting. She suggested planning a more structured and varied day and asked me to help him, each evening, to come up with a timetable for the following day. I wondered where on earth she thought I would find the time to do that, and I knew that Daniel would resist. Nevertheless, we agreed and did attempt it for a week or so, timetabling exercise, meeting a friend, spending time with the family, meeting Adam for lunch, going for a walk, visiting a church and so on with only two hours allocated each day for job-hunting. But the reality was that all of these activities required a degree of motivation that Daniel simply didn't have. I would try to cajole him, but it was futile, he could not focus on anything other than finding work.

His sense of self-worth, built on his work success, evaporated and his relationship with the children, especially Theo, continued to deteriorate. Theo and Daniel were so alike, live wires but also deeply sensitive. As Daniel began to loathe himself, he saw in Theo a mirror image and his intolerance intensified. Theo absorbed all the tension in the house and acted it out in increasingly disturbed and challenging behaviour and it became a vicious cycle.

One morning in mid-October I left early for work. As usual in my lunchtime break I phoned Mum to see how they all were. She said the children were fine but that she was worried because Daniel had gone out a couple of hours earlier and not returned.

Daniel rarely left the house when he was very low except to attend his mental health appointments, so my immediate thought was that he had gone to Beachy Head. I phoned him and got no answer. When I called again he answered the phone and said, 'baby, I've got to go into hospital for a while, are you OK with that? I'm sorry'. He was on a train with the manager of the crisis team who had collected him from Beachy Head and was escorting him to a psychiatric hospital.

I phoned the crisis team and they told me that somebody had seen Daniel at the cliff edge, looking distressed, and had phoned the police. An officer went to find him and helped him to phone the crisis team. I got the details of the hospital that Daniel was in and said that I would visit later that evening. How I managed to stay at work that afternoon, I don't know, but I didn't feel I could tell my colleagues what was happening at home and I didn't want to lose my job, so I put on my professional head and got through it. I reassured myself that at least Daniel was safe. On the hour-long journey home, I cried all the way.

After the boys were in bed I headed for the hospital where a staff nurse ushered me into an office and told me that Daniel was under close observation. I found him playing table tennis with other patients. I was stunned to see him being active and sociable, but once we were alone together he became very anxious. He was feeling ashamed and guilty and kept saying sorry and that he didn't want me to see him in hospital. I started to cry at the thought of him coming so close to taking his life. They were tears of relief that he was still here and was now being looked after. But my tears just added to his anxiety, he started pacing the room and told me to go home. Without arguing, I left. I could see that my presence was making him feel worse. He felt mortified by the idea of being in a psychiatric hospital and could just about deal with it if he kept it totally separate from his life at home.

On the way home I phoned Tania. She had married a lovely man named Marcus and had two children. They had moved to Dorset, so I didn't see her often, but we spoke on the phone and she had been a huge support, listening to the whole dreadful saga as I poured my heart out each week. Her husband Marcus had become a good friend of Daniel's and he came on the phone to say that when Daniel was well, he would offer him a job in his recruitment company. This was good news, it was what Daniel desperately needed, and I hoped it might provide a lifeline for him.

It was good to have a break from looking after Daniel at home, from constantly worrying about what he was doing, having to supervise him with the boys and trying to moti-vate him and lift his spirits. Living with a severely depressed person is draining; the gloom settles like a mantle over everyone in the household. An oppressive atmosphere had become the norm in our house and I felt as though I was struggling to pull Daniel out of the black hole he was in whilst trying to keep my footing and not slip in myself.

He settled into the hospital regime, running in the morning and playing table tennis and chess with the staff.

He was getting a break from job-hunting, from the stresses of family life with a baby and a toddler and from all our financial worries and, free from the pressures, he was slowly getting better. His mum and brother visited him frequently and I took Theo and Milo in to see him three times a week. Daniel was always pleased to see them, and enjoyed introducing them to the staff, he was proud of us. But in the family room he would sit on the sofa looking awkward and vacant while I was on my hands and knees entertaining the boys.

Daniel had not been sectioned, he was a voluntary patient and was free to leave at any time and after two weeks he came home, insisting that he was now better and ready to face the world. As I drove him home, his anxiety and tension were palpable, as was his intense irritability. He criticised my driving and cursed other motorists for the whole 30-minute journey. As soon as we got home Daniel rushed inside to tend to his plants. He became angry that his precious lime plant was looking dry and accused me of neglecting it. It was hard for me to conceal my disappointment and I was wounded by his complete indifference to Theo and Milo, who had been so excited about Daddy coming home.

He began pacing the kitchen with his head in his hands, looking very distressed and fearful and I was terribly worried that he was now back under my watch when he was so clearly still very unwell. After I got the boys to bed we talked and he admitted that he had come out of hospital against professional advice. He had so wanted to be well and back home, he hated the idea of being in hospital, although the reality was that it had been good for him.

The following morning I phoned Nathan and let him know that Daniel was not coping at home. Nathan arranged a meeting with him which resulted in Daniel coming home, packing his bags and returning to hospital. I was proud of him for finding the courage to return, it was the last place on earth that he wanted to be.

Once again he began running, playing table-tennis and chess during the day and we talked every evening on the phone. The boys and I continued to visit him three times a week and I took Ella and Hannah in too. Daniel was ambivalent about this, he wanted to see his girls but it upset him that they were seeing him in hospital. All six of us crowded into the family room and although the atmosphere was thick with unspoken emotion, the children sat on the floor and played. The girls thrashed out some tunes on the organ, read to the boys and helped them with the train tracks and Daniel was touched that his family were all there.

When the time came to leave, he looked agonised and Ella also looked desperately troubled. She was twelve, old enough to understand what was going on, and she was also deeply sensitive and adored her father. She hovered by the doors and for a second I thought she was going to run back to him. As we walked away, I put an arm around her but she stiffened. She didn't want to be comforted. It was all so dreadfully sad and shocking. Daniel had always been the life and soul at the heart of our family; it was incomprehensible to all of us that he was here, so vulnerable, fragile and shrunken.

In the weeks that followed, Daniel was committed and studious about getting well, keeping up his exercise and his cognitive behavioural therapy. One afternoon when we were all in the family room, I noticed that he seemed more involved with the children; he tenderly lifted Theo onto his lap and read him a story and got down on the floor to help the boys make a train set. His eyes were changing too, the sparkle I loved so much and which had first drawn me to him, was coming back. I felt full of hope.

He stayed in hospital for six weeks and before being discharged, he came home for an afternoon, then a day and then a weekend. This gradual transition seemed to work well and when he finally came home, the day before Theo's fourth birthday, he appeared to be so much better that, for a little while, it really did seem as though we had the old Daniel back.

CHAPTER ELEVEN

For the next few weeks Daniel seemed strong, positive and hopeful. He was grateful for Marcus' job offer but he knew it would mean a lower salary and relocating to Dorset so he threw himself back into job-hunting and managed to set up an interview for a very good job for early January. I was delighted that for the first time in eight months, he wanted to be more involved with the children. He started by taking Theo over to the beach for ten minutes and graduated to taking him swimming, to a soft play centre and, when we woke to an overnight fall of deep snow, sledging down the beach. It was thrilling for Theo to have his daddy back. Daniel took over reading his bedtime story at night and began to share the early mornings with me, allowing me to lie in some days. It was blissful.

One evening, just a few days before Christmas, I was wrapping Daniel's present when it hit me how close we had come to losing him and I became overwhelmed with emotion. I went downstairs to find him, put my arms around him and told him that I was so relieved and grateful that he was still here. I asked him if he could imagine the Christmas that we would be having without him. He said that he could now see that it would have devastated everyone but that at the time his own pain had felt too unbearable to live with and he hadn't been able to see any other way of freeing himself from it. He had felt he was a terrible burden to everyone who loved him and had been convinced it would be better for us all if he just disappeared. He said it was like being in a very dark tunnel with blinkers on. We hugged and he said that he never, ever wanted to feel that low again.

That brief, poignant conversation has played over and over in my head many times since. At the time I felt reassured that Daniel was past the nightmare and was recovering. I couldn't have known then how brief the respite would be.

Daniel always preferred to be at home at Christmas, with everyone coming to us. He was happiest being the host; king of his palace. He liked all celebrations to be in our home and if we were invited anywhere, he would often suggest that they came to us instead. I found this exhausting, so when it was my turn to choose what we did, I always opted to go to my parents. I relished their help and support, but for Daniel Christmas at my parents' house was difficult and he seldom concealed his misery. He found their house small and cramped and the village that they lived in oppressive and uninspiring. Because of this we usually only spent Christmas and Boxing days there, but this year I was feeling tired and was battling a throat infection and Milo had been ill with another ear infection, so I really needed a break. I told Daniel that the boys and I would be staying on and that he could stay with us or spend some time with his family. He decided to visit Adam and Imogen who would be staying close by with Imogen's family, and then go to see his mother in Dorset. He said he would return to collect us on December 30th.

By the time we got to Wiltshire on Christmas Eve I had become aware that Daniel was not as well as I'd hoped. He was irritated by the interruption to his job-hunting and was snapping at Theo and finding excuses to avoid being around the children. On Christmas day he became annoyed when Theo played with his new toys too loudly, disrupting his attempts to watch the television. I could see Theo's hurt and I felt protective of him and terribly disappointed. On the surface Daniel appeared to be his old jovial self, so it was hard for us all to understand why he was so disinterested in, and irritated by, his children. Later I came to understand that he was still very ill and was simply unable to cope with family life.

He left on the 27th and when he returned he brought his mum, who travelled back to Sussex with us. On New Year's Eve, Maggie left soon after breakfast to babysit for Adam and Imogen, while I spent the day unpacking and trying to find places for all the new toys. That evening, after the boys were in bed, Daniel and I watched a tacky psychological drama. He was always able to escape with television and watching it with him that evening gave me a rare feeling of togetherness. We went to bed before midnight; both too exhausted to stay up and see in 2011.

I woke on New Year's Day with a vicious sore throat. Despite a course of antibiotics, the infection I'd been trying to fight off was back with a vengeance. I knew the root of it was stress; I was extremely tired and run-down.

Later that morning Adam arrived with two year-old Ava and Maggie. Ella and Hannah arrived too, full of excitement. Daniel had been looking forward to seeing the girls, who were going to sleep over for the first time in eight months. It had been hard for them to see Daniel morose and introverted, so unlike the carefree father they had known before, but now they too believed he was much better and they were looking forward to staying with us.

I had planned an outing to a quaint nearby town; just to look around a castle, have a walk and then have tea and cake, so I was disappointed that I was feeling so ill. Adam and Ava left before lunch, and Maggie and Daniel offered to take the children to the castle and give me a rest. I knew it would be a big thing for Daniel to take all four children out; he hadn't done that in a long time, but as Maggie was with him I put aside my unease and agreed.

A couple of hours later they were back, and the tension that hung over all of them was palpable. Daniel was clearly enraged and it soon became apparent that he and Maggie were not on speaking terms. Milo's buggy did not come back with them and Theo was being overly boisterous and chaotic, no doubt disturbed by the toxic atmosphere. I had no idea what had happened and it wasn't the right time to ask, so I tried hard to keep things jolly as we sat down for tea. Ella joined me in my attempts to lighten the atmosphere and after the meal, while Maggie retreated to her room and Daniel to the TV, I managed to get the boys through their evening routine.

Once they were in bed, I tried to piece together what had happened. Maggie was feeling hurt and told me she understood how hard it was to live with Daniel whilst he was ill, while he launched into a tirade against her. It was Ella who, diplomatically avoiding getting anyone into trouble, gave me the fullest story. She told me that after they had been to the café, Theo ran off which had alarmed them all. It seems that Daniel felt this was Maggie's fault and he had become very angry. I imagine he was frightened by the incident and the whole outing was too much for him, it would have been a horrible realisation that he was unable to look after his children. I never did find out what happened to the buggy but Daniel was clearly not as well as I'd thought.

Over the next few days I felt him slipping away. He was physically present but his mind and spirit were elsewhere.

When he was well he and I were close, we were companions and partners, working through things together. But as his mental state deteriorated, his connection to the present, to his family and to me, ebbed away. I tried so hard to keep him with us, but I couldn't reach him.

In the early days of January, as his behaviour became increasingly odd and inappropriate, I began to suspect that he was becoming high again. I went back to supervising his interactions with the boys closely; the brief moment in time when they were safe with him had passed.

One evening Daniel announced that he was going for a run. I was pleased; running had helped his state of mind when he was in hospital, but he had stopped after he was discharged. Off he went, promising to be back in an hour.

Three hours later, at 10pm, there was no sign of him. I tried calling him, but his phone was switched off. This was confirmation, beyond doubt, that he was hyper-manic again and I felt heartbroken. Why was this happening? Why hadn't his medication kept him stable? I lay in bed waiting for him, wide awake. Around midnight I heard him come in and he was not alone, there was another male voice. I could hear them in the living room, talking about kite surfing and looking at our family photos. I felt very vulnerable with a stranger in the house and sat at the top of the stairs in my pyjamas, guarding the children's bedrooms like a lioness.

Finally the man left, with Daniel seeing him out like an old friend. Relieved, I slipped back to bed. The following morning Daniel told me that the man had been a taxi driver who had brought him home. Unable to pay the fare, he had invited the driver in to give him one of his surfing kites. He didn't know where he had been for the evening, dressed in his running shorts and vest, and he saw nothing unusual or risky in inviting this man into our home late at night or giving him one of his treasured kites.

Over the following days, as Daniel's grandiosity returned, along with alarmingly raised anger and irritability levels, I felt utter despair. We were back to square one of this horrendous journey and I didn't know if I could go through it all again. My own health was suffering; I still couldn't shake the throat infection I'd had over Christmas and the asthma that hadn't troubled me for almost thirty years had returned so badly that I was dependent on my inhaler. I felt I was suffocating.

Just as it felt that life could not be any harder, Mum was diagnosed with a brain aneurysm (a bulge in a weakened blood vessel). She had been suffering from double vision and headaches for four years and specialists had told her this was a mechanical problem rather than a neurological one, but at the end of 2010, an optician who examined her eyes disagreed and wrote to her GP, which resulted in a referral to an NHS neurologist. Brain scans revealed that she had a large aneurism pressing on vital nerves in her brain. As she still had private health insurance, she was referred to a private neurological hospital in Oxford. The whole family was desperately worried; if the aneurysm ruptured, it could be fatal. She would possibly need surgery, but we would have to wait to find out. I felt very conscious of the worry that my parents felt over what was happening to Daniel, and I hated adding to Mum's pressures in this way and felt deep concern for her.

By late January all Daniel's self-doubt was gone; he had lined up two job interviews in London for the following week and he was buoyant and overly confident that he would be successful. He was going to stay with his father and stepmother and I asked him to stay on there after the interviews for a few days. It was exhausting constantly worrying about where he was and what he was up to, especially as by this time I was barely sleeping. Daniel seemed happy to agree. I felt bad that he knew that I needed a break from him, yet in his buoyant mood nothing appeared to bother him. He took his saxophone, with the intention of having a good old sing-along with his dad. He hugged us all before he left and I asked him please to remember his medication and not to be tempted to drink alcohol. He looked into my eyes and said, 'of course'.

When we spoke on the phone each evening he sounded very distant. He seemed to be out and about, catching up with old friends and socialising and I was worried because I knew this meant that he was probably drinking. I asked him not to spend too much money; we were living from hand to mouth, but he assured me that he wasn't spending much and had not touched alcohol.

On the fourth evening I had a late phone call from Adam. Their father had rung him to say that Daniel was in a bad way. He hadn't taken any medication to London, had been binge-drinking all week and had vomited in his father's home. Daniel's mental health had apparently totally deteriorated, Adam thought he was psychotic and his relationship with his father was strained.

I was deeply alarmed. Adam said Daniel would be heading home in the morning, but I knew I couldn't have him home in that state. After a sleepless night I gave the boys breakfast and put them in front of the television before phoning Daniel. As diplomatically as I could I told him that I knew he'd had a bad week and had not taken his medication and asked if he would go straight to the Community Mental Health Unit when he got off the train.

To my relief he seemed receptive. Goodness knows what he was feeling but he seemed to know he needed help. Then he paused. 'Who's that?' he said, 'I can hear a man with you'. He must have heard the voice of one of the children's television presenters and in his paranoid state believed I was entertaining a lover. He became furious and refused to listen to my explanation, insisting he was coming straight home to see what I was up to.

I was very frightened. His anger and paranoia had escalated dramatically. I dropped Theo off at nursery and then tried to phone Nathan. When there was no answer I put Milo in the car and drove to the unit. I knocked on the door in tears. I had Milo in my arms and he was picking up on my distress and howling. I was ushered quickly into a room where I was seen by a female duty officer I hadn't met before. I told her the situation and said that I was frightened and that Daniel needed to be in hospital to be stabilized. She explained solemnly that it was a very serious thing to do to take away somebody's liberty. Of course I knew that, it tore at my heart to be begging to have Daniel sectioned, but I honestly felt there was no alternative. She told me it wasn't possible and suggested that if I felt afraid of Daniel I should go home and change the locks and then call the police if he caused any problems. I looked at her in disbelief. She was telling me to kick him out. It was an outrageous suggestion.

I said I wouldn't do that. I didn't want to cause him distress; I wanted to help him get better.

Reluctantly, she agreed to phone Daniel and ask him to go straight to the unit when he got off the train. I doubted he would agree, and even if he did, what could she do if they wouldn't hospitalise him?

I left in despair and phoned the psychiatric hospital where Dr Anton worked and I was told that he was in meetings. Back at home I felt I had run out of options. No-one was listening, and Daniel would be home soon. I felt a strong sense of protection towards the boys and knew that they couldn't be exposed to Daniel in his current state, he was desperately unwell and I didn't know what he was capable of doing. I was very scared.

Weeks later his mother told me that he'd phoned her twice during those three days in London expressing extremely violent thoughts. Hearing this confirmed what I had known instinctively at the time; that Daniel, who before his illness would have done anything to protect me and the boys was now the danger we faced.

I felt I had no choice but to leave and take the boys to the safety of my parents' home.

I ran upstairs and packed clothing, toiletries and the children's bedtime comforters into a couple of bags. I picked Theo up from nursery and headed for Wiltshire. Theo was very aware that something unusual was happening. He knew that we didn't normally go to Grandma and Grampy's house without me talking about it beforehand. He kept asking me 'why are we going?'. I told him that Mummy needed a rest and that Daddy needed some time at home to get better.

It was a huge relief to get to my parents' house. My parents took over, feeding and playing with the boys, who immediately settled in the calm environment.

Daniel had gone to the unit where a different psychiatrist saw him. This psychiatrist phoned me after their meeting and said that Daniel had admitted that he hadn't taken any medication since he'd left hospital at the end of November. He had referred Daniel back to the crisis team, who would be caring for him at home. I was horrified. For the previous six weeks I had thought Daniel was taking his medication and recovering, while, believing himself to be well again, he had simply discarded it. No wonder he was in such a bad state.

I called Daniel, who was at home and very angry that we'd left. I explained that I wanted him to go back into hospital and take his medication. He told me loftily that he didn't intend to take any more psychiatric drugs. He was grandiose and paranoid and said that he would comply just enough to keep the professionals off his back and was clever enough to do just that. He was very, very unwell and unable to see it.

The following day I wrote to the mental health teams explaining that I had temporarily left our family home, to keep our children safe. I explained the risks that Daniel presented to the children when he was hyper-manic and I detailed several incidents that had occurred during his last manic phase that had put the boys at risk. I said that we wanted and needed to return to our home as soon as possible and requested that they consider hospitalisation for Daniel while he posed such risks to his children. I sent copies of the letter to Dr Anton, the crisis team manager and our family GP, Dr Shank. Dr Shank phoned me the day that he received the letter to check on our welfare and alerted social services to our situation. Neither Dr Anton nor the crisis team responded. A few days later, I received a phone call from social services. I explained that I had taken the boys to stay with my parent's to protect them from Daniel's illness but that I wanted him to be treated in hospital and for us to return home. After that brief phone call they made no further contact.

The crisis team were, as far as I knew, seeing Daniel at home twice a day. Although they, along with Dr Anton and Nathan, had been instructed by Daniel to not give me or his family any information, I stayed in contact with all of them. Friends who went to see Daniel kept me informed and told me that he was burning candles in the house day and night

and told them that I had gone away to have a 'boob job'.
I told the crisis team that I was worried he would set fire
to the house or harm himself in some way, but they didn't
appear to take my concerns seriously.

Daniel and I still spoke every day. I told him that I wanted
to come home, but needed him to take his medication and
stabilze first. He was delusional and veered between begging me to come back and telling me he would never need
to work again as he would find a wealthy new woman to
live with. I felt helpless, frustrated and stuck. How could I
go home with Daniel in such a bad way? Why wouldn't the
mental health team take him into hospital?

Daniel told me that he was never going to leave our
house, that he wouldn't agree to sell it and that he planned
to stay in it until it was repossessed. He said he had been
far too generous to his first wife and that he wasn't going to
make that mistake again. He was hurt and angry and I was
his target.

I began to understand that the crisis team viewed our
situation as a marital dispute. No doubt Daniel was informing them that I had left him and that we were divorcing
and it seemed they were accepting his version of events and
encouraging him to protect his rights and hang onto the
family home. Daniel had told them that I worked in mental
health and I believe that this caused some members of the
mental health teams to feel threatened by me or to view my
input as that of a know-all. Their assessment of my relationship with Daniel was grossly inaccurate; it appeared that
they did not view Daniel as being a risk to himself or others
and my concerns were often dismissed. In one telephone
call to a member of the crisis team I was grilled about my
job and my knowedge of the Mental Health Act. It was clear
that this person suspected me of reporting my concerns

about Daniel in an attempt to get him sectioned so that I could have the house.

The injustice of this was deeply hurtful and painfully frustrating. I wanted Daniel sectioned because I knew that he was spiralling out of control and I was frightened for him. I had a terrible feeling that something really dreadful was going to happen. He was heading towards catastrophe, but no-one was listening to my fears.

CHAPTER TWELVE

I was terribly worried about money. We had been living with Daniel's unemployment for nine months and were just about keeping our heads above water. The boys and I were living as frugally as possible, but I was afraid that Daniel, formerly so wise and practical about money, would blow the little we had left.

I could see from our statements that he'd spent an awful lot during his few days in London, so I asked the bank about putting a limit on withdrawals from our joint account, or even cancelling his card. I was told that I couldn't do either without his signature unless I had a power of attorney, which would mean seeing a lawyer.

One cold winter afternoon I took the boys to a nearby town, just to get them out and to give my parents a break. We went to the park and I wanted to take them to a cafe but when I stopped at an ATM for some cash, the machine gobbled up my card.

I was stunned. We'd had £6000 in our account when I'd last checked, the remains of our savings, that we were using to top up our benefits and my earnings.

I managed to see an on-screen balance. There was nothing left. I felt furious with Daniel.

The next day I went into the bank and made sure that my wages, our tax credits and the child benefit were paid into my account. To do this I had to formally state that we were separated. I hated doing that, it wasn't what I wanted, but I had to think of the boys and our survival. Daniel was on self-destruct and I was trying to minimize the damage.

Later I found out that he'd spent the money on a seemingly random list of things that included a motor bike, a helmet and leather clothing, an electric guitar, a crossbow and a sewing machine. I felt desperately sad. This was so unlike Daniel; always so financially astute and careful with money. This was the man who used to monitor our gas and electricity expenditure each day to ensure that we were living within our means. He had always taken care of the finances and I'd trusted him to look after us. His whole sense of self worth and his identity, pride and dignity depended on his role as our provider. When he lost that, he lost himself.

With a heavy heart, I went to see a lawyer. I knew that I had made myself and the boys unintentionally homeless and it seemed that Daniel was determined to keep the house; I needed to know where we stood. I was told that because the interests of the children always come first, I could take out an order which would mean that Daniel could be forced to leave the house within days. I was also advised to file for divorce as soon as possible as this was the only way that I could separate myself financially from Daniel.

I couldn't do it. I loved and cared for Daniel and desperately wanted him to get well. Making him homeless and confronting him with divorce was only going to add to his turmoil. And besides, I didn't feel that our marriage was over. I wanted Daniel back, I wanted our life back, and I still hoped that might be possible.

I really had no choice but to stay at my parents house and ride it out. I had no idea how long it would take for Daniel's mood to alter or how much longer he would continue to self-destruct. I knew that we would lose our home and I had no idea where or how we were going to live. I started obsessively looking into estate agents' windows, wondering where on earth the boys and I would end up. Theo was due to start school in six months time and I'd put a lot of care into finding the right one for him. Now I didn't know if we would be back at home in time or not. I'd put him into a pre-school near my parents, but I didn't know if I should now apply for a school there too. Everything was so uncertain.

It was a deeply frightening and unsettling time. Daniel was like a loose cannon, hurtling out of control and I had a dread, an intuition perhaps, that something terrible was going to happen. I continued to speak to Daniel every day, trying constantly to gauge his mental state. If I couldn't get hold of him, I feared the worst. I knew he wasn't suicidal when he was high, but I was afraid that he'd have an accident riding his motorbike recklessly or set fire to the house or in some other way injure himself.

Throughout this awful time I continued to work two days a week. I would leave the boys with my parents and commute back to Sussex; staying overnight with a friend, Clare or, if she was away, Helena. It was exhausting but I couldn't afford to lose my job. I was working with people who were sectioned because of the risks they posed to themselves or others. The only way I could manage it was to put on my professional head and separate it from my personal life. With the exception of two close colleagues, no-one at work knew about my situation.

The two to three hour commute was physically exhausting. I knew that I looked underweight and drained and I relied on a lot of coffee to get through the day. I was aware that I was just about surviving both physically and emotionally and so began to see a therapist, Roger Squier, for some support and guidance. This gave me a space in which I could pour out my turmoil, enabling me to compartmental-ize it so that I could continue to function.

One day I decided to pop back to the house after work for some of our things. We had left with a couple of bags, hoping to be away for just a weekend. We needed clothes and I felt that the boys needed some familiar toys and books around them.

I chose the time when I knew Daniel would be seeing his counsellor, Tuesday evening at 6pm. I found the house in a terrible state; dirty and messy, with scorch marks on the walls where he'd had candles constantly burning. I felt desperately sad, but I didn't dare stay for long. I rushed about filling two large bags with clothes and toys. I had also brought two empty cardboard boxes to fill with photo albums. I had always loved putting together albums of our special times; our wedding, holidays, the children's land-marks. Daniel would tell me that I was wasting the planet's resources because the photos were on the computer, but I loved them. I piled them all into the boot of the car, along with the boys' baby memory boxes. I feared that something terrible was going to happen and was trying to salvage some precious items from the potential wreckage.

Just as I was about to leave I heard Daniel's key in the door. He was home early. I was rigid with alarm, but he seemed pleased to see me and greeted me warmly. We sat down in the kitchen to have a cup of tea and I asked about his treatment. He said he wasn't taking his medication and had no intention of ever taking it.

I changed tack and asked him if we could put the house on the market, we couldn't possibly afford the mortgage payments. Daniel became agitated and his whole demean-our changed. I knew that he couldn't bear the idea of losing our house and all that it symbolised to him, he saw it as a connection to me and the boys. I think selling it felt like a very public display of his failure, besides which he knew that his being in our home gave him power and I imagine he was feeling utterly powerless about everything else in his life.

He began accusing me first of throwing away his coats, then of squandering our money on a 'boob op' and finally of refusing to come home because I had found somebody else. He put his face up against mine, his eyes wild and menacing. He seemed possessed. He laughed angrily and said 'I smell fear'.

He was right, I was terrified. Trying to appear calm, I said, 'you're right Daniel, it's too early to sell the house, I'm sure you'll get a job soon'. I suggested he make us some more tea while I went to get something I'd left in the car. He was suspicious, but he let me go. I leaped into the car, locked the doors and started the engine. Before I could move the car Daniel appeared, he hit the back of the car and as I pulled out of the drive he held his hands out as if to say 'why?'

I was staying at Clare's and when I arrived I found furious texts from Daniel, accusing me of being insane. There were also a couple of messages from Mum; she'd had a feeling that something was wrong. I rang and reassured her, but I was left very shaky. Daniel was very sick and he was dangerous, he desperately needed help – why was no-one doing anything?

Clare was kind and supportive that night and the following morning I left at 7am for the hour-long drive to work. When I arrived I phoned Daniel to check that he was alright. He asked me why I had left the previous night and I told him that it was because he had seemed so unwell that he frightened me. Again, I asked him to start taking the medication and to co-operate with the mental health services. I was expecting a defensive reaction but this time he appeared to be listening. Perhaps he had scared himself too.

An hour later I slipped out of work to sit in my car and make a phone call to the crisis team. The team member I spoke to questioned me about exactly what had happened the previous night; did Daniel physically hurt or intimidate me? Did he actually say that he would kill or hurt me? Had he been violent? Of course I answered no to all of these questions. Daniel didn't lay a finger on me. I explained that his behaviour was extremely intimidating and threatening, that he'd wanted to frighten me and that he had appeared psychotic and out of control but I felt that I wasn't being taken seriously.

I had no choice but to get on with my day at work before the two and a half hour drive back to my parents' house. It was always so lovely to arrive back there after my night away each week. The boys would be bathed and in their pyjamas, happy and full of laughter and so pleased to see me. They were having a lovely time being spoilt rotten by their grandparents and I would read them a bedtime story while Mum prepared some food for me. This homecoming was a real moment of happiness in the turmoil that was our lives.

The following day I received a call from a social worker in the Community Mental Health Team; someone I hadn't spoken to before. She told me that they had attempted to section Daniel the previous day. I had always felt that Dr Anton took my input seriously and he, along with a police officer and this social worker had assessed Daniel and all agreed that he should be sectioned. She told me that Dr Anton was worried about my safety and she urged me to stay away. However, a second independent psychiatric opinion was needed, and the psychiatrist who assessed him later in the day felt that he did not meet the criteria. The social worker told me that she had been present both times and Daniel had presented completely differently in each assessment. In the assessment with Dr Anton he had been angry and paranoid, confrontational and intimidating and had refused to agree to take his medication. With the second psychiatrist he had been calm and charming, talking about his 'wonderful wife and children'. He had agreed to take his medication under supervision every day and not to ride the motor bike. He would be seen by the crisis team twice a day and if he broke the agreement he would be sectioned.

I felt bitterly disappointed. I knew that once he started taking his medication he would inevitably have an almighty low after this high phase and I felt that it would be far safer for him if this mood drop could be managed in hospital. As ill as he was, he was a very clever man, always one step ahead of the professionals. It was a cat and mouse game for Daniel and he was winning. It was no surprise to me that he was able to pull the wool over the eyes of the independent psychiatrist but Dr Anton had been his psychaitrist for almost a year and knew him well. If he felt that Daniel needed to be hospitalised, why wasn't the second psychiatrist supporting this? It seemed that the decision was based not on the experience of people who regularly saw him or on his recent mental health history, but purely on how Daniel was presenting in that brief meeting.

I continued to phone Daniel daily and less than a week later he told me he had just been to London on the motor bike to see an old friend. I phoned the crisis team. He had broken the conditions of the agreement, so should surely now be sectioned. Unfortunately, the phone was answered by the team member who had formulated a view of me as a bitter wife wanting to get her husband out of their home by any measure. He simply said, 'thank you for informing us' and hung up. Later I learned that Daniel had been warned to not ride the bike again and that was it. I believe that if Daniel had been sectioned at that point, so that the inevitable low that followed the high could be properly managed, his death would have been prevented. But no-one was listening.

CHAPTER THIRTEEN

A couple of weeks later I had a strong sense that Daniel's mood was coming down. I knew that he had been taking his medication under supervision in a form that melted on the tongue and was impossible to hide, and in our calls he sounded calmer and more reasonable.

As he came back into reality he was deeply remorseful and he pleaded with me to come home with the boys. I decided to go and see him one Tuesday evening after work before I considered taking the boys back home. He was pleased to see me, he'd tidied the house and got some salads for us to eat. He was reasonable and talked about our financial situation and how we could resolve it and I felt completely safe with him.

We agreed that we would have to sell the house and I told him that when we did I wanted us to live separately until he was better. I wanted him to have his own space in which he could concentrate on getting well, and I wanted to have my own space with the boys; stable, peaceful and shielded from Daniel's illness. I would still support him and we could see each other daily, but I didn't feel that I could take any more of his illness or put the children through it any longer. The boys and I would be better off financially if I claimed tax credits as a single working mother and Daniel could claim benefits until he was well enough to work. I had reached the end point of my endurance and I could see how much his illness was damaging our boys. I needed to draw a line. Daniel understood and agreed. He said I could take the equity from the house and buy a small flat, in our joint names, and he would claim housing benefit. I felt terribly sad, I didn't want to hurt him, I just wanted to find a way to cope and to care for the boys.

A week later, at the end of February, I took the boys home. My parents were deeply concerned about this decision. My dad, who usually took a neutral stance and who always encouraged my independence in decision making, openly voiced his fears about me taking his grandsons home. He could see that they were happy and stable and was worried that they would go back into a very tense and unpredictable environment. And he was worried about me too. I had arrived at my parents house two months previously looking thin, exhausted and strained. But I was now feeling physically and mentally stronger and I knew the time was right to go back. I had prayed a lot in the preceding weeks, asking God for guidance and it felt like the right decision. I am now so pleased that we did go home then. I will always be thankful that we were there, with Daniel, for his final weeks.

When we arrived home he was pleased to see the boys and he made an effort to be with them. A couple of hours later we had a meeting with Dr Anton and a member of the crisis team, so we left the boys with Mum, who had come back with us to help. As we walked to the meeting I could see that Daniel was struggling and he admitted that he was feeling very low and hopeless. In the meeting, of course, he presented a different version, saying that he felt alright. But I voiced my concerns about his plummeting mood and Dr Anton increased his anti-depressants. The crisis team member was the one who had often been so unhelpful over the phone. He seemed very surprised to see me supporting Daniel, having assumed that we were having acrimonious marriage issues.

Over the next couple of weeks Daniel's mood sank even lower. During the previous low I had tried to motivate him, to give his day structure and to encourage him to do things. That hadn't worked so this time I accepted it when he stayed in bed all day. I went to sit with him, take him food and talk. But each day he was becoming more unreachable.

Theo adapted very well to returning home. He was just recovering from chicken pox, but he was past the infectious stage and was very pleased to be back in his old pre- school. Unexpectedly, it was Milo who was clearly unsettled. He was usually such an easy-going toddler, but not this time; he was uncharacteristically fretful and clingy and then he developed chicken pox too. He was absolutely covered in spots and very itchy so he was up for most of the night and we were housebound during the day.

Milo was sleeping in my bed, while Daniel slept in the girls bedroom. Milo being unwell softened Daniel. He hated seeing any of the children ill or unhappy and couldn't bear it when they cried. He was such a big softie. I think their suffering resonated with something in him; it stirred up his own pain. He felt helpless as Milo just wanted to be in my arms. One evening, I wanted to have a shower and tried to pass Milo to Mum but he wasn't having any of it so I sat back down with him. After a short while, I tried passing him to Daniel. Milo fussed for a few minutes but then settled in his arms and Daniel was thrilled. Despite the fact that he had been unwell for most of Milo's life, and so much less involved than he had been in Theo's babyhood, they had a bond. When Daniel lay in bed all day, eighteen month-old

Milo would go in to him and kiss his head and Daniel would kiss him back. Milo melted Daniel and could get him to smile, even on his darkest days.

Daniel was now consumed with desperate guilt and self-loathing over the way he had behaved when he was high. It was all so out of character. He was also upset that he had not seen his daughters as Beth had also drawn a line and said that she didn't want them to have contact with him until he was stable. The children had to come first.

Through everything, until now, he had kept on looking for work, and he'd come so close. But now he stopped trying. He lay in bed, coming down in the evenings, after the boys were in bed, to watch television.

I felt frustrated that Daniel had begged and pleaded for us to return home but was now having little to do with any of us. One Sunday I made a roast dinner, Daniel's favourite, and insisted that he come downstairs to share it. To please me, he made a huge effort and came to the table and after the meal we took the boys to the park and then went to a cafe for hot chocolate. He appeared to cope well and it was lovely to have him with us. But that evening he told me he had felt he had 'unemployed' written across his forehead.

He felt hopeless about ever getting a job again and very guilty about all the money he had spent. He felt that he had destroyed everything that he cared about. He tried very hard to rectify the damage. He began putting all his frivolous purchases on e-bay; the motorbike and leather biker boots and clothing, an electric guitair, kites and boards and other smaller items. This gave him a purpose each day and as the money came in, he gave it straight to me.

His memory of what he'd done when he was high was patchy. He asked me lots of questions about how he had behaved and what he had said. It was like someone sobering up after a drunken night out. He was concerned about others' perception of him and he felt ashamed and humiliated. I think he was scared too; realising that you have lost your sanity, even temporarily, must be terrifying.

This was the first time that Daniel really acknowledged that he was unwell; until this point he'd seen himself as an unemployed man, trying to find a job. Now he realised he was a mental health patient with a serious disorder, and he hated it.

He should have been in hospital. Being at home with us constantly reminded him of his inability to be the husband and father that he wanted to be. The pressures of family life and our finances were in his face. He needed time away, treatment for his illness and a chance to rehabilitate. Isn't that what psychiatric hospitals are for? Of course he wouldn't go willingly; denial and resistance to treatment are part of the symptoms of mental illness. He should have been detained and I should never have been left to care for him alone. But no-one was listening.

Everything had been calm and peaceful between us since the boys and I came home. Daniel and I were opposites who had been drawn together. In some ways we were not at all compatible, but we loved each other deeply and both had an absolute commitment to one another and to our family. Because we saw things so differently we'd always had to barter and negotiate with each other. But not any longer. He was so ill that I had to let go of all expectations. When he wasn't in bed he was in front of the television, barely present and only distantly aware of the family around him.

A couple of weeks after we came home I drove the children back to my parents' house. Theo had been invited to a Sunday afternoon party by one of my old school friends in Wiltshire and I decided to take him. Weekends with the boys on my hands and Daniel in bed were a struggle, so I looked forward to any break in our routine.

We arrived back home on the Monday evening and Mum came with us. I'd ordered a Tesco shop online and Daniel was out of bed unpacking it when we got home. Milo was still spotty and itchy, clinging to me and refusing to let me put him down but as with the previous time, he didn't protest when I handed him to Daniel and I could see that it meant a lot to him that he could comfort Milo. He felt so castrated and useless in every other way.

On Tuesday morning, March 15, I was up at 5.30am, after being woken every hour by Milo scratching. I felt exhausted but I'd got used to functioning in this state. I gave the boys their breakfast and got Theo ready for nursery. He asked where Daddy was, it was hard for him to understand Daniel's lack of involvement. I went into Daniel's room and found him lying in bed listening to music. I said little, but Daniel knew what I was thinking and he got himself downstairs and sat like a zombie with Theo on the sofa. He had developed a sty on his eye and looked awful. I suggested he go back up to bed and he looked relieved and retreated back upstairs.

After taking Theo to nursery, I went up to talk to Daniel. He admitted that he was having suicidal thoughts again. He knew I would be straight on the phone to Nathan, so I wonder if he still wanted to be saved at that point. He told me that the previous day he had told Nathan that he was feeling suicidal and that Nathan had scheduled an extra meeting for Thursday. I tried to convince him that he needed to go back into hospital, pointing out that it had helped him last time. But he didn't remember that, he was convinced it would only make him feel worse. I was relieved that at least there was another meeting with Nathan in two days' time; I could monitor Daniel until then and phone Nathan before the meeting.

Mum went out to buy Daniel some cream for his eye. I knew that my parents felt angry towards Daniel for the pain he was causing me and the children, but they were also deeply fond of him and were always kind and compassionate towards him. Mum made a big effort to cook him nice meals and despite his depression Daniel didn't lose his appetite or his enjoyment of food. He usually came downstairs to eat and always expressed his gratitude.

After the children had gone to bed that evening Daniel came and sat, as he did most evenings, unresponsive and silent in front of the television. Television seemed to give him some comfort and watching it together was the only way I had left to connect with him. We would sit peacefully side by side and sometimes talk about the programme. I had got him into watching my daily soap, 'Home and Away', something he would never have done when he was well. He used to rib me constantly over watching something so trashy and mindless, yet he'd come to enjoy the escape it provided and he looked forward to watching it with me.

The following day was my long work day. I often worried about Daniel on Wednesdays when I was away and not able to keep an eye on him. But that day I was less worried; Mum was there and Daniel's mum was coming to Brighton to stay with Adam and would be over in the afternoon.

When I came home from work, Daniel was downstairs watching his mum play with the children. This was the first time that she and I had seen each other properly since I had left the house and things felt slightly tense. I think Daniel's family viewed us as a couple who had separated but were oddly still living together. It was hard to convey to them, just as it had been to the crisis team, that to me this was not the end of our marriage. I still loved Daniel but I had reached a point where I could not go on living with him whilst he was so unwell, and more importantly, I couldn't put the children through it any longer. If I struggled to keep looking after Daniel and managing the situation I was going to crack and I couldn't let that happen, the boys needed me. But for me this was not a marital breakup; it was a mental health crisis. I always intended that, when Daniel got better, we would be back together as a family.

Maggie and I were pleasant to one another and she joined us for the dinner that Mum had cooked. But she kept saying that Daniel seemed better than when she had last seen him and I felt frustrated because I knew that he was lower than he had ever been. He was only out of bed and interacting with the children for a brief time for her benefit and the minute she left he went back to bed. Daniel always managed to put on a show for others and I think that's why nobody else accepted how unwell he was. Maggie so badly wanted to see her son getting better, it must have been hard for her to acknowledge how severely depressed he really was. Daniel always gave his family an extremely edited and minimised version of how he was doing. He was a proud, proud man; he didn't want to trouble anyone and he couldn't ask for help.

That evening Dad arrived to collect Mum and they took Theo back to Wiltshire with them for a couple of days. The plan was that Milo and I would stay so that I could clean the house ready for a couple of viewings on Thursday afternoon – I had put it on the market a few days earlier – and then join them on the Friday for the weekend. Mum's neurology appointment to discuss treatment for her brain aneurysm was on the Saturday and I'd promised to be there.

On Thursday morning Daniel was extremely low again and unable to get out of bed. I hoped that in the meeting that day Nathan might see how bad he was and either persuade him to go into hospital or get him sectioned. Daniel had not showered all week and I didn't remind him to, I hoped it would be an indicator to Nathan of how ill he was.

Daniel got up for the meeting without any prompting; he was still able to get himself to appointments on time. He left at midday and as soon as he'd gone I pacified Milo with a biscuit and phoned Nathan. I told him that Daniel's mood seemed lower than I had ever seen before, that he seemed to have given up on everything and that he had been voicing suicidal thoughts. I also told him that I was concerned about leaving Daniel for the weekend and that I wanted him in hospital. He said he would suggest hospital to Daniel again and suggested that I ask Daniel's family to spend some time with him while I was away.

Daniel was home again by 12.40 and I was disappointed by how short the meeting must have been. He told me that Nathan thought he should go into hospital but he said there was no way he was going. Clearly Nathan didn't share my concerns about Daniel's risk as no action was taken. I kept questioning my instincts; was I over-reacting? But I couldn't shift my worry. I knew Daniel and I knew that he had given up.

That afternoon we had to go out because we had arranged the house viewings. It was the last thing that Daniel wanted to do, but he came with us to a cafe where he had a hot chocolate and I had a coffee. Afterwards he waited in the car while I walked around with Milo, killing time until we could go home.

When we got back Daniel stayed downstairs at the desk in the office while I fed and bathed Milo. Surprised that he hadn't gone back to bed, I asked what he was up to and he said 'looking for jobs but there's nothing out there'.

A little later he overheard me talking to my old school friend, Sarah, on the phone. She had asked me what my plans were for my 40th birthday in a few weeks' time and Daniel said he felt guilty that we wouldn't be doing anything nice for my birthday and that he appreciated the party I had surprised him with for his 40th. I told him that I was happy to put off turning 40 and that we could plan to do something special the following year. I wanted to give him hope, to show him that I still believed we could be together, once he was well.

After Milo was in bed I had what was to be my final evening with Daniel. I'm thankful that it was peaceful; we spent it watching television together on the sofa. Daniel barely spoke but sitting together and sharing a snack felt like small ways in which we could connect.

The following morning Milo and I left for Wiltshire. We waved Daniel goodbye, for the last time.

CHAPTER FOURTEEN

The events surrounding Daniel's death still seem unreal, even after all this time.

I've tried many times to piece together what happened; when he made the decision, where he got the pills, when he took them. I'll never really know, but I believe he was probably out buying the aspirin when I spoke to him from Reading Services on the Friday afternoon. He would have needed to go to several chemists. Our shared laptop revealed that 'aspirin overdose' was the last thing to be entered in the search engine.

He saw the crisis team member at six and convinced them he was fine. Then he spoke to his mum at seven. I think he must have taken the pills sometime after that. That's why he didn't answer my calls; he knew what he was going to do, and perhaps he knew that I was the one person he couldn't fool.

Daniel must have been as strong as an ox to be able to walk to the ambulance at around 2pm the following day. He died between 5pm and 6pm, while I was on the motorway. My decision to delay cost me the chance to say goodbye to him and I have tortured myself with it. But sometimes I feel that it was better that I didn't witness his final suffering and have that etched on my memory as his mother and brother must have. I know Daniel didn't want me to see him die.

After Adam broke the news to me, he told me that the priest was coming to bless Daniel. I was on the pavement, shaking and asking questions, most of which Adam couldn't answer, although he tried, his voice breaking. I asked him please to wait for me, to make sure they didn't take Daniel away, I needed to be with him.

Mum had phoned Dad, who told us to go back to the services we had just passed and that he, Sam and Katie would meet us there. I managed to compose myself enough to drive there and, in a falsely chirpy voice, I explained to the boys that Daddy had gone to hospital, that I needed to go and see him and that they would go back to Grandma's.

I felt desperate to get to the hospital and during the 45 minute wait for Dad, I threw up in the toilets and paced up and down, agitated and distracted.

Sam came with me to the hospital. It took us two hours to get there but felt much longer and yet despite my sense of urgency, I kept telling Sam to slow down. I don't know if he was really driving fast or if I was just feeling vulnerable. I had an immediate, powerful sense of sole responsibility for the boys – if something happened to me, who would look after them? From the moment Daniel died I felt that the world was unsafe and unpredictable. Terrible things could happen unexpectedly and shatter your life.

The hospital was the same one in which our sons had been born. Until that moment their births were the only times I'd ever had to go there. As Sam and I walked into the reception, my older brother, Tom followed us in; he'd been told the news while visiting his girlfriend in Essex and had jumped straight into the car to come and meet us. I deeply appreciated both my brothers coming to be with me.

We were ushered into a small room and after a few minutes Adam and Maggie arrived. It felt surreal yet comforting to see them, as if suddenly I was not alone in this hell. They took me into the room where Daniel was and left me to spend some time with him alone.

I still felt very shaken, the room started spinning and I thought I might faint, so I sat on the floor. I've since questioned why I didn't sit on a chair – surely there must have been one – and wondered if I had a primitive need to feel the ground beneath me. After a few minutes, I gave myself a stern talking to; I knew that this was my last chance to be with Daniel again and felt I should be cherishing these few minutes. I got up and looked at his familiar bulky body. He looked peaceful, but I could see that nothing of Daniel was there, he had gone. His soul and spirit, all that I loved, was somewhere else.

His eyes were closed and I looked for the last time at his beautiful eyelashes that I'd always both admired and envied. They were thick and long; Theo has them too. I put my hand on his chest and told him that I loved him and that I was so, so sorry.

I looked at those enormous, cartoon-like feet that had always made me smile. How could our life together, full of so many hopes and dreams, have come to this? How could this vibrant character, always laughing and searching for fun, have become so low that he would choose to end his life, leaving his wife and four beautiful children behind?

After about ten minutes I left the room to find Maggie and Adam. They were sitting in the nurse's office. I remember sitting there feeling as if I had been run over, utterly shocked. Adam looked very white, strained and suddenly much older, but Maggie was strangely cheerful. She told me later that she had an almost manic, defensive response to the trauma.

After Adam and Maggie left to go home, Sam, Tom and I sat together in the relatives' room for some time, wondering what to do next.

There was a young Thai girl mopping the floor outside the room. The door was open and she came in and put her hand on mine and, in broken English, told me that she had lost many loved ones, that she knew my heartache and that it would get better. I was touched and grateful for her kindness.

I couldn't face going home so Tom offered to go back to our house to see if Daniel had left a note and I asked him to remove the covers from our bed and wash them for me, as if they were contaminated with death. Sam said he would drive me back to Wiltshire and we arrived back at my parents' at about 2am. I went straight upstairs to look at the boys and felt comforted and relieved to see them sleeping peacefully. Alongside the grief and shock and sense of loss, I realised the relief I felt was overwhelming.

This made me feel very guilty, but I came to understand that it was a by-product of the unbearable fear I had been living with for such a long time. I hadn't really dared to acknowledge it, but I had been terribly afraid that Daniel might harm the boys. Not intentionally, but in his hyper-manic phases he was reckless and incapable of keeping them safe. It had been an enormous strain on me.

I had also, in my deepest nightmares, been afraid that he might, in his altered state, decide to take us all with him. There had been a lot of terrifying reports in the press of parents who chose to end the lives of their whole family.

I fell into bed and woke a few hours later to hear the boys tearing around the house, unaware of the tragedy that had enveloped us all. Sam and Katie offered to take them out for the day and I was grateful. At that moment I felt too weak to look after them and it frightened me. I packed their bags and watched as they went off, full of excitement.

As I waved them off my thoughts turned to Ella and Hannah. Daniel adored his girls. How could he possibly have done this? How had Beth managed to tell them? I couldn't face phoning, but I sent Beth a text, sending love.

I stayed upstairs crying for the whole morning. My parents were ashen-faced and helpless. They had their own feelings of loss to deal with, as well as their concern for me and their grandchildren.

A couple of friends phoned me, unaware of what had happened. I heard myself telling them that Daniel had died and heard them both cry out, but that didn't make it feel any more real. I sent a text to Ann, Theo's play therapist, asking for advice on how to tell him and she called me back straight away. She was shocked but calm and practical and talking to her helped.

I had been trying to phone Tania all morning but couldn't reach her, so at lunch time I phoned Sarah, my old school friend who lived close to my parents' house. When I told her what had happened she said 'I'm coming over'. I didn't think that I was up to seeing anyone, but actually I was glad to see her. I had first met Sarah when we were fourteen and she had been there through all the ups and downs of my life. She was in the midst of her own tough times after being diagnosed with breast cancer the previous year, which made her response all the more generous. We went for a walk and as we reached my parents' local church, I felt that I had to go inside. Being inside brought me closer to Daniel, I felt as though he was beckoning me in. As soon as we sat down in a pew at the back, the floodgates opened. Sarah just sat beside me and allowed me to cry and the peace and calm there helped.

As we walked back towards my parents' house, a passing man took one look at my swollen face and said 'cheer up love, it may never happen'. It was a horrible moment. I'm sure he meant well, but the worst *had* happened and his thoughtlessly flippant comment hurt.

The walk with Sarah and the emotional release in the church helped me to feel up to telling Theo what had happened. I didn't sit down to tell Milo in the same way because he was so young, although later I regretted it and felt I should have. I thought that at 19 months and not yet talking he wouldn't understand, but his behaviour in the weeks that followed showed me that he understood so much more than I had thought possible.

I took Theo upstairs and sat with him on the bed. I told him that a very sad thing had happened; his Daddy's illness had got worse and the doctors were not able to make him better, so he had died and was now in heaven. Theo looked at me and said, 'can I tell Uncle Sam?' I said yes and he flew down the stairs and told Sam that his Daddy had gone to heaven. Sam said that he knew and that it was very sad. Theo asked, 'how did he get there?' And then he answered himself, 'I think the wind blew him there'. Sam was choking on his tears and we all felt shredded.

Later I phoned Beth who told me that she and the girls, along with Pete and their younger half-brother, had all slept together in one bed for comfort after being given the news the previous evening.

In the days that followed Theo asked a lot of questions about heaven. He wanted to know if we had all known that this was going to happen. And, like me, he was clearly grappling with the suddenness of it all and the inability to say goodbye. He kept asking, 'why didn't Daddy tell me that he was going to heaven?' He also became fascinated by the concept of heaven being way up high above the world and frustrated that he couldn't see it. He would tell me that he was going to get a ladder so that he could see heaven, or that he was going to eat all his dinner so that he would grow tall and his head would be in heaven. It was excruciating to hear his innocent yearnings for understanding and his desperate need to see Daniel again.

By the second day the phone was ringing continuously, as friends heard the news. Sometimes it helped to talk, at other times it felt incredibly wearing. I was surprised by the way I was able to talk about what had happened quite rationally, but it was draining having to repeat myself over and over again.

Two days after Daniel died I realised I could no longer cocoon myself at my parents' house. I had to face going home so that I could help Daniel's family arrange the funeral. Mum came with us and I was extremely grateful; I couldn't have managed without her.

As we approached the house I felt myself growing tense. It had not been a happy place to be for at least a year and my hopes and dreams of our family life there had long since been shattered. But the feeling I had now was worse than anything I could have imagined. Entering the house in which Daniel had lain dying was indescribable. Apart from telling Theo that his daddy had died, it was the hardest thing that I've ever had to do. I felt weak and sick and my limbs hurt. Nothing seemed the same. People had been all over the house and it didn't feel like our home any longer. The area round the kitchen bin had been sealed by the police; I could only think that Daniel must have thrown the aspirin packets there.

I couldn't face going upstairs; we put the bags in the hall and Mum and I tried to normalise things for the boys, getting them something to eat. Tania arrived about half an hour later and I was incredibly glad to see her. She lifted the atmosphere and soon had the boys chasing her around the house, squealing and shrieking with delight. They were happy for a couple of hours in her care and it freed me to go up and face our bedroom alone.

Daniel had been found lying on my side of the bed, and when I walked into the room, I felt dizzy. I sat on the floor and wept. I had to get out, so I went into Theo's room. Daniel's phone was there and I could see that he had been sleeping on the top bunk; his trousers and jumper were still up there. This still puzzles me now. Daniel had slept there before, in order to avoid having to make the bed neatly in our room for house viewings. But surely he wouldn't have done that on the Friday after I left, because he took the overdose that night and wouldn't have been concerned with bed-making. Perhaps he slept up there in the afternoon and then decided to take the pills after his visit to the day hospital? Had something there made him lose any glimmer of hope that he may have had? Or maybe he had planned his overdose beforehand and got into Theo's bed before deciding to go into our bed to ensure that he was found? I feel certain that he planned to be found by the estate agent and not by me. When we'd talked at Christmas he had confessed that the only reason he'd chosen Beachy Head was to spare me and the boys from finding his body.

Mum came up to tell me that she was going for a walk; I think she felt like a bit of a spare part now that Tania had taken over the boys, but I panicked and begged her to stay. I felt weak and faint and unable to cope. It was nice to hear the boys laughing but it was stressing me and I knew I wouldn't manage to get them through the usual feeding, bath and bed routine.

All my energy seemed to have ebbed away and I felt afraid that I was never going to find the strength to look after my children. Mum stayed and between all of us we managed to get the boys calm and ready for bed. As I was reading Theo his bedtime story, the phone rang and Tania answered. It was Dr Shank. He had just heard about Daniel's death and was phoning to say how sorry he was. Dr Anton also phoned to say he was sorry.

After the boys were in bed I was too tired to talk, but I was comforted by having both Mum and Tania there. We had to figure out sleeping arrangements; I didn't want to sleep in our bed, but Tania encouraged me to be brave, reasoning that I had to live in the house for a while so perhaps it would be easier to just face it the first night back. I did somehow manage it by numbing my emotions and cutting off all thoughts of Daniel.

The next few days passed in a haze. It helped to focus on keeping things normal for the boys and being with them in the present. Theo went back to his pre-school and I explained what had happened to Mrs Hodson. She promised to keep an eye on him and reported that he seemed to be coping well; perhaps pre-school provided the sense of normality and security that he needed.

Two days after returning home, I went to see the girls. It was terribly hard. I couldn't bear to see their pain and it seemed to bring home the finality of it for all of us. I wanted to give them something but what could I possible give them that would comfort them? In the end I took them each a colourful plant. We just sat together, huddled on their sofa. I told them how much Daniel loved them and Hannah cried, but Ella remained dry-eyed and white-faced. They wanted to know what would happen to the boys and me, what would happen to the house? I answered honestly with 'I don't know'. But I reassured them that we would always remain a family. The visit was a comfort to me, and Beth phoned later to say that it seemed to have helped the girls too.

Daniel's family took over planning his funeral and I was grateful as it enabled me to focus on the boys. Adam kept me informed and if there were a few occasions when I felt overlooked, I let it go. I knew that once the funeral was over I had a huge task ahead of me sorting out our finances and Daniel's things, going through probate and selling the house. For me this was more important than the funeral and I was bracing myself for it.

A week after Daniel died I spent the day feeling very low and tearful. I was having frequent dizzy spells, feeling faint and having to sit down, sometimes on the edge of the pavement if I was out. I had a constant sensation of the world spinning around me. Everything was hazy and dreamlike and I felt as light as a feather as if I were floating. I also felt constantly queasy and struggled to eat. I knew it was shock; I was struggling to take in Daniel's loss and its consequences. I was a single parent now, a responsibility that I would never have sought or wanted. And I would have to help my boys come to terms with the loss of their father, now and forever.

I was haunted by regrets. If only I'd come home in the morning, been more forceful in asking Adam to check on him, called the police. I revisited the days before his death over and over, torturing myself with 'what ifs' and 'maybes'.

That afternoon Adam came over to talk through the funeral arrangements. He gave me a CD that he had made of Daniel singing tracks that he had written years ago when he'd been in a band. They planned to play two of Daniel's tracks in the church. I couldn't listen to them and it would be three months before I managed to play the CD.

As we sat in the garden, finalising the preparations, Daniel's Irish 'Uncle David' phoned Adam. He asked to speak to me. I was a little nervous, as I barely knew him. He said that he was terribly cut up about Daniel's death, mainly for me and the boys. He said that I had given Daniel his best years and that he knew that I had done everything I could for him. His words meant everything to me that day and still do. In all of the doubts, recriminations, and tearing apart that arrive in the wake of a death like this, his words gave me something to hold onto.

I had made a decision not to take the boys to the funeral. It was not going to be a funeral centred on the needs of children but one for adults and I felt that Theo, particularly, would not be able to cope with the tension and the high emotions of many people there, including me. Instead I planned a little ceremony on the beach for the children.

After Adam's visit, Sam and Katie, who had come for the weekend, took the boys out while I took Katie's car to pick up 20 helium balloons that I had ordered. The car was full of sports kit, so it was quite a struggle fitting the balloons in and I had to drive home with some hanging out of the window, tied to the gear stick. It looked unintentionally celebratory; I got a lot of well-meaning honks from other motorists, but I just wanted to shout at them to leave me alone.

The next day was a Sunday. I had planned the beach ceremony for the afternoon but the weather was looking a bit iffy, the sky filling with ominous grey clouds. I prayed for it to stay dry. The girls arrived at lunchtime. I had laid out some art materials on the kitchen table and I suggested that they might like to draw a picture or write a note for their dad, to send off with the balloons. They all ignored my suggestion and went out into the garden to play. Perhaps, it was too difficult to think about sending something to

Daddy. They chose to kick a ball around and jump on the trampoline instead. I have since learned that, for Theo at least, it is intolerable to process grief in a direct way, but he is able to do it metaphorically through stories and play. It's less engulfing that way. As a therapist I should have known this but as a parent I couldn't help wanting to encourage the children to get on and deal with it, fearful about how it might emerge in later years.

When they came in from the garden we all headed over to the beach. Each child carried a balloon they had chosen, and I took the rest. Sam and Katie came too, with Sam lagging behind us to record it all. Amazingly, as we walked across to the beach the grey clouds parted and bright orange rays of sun poked through.

I felt conscious of the huge void in our family as we reached the beach. It was unheard of for us to go without Daniel. It was his place; he was always the instigator for time on the beach and was over there in all weathers, any time of the day or night. It felt odd and wrong that he wasn't there.

We found a spot in front of the sea and kissed our balloons and said goodbye before releasing them together. They really did look spectacular as they drifted off into the sky. We stood and watched, mesmerised. It didn't take long for them to disappear and then Theo, Hannah and Milo were off, running across the beach. Ella and I shared a hug, but there were no words that could possibly connect or comfort us.

We walked to the water's edge and I felt an indescribable sense of peace. I have never seen the sea looking so calm and tranquil, mist rising from its pond like surface. In that moment, I really felt that Daniel was with us and that he was at peace.

CHAPTER FIFTEEN

The funeral was a fitting tribute to Daniel; a big send-off for a very popular man and a powerful reminder of just how many people loved and cared for him.

I took Theo to nursery as usual that morning. He had been told that all the grown-ups were going to church to say some prayers for Daddy and that after lunch he and Milo would be going to play at a friend's house. He was happy with this plan and very excited at the prospect of being collected by Uncle Sam.

Unconventionally, we were going to the crematorium first and then having a three hour wait before going to the church. I'd been involved in planning the church service but had no idea what to expect from the morning service at the crematorium.

I had told everyone that the dress code was 'not black' because I knew Daniel loathed convention and formality. I'd bought a purple dress to wear, but it was a cold day and the dress was summery. It needed a jacket, and the only one I had was black. As I hesitated over what to do, Tania arrived. She was just what I needed that day. So many people had been tip-toeing around me in the previous few days, but Tania, direct, funny and no-nonsense, treated me just as she always had. She strode in, took one look at me and said 'For god sake Louise, you look like you're going to a summer ball. Wear the jacket'.

Sam and Katie stayed with Milo while the rest of us went to the crematorium. I knew that managing the day would be an ordeal. I didn't want to break down, Daniel's loss still felt so raw and shocking and I didn't feel ready to say good-bye to him.

Ella and Hannah, with Beth and Pete, arrived at the same time as us. We huddled together outside for what seemed an age and as guests gathered I did my best to greet people, although all I could manage was 'thank you for coming'.

I noticed Beth usher the girls around the corner and turned to see the hearse arriving. I felt I could barely breathe, I was dizzy and light-headed. I watched as Daniel's brother and father, my brother Tom and three close friends of Daniel's heaved the coffin out of the car and onto their shoulders. It was this evidence of its obvious weight that brought home to me that Daniel was inside. 'What the hell are you doing in a coffin?' I wanted to yell.

Daniel's family did him proud with a unique and memo-rable service. My heart lurched when they played Daniel's party piece, Caro Mio Ben (My Dear Beloved) by Giuseppe Giordani. He had sung it to my bump during both my pregnancies and to the boys as babies. Theo would stop crying as soon as he heard it and would become mesmerised, staring at Daniel with glazed eyes. Maggie, Adam and Lottie, who flew over from New York, where she was working, all gave speeches and Maggie sang something very beautiful. But most of the content of the ser-vice was lost on me because all I could focus on were Hannah's heart-wrenching sobs in the row just behind me.

They played Daniel out with 'Hello, I Must be Going' by Groucho Marx. It was very unconventional, very comical and very Daniel. Afterwards I made a polite but hasty exit. I just wanted to get home, re- compose myself and mentally prepare for the church.

Sam and Katie had collected Theo so we arrived home to find the boys racing around, which was a relief after the sombre mood of the morning. My parents, brothers, their girlfriends, Tania and I all sat around the kitchen table eating the fish and chips we'd collected on the way home, while the boys played in the living room. Most of us felt lost for words and the atmosphere was gloomy, until the door was flung open and Theo burst in singing 'I Like to Move It, Move It' from Madagascar. He sang at the top of his voice, while bumping and grinding round the table. It was so unbelievably comical that nobody could fail to laugh. He is his father's son.

After lunch, people started arriving at the house. My dad's three brothers and their wives all came. His oldest brother was in his mid-seventies but still endured a six hour journey to be there before driving back home the same day. They had only met Daniel a handful of times but came to support me and to pay their respects. Two of my old school friends Sarah and Nik travelled from Wiltshire for the day and many of Daniel's Irish Aunts, Uncles and cousins had flown over. The fact that so many people were willing to arrange time off work, childcare and then travel to be there meant a lot to me and gave me strength; I was touched and comforted by their presence. And it meant a lot to me that they all came to the house, Daniel's home was so important to him, he'd have loved everyone gathering there.

The boys were in high spirits. Just before we set off for the church Sam took them over to a friend's house where a couple of my friends had arranged a play afternoon for them. We walked the short distance to the church and many of our neighbours joined us, smiling hello and falling into step, all of us heading for the same destination. There was a collective sense of anticipation, a feeling that something big was happening in our otherwise quiet part of town. Daniel deserved that. He caused a commotion in his life and it was appropriate that his send-off should cause another.

The church was packed and as I walked towards the front, I was touched to see two friends, Linda and Helena, sitting together. I hadn't expected Helena to come, as she barely knew Daniel, but she was a true friend to me and was there to show her support. It can be hard for people to know how to help in the wake of tragedy, but seeing that people cared enough to be there really did help. I took their hands as I walked past them.

The service was both heart-breaking and joyful. Many of Daniel's friends got up to pay warm and affectionate tributes to him, telling funny stories and talking about how much he had meant to them. One of Daniel's close friends, Eddie, whom I had never met, spoke about his regret that he had not stayed in contact with Daniel and had not been there for him at the end. It was brave of him and I think his words resonated with many people there. The sadness and sense of disbelief in the room was palpable.

I had written a speech, but knew I would not be able to speak about my love for Daniel and remain composed, so Tania read it for me:

'It is impossible to put into words the enormous gap that you have left in my life. Everything about you was larger than life and the imprint that you have left in my heart parallels that. From the moment I met you, I knew that my life had changed forever. You lived life in the fast lane and burned the candle at both ends. Yours was a life cut short but lived to the full. You had a magnetism and irresistible charm that touched the lives of many. Your all-time

favourite word was equilibrium. How ironic that this was some-thing that you could not find in life.

Underlying your strength and immense capability was a fragil-ity and vulnerability that you could not share with others, your warm, generous and empathic nature meant that you were always giving, helping and wanting to rescue others yet you were unable to receive help for yourself. Your mind was ravished by a terribly cruel illness. I know that you understood that my loyalty to you was sometimes compromised by my duty to protect our children from that illness. I also know how agonised you were because you could not provide financially and emotionally for the family you loved so much and that this crippled you mentally.

In our brief time together you gave me everything that I always wanted and I will be forever grateful for the two beautiful boys that we were blessed with. I also now have your two lovely daughters in my life and I promise to cherish and sustain the bonds that we have as a family in your absence. You will live on Daniel in those four special children who all adored you. You will always remain in our thoughts and hearts, never forgotten.'

I shed a few tears, but there wasn't the outpouring of emotion that I'd feared; mostly I felt numb. I hadn't stopped shaking since I'd arrived at the crematorium that morning; people kept offering me their jackets, thinking I was cold, but I was just in shock.

As I left the church I had a flashback to our wedding. One of Daniel's kite-surfing friends, Marcus, had referred to our wedding in his speech and walking past all our friends and family took me back to it. Could it really have been less than three years earlier? There were a lot of people there that I hadn't seen since our wedding day and this only com-pounded my sense of disbelief.

Crowds were gathering outside the church and I felt I should stay, but once again I just wanted to get away. Most people were making their way to the local pub, where the wake was being held and I knew I'd need to go, I didn't want my absence to cause offence. But I needed a break at home first so, while Sam shot off to collect the boys, I said goodbye to Ella and Beth as they were rushing back home to Hannah who had not felt able to face the church service, and made my way home.

When I reached the house Dominic, an old friend of Daniel's, was standing outside. I'd only met him twice before; once when he came to stay with us and the second time at our wedding. He looked utterly shell- shocked. I invited him in for a cup of tea and he told me that Daniel had gone up to London on his motorbike and stayed with him after a night out the previous month. He said that Daniel had appeared to be in good spirits and hadn't told him about his illness or his unemployment. No wonder Dominic looked so shocked. It was hard to imagine how somebody who had been so full of life could sink so low that they would take their own life just a month later. It's hard for those who haven't witnessed it first hand to understand how an illness such as bipolar can alter someone's mood and mental state to such an extent that the personality, behaviour, outlook, opinions, abilities and level of competency can become unrecognisable in a very short space of time.

Sam and Katie offered to stay with the boys while the rest of us went to the wake. I didn't want to go; it took a huge effort to get myself there. I said hello to everyone and then went to sit with my friends and family in a quiet area of the pub. I was exhausted and burnt out and as the party got going I felt disconnected from everything around me. In my own bubble, I remember thinking that I needed to get home to apply Theo's verruca cream before he went to bed. It's amazing what the mind conjures up to defend against a brutal reality.

I probably stayed about an hour. I've no doubt that a lively Irish knees-up went on into the small hours, the kind of party that Daniel would have loved. And I didn't want to upset anyone by leaving, I was simply overwhelmed.

I got home in time to bath and put the children to bed. They seemed happy and oblivious to the momentous events of the day and went easily to bed. After a glass of wine with Tania, Mum and Dad, I went to bed myself. I was utterly exhausted, but I couldn't sleep. Consumed by guilt that I had seen what was coming and yet not been able to save Daniel, I went over and over his last few days. Why had I left him at home alone? Why hadn't I managed to get him into hospital? Why hadn't I realised what was happening on his last night and driven home when he didn't answer the phone?

Desperate to comprehend what had happened and to feel connected to him, I wrote him a letter.

Dear Daniel,

I think you would have loved the send-off we gave you today. As I write this, after putting the boys to bed, so many of your friends and family are still in the pub with you in their hearts and minds. I hope that you're there with them; I know that you would cherish having so many of the people you loved gathered together and you would be the last to leave.

I am trying so hard to stay buoyant for the boys. I keep waiting to wake up from a terrible nightmare with you beside me, comforting me and telling me that the last year has just been a horrific dream ... I never let go of my hope and belief that you would come back to us.

My guilt and regret are so intense; I feel I should have saved you. Why didn't you pick up the phone? It must have been ringing beside you. You would have known that it was me.

I know that you were not in that coffin today, you are far away and I just want to know that you are OK. I felt that you were on the beach on Sunday, letting us know that you are at peace. I do hope that you really are.

In the days that followed the funeral I felt numb and exhausted. I wanted to hide under the bedcovers and not have to come out. I functioned because I had to, for the boys. They needed the stability and reassurance of 'things as normal' and that need to keep them in their usual routine was what got me through. Of course nothing was normal, and I felt it never would be again, but I knew that I had to make sure that, at least in the mechanism of our lives, things continued in ways that the boys understood. And though I didn't realise it at the time, that consistent structure was key to my own survival too.

A few days after Daniel died I received a text from a friend whose sister died under similar circumstances years before. He simply said, 'Louise, just keep on going'. At the time I thought this was a little cold and lacking in sentiment. But as it turned out, it was probably the most helpful thing that anyone said to me.

Guilt was the only feeling that seeped through my numbness and it was all-encompassing. I felt I was somehow to blame for Daniel's death; I didn't do enough for him, prioritised the children over him, abandoned him and failed to stop him taking his life. These thoughts played in a continuous loop in my mind. I would see pity in people's eyes and feel detached from it because I didn't deserve it.

As soon as the boys were in bed each night I busied myself with the mountain of practical tasks that I had to sort through. Daniel was a hoarder, he had every bank statement, letter and credit card bill he'd ever received, along with a mountain of other miscellaneous files and pieces of paper that I needed to sift through, trying to keep anything important and throwing the rest away.

A couple of days after the funeral, I had a visit at home from a coroner's assistant. My recollection of this meeting is fuzzy. I do remember that she was very kind and she asked me a lot of questions. I had to go over, in minute detail, the last forty eight hours of Daniel's life. I was told that the purpose of the inquest was to ascertain exactly what happened in order to formally state the cause of death. It was not to direct blame anywhere. After what seemed like a very long and painful meeting, she told me that I had a right to complain about Daniel's treatment but that this would be a separate process to the inquest. What I didn't realise was that the information that I'd given her would be compiled into a formal statement that would go to the police and the coroner's office and that I would be obliged to read that statement in a full courtroom at the inquest.

In hindsight, it seems extraordinary to me that, at this stage of my bereavement, despite the contact I'd had with the coroner, the calls from Dr Shank and Dr Anton and the evidence that the police had been in my home the night that Daniel died, I had not been offered any information on possible avenues of support. In parallel with my experience when Daniel was ill, I was just left to get on with it. I had to inform so many official people of Daniel's death. I realised that all our bills, credit cards, insurances, bank accounts and debts were either in his name or in our joint names. And I was told, by each company I contacted, that I couldn't access them without providing Daniel's original death certificate which I wouldn't have until after the inquest. It also meant I'd either have to take it to them personally or send it and wait for it to be returned before sending it on to the next one. I felt lost in all the red tape.

Soon after the funeral, three of Daniel's friends spent one Sunday clearing out our garage. He had so much stuff; kite surfing equipment, wetsuits, life jackets, tools, bicycles, bits of furniture and even computer parts that he brought home from work when they were having a clear-out. We had a double garage and it was full of the things Daniel had hoarded. His friends, Richard, Marcus and Roger cleared it out, taking away anything valuable to sell on eBay for me and making numerous trips to the tip. It was a huge help and I was grateful.

I knew we would have to move as soon as possible, so I rooted through every drawer and cupboard sorting out the contents and piling things to go to the dump or to charity shops. I was so tired that I could barely think but, fuelled by shock and adrenalin, I continued to function on empty.

While I was able to keep my demons at bay during the day by occupying every moment with the boys and the sorting out of the house and paperwork, nights were a different matter.

Once I had fallen into bed at the end of each long and weary day, I was no longer able to distract myself from my inner turmoil. I was exhausted, yet I lay wide-eyed, staring into the darkness, unable to sleep, tormented by thoughts of Daniel and of how I was going to manage financially and bring up our sons alone.

I had got into the habit of bringing Milo into my bed while he had chicken pox, as he woke every night at midnight, miserable and scratching. Once he recovered he continued to wake around midnight each night and I would guiltily bring him into bed with me, grateful for his small, warm, breathing presence helping to fill the huge void on Daniel's side. I even took to lifting him out of his cot and in with me when I went to bed, without waiting for him to wake. It was an indulgence, but it made going to bed less painful. It was so comforting to hear his breathing while I was lying there unable to sleep. It helped me to feel less alone and frightened and I think it probably gave Milo a sense of security amid all the grief and confusion that he must have been absorbing.

The only way I could sleep was by taking sleeping pills the doctor prescribed for me. I began to feel dependent on them, which scared me. And as I struggled, in the bleakness of the night, to make sense of what had happened, I continued to write to Daniel.

Why do I feel so frightened Daniel? I am scared of the responsibility that is now solely on my shoulders. How am I going to provide for these boys? I am trying not to think about finances but I know my dad is worried about it all. And I am so fearful about the psychological harm all of this will have on our little urchins. Theo is so mixed up. How is this all going to impact on them in later life? I feel so helpless about that and feel that I have failed them somehow. I want to make it all better for them but know that I will never be able to do that.

The boys, each in their own way, attempted to make sense of their father's disappearance.

Theo asked a lot of questions about heaven and it was terribly hard to have to keep reiterating the finality and permanency of death to a four year old. Theo worried about Daniel too. He was confused about why he didn't take all his belongings with him and worried that he would need his clothes. And he was beginning to develop a state of high anxiety, afraid that I would die too and increasingly unable to let me out of his sight.

As for Milo, most days he would go into our bedroom and round to Daniel's side of the bed where he would pull back the covers. It was as if he kept hoping to find his daddy there. After checking under the covers he would look under the bed before giving up. He was just a baby but he felt Daniel's absence as deeply as the rest of us.

There were memories of Daniel in every corner of the house. I would walk into the kitchen and see him hovering over the chopping board with Theo, the two of them stuffing themselves with taramasalata and crackers. He was always snacking. I would nag him to sit down and eat but I think he felt that if he had a sneaky graze standing up, it didn't count. A few days earlier Theo had asked if you could get taramasalata in heaven. He worried about whether Daniel had everything he needed and kept talking about going up to visit him by plane or air balloon. I explained that it wasn't possible to go to heaven until you had died, but Theo continued to speak about Daniel as if he was simply staying somewhere else. He would try to barter with me and get me to agree that Daniel would phone him instead of seeing him. As if somehow it was up for negotiation.

I contacted the children's bereavement charity; Winston's Wish, to ask about how I should talk to the boys and bought some age-appropriate books about death. When we read them Theo asked me if I had known that his dad was going to die. I knew that it was best to be honest with him about what death meant, but I also felt that I needed to be intuitive about what he could handle and understand. It felt as if I was giving him tiny chunks of the cookie, as he was able to digest them. I could only hope and pray I was doing it right.

I didn't explain it all to Milo in the same way as he was so young, but one day he absolutely amazed me. I eventually plucked up the courage to listen to the CD of Daniel's songs that Adam had given me and as soon as he heard his father's voice, Milo flew into our bedroom, went straight over to my bedside table and got out a framed photo of Daniel that I kept there. He took it to the window, pointed and said 'Daddy, house, sky'. He had taken it all in.

Did you send me a dream last night? I'd like to believe that you did. You knew that I was in need of reassurance and that I was grappling to comprehend what has happened to you. In the dream we arrived together at some family occasion in a pub. We walked through the car park and as we entered the pub you took my hand and we were floating upward. We stayed together, hovering on the ceiling, looking down on all the people below who were unaware of our presence. I felt free and happy up there.

I am going to interpret it as a message from you. Perhaps, you were showing me where you were; above all your loved ones looking down on them feeling happy at last.

Thanks Daniel, I feel less wretched today. It was lovely to be together in the dream.

One of our neighbours gave me the number of a financial adviser, urging me to see him as soon as possible. I knew he was right, I had to sort out our finances, but I dreaded it. Daniel had always taken care of that side of things; paying bills, sorting insurance, dealing with the mortgage.

The adviser told me that because there were no assets other than the equity in the house, I shouldn't have to go through probate. However I couldn't legally sell the house because I only owned half of it. I would have to apply to the local land registry to change the ownership to my name and would only be able to do that with an original death certificate. I was stuck in limbo until the inquest was out the way.

He also confirmed what I had already feared; that we were in a bad financial situation. He told me, bluntly, that even if Daniel had continued with his life insurance payments – and I didn't know whether he had – I didn't stand a hope in hell of getting a pay-out. He said that in his entire career he had never known an insurance company to pay out after a suicide. He also told me that I would be liable for the debts that Daniel had run up on our joint credit card and bank account.

It all felt so bleak and uncertain. I had no idea where or how we were going to live, and I was scared.

CHAPTER SIXTEEN

E aster fell in late April and with it came the sun. It was scorching, the beach was packed and the boys, in shorts and t-shirts, splashed happily in the sea.

It was always my favourite time of year. Daniel's too. We used to count the days down in February and celebrate the first of March. As I watched the crowds of happy families flock to the beach I kept thinking, if only he could have hung on a bit and let the bleakness of winter pass. Though I know, really, that even spring arriving wouldn't have helped him.

Sam and Katie came for the Easter weekend and took the boys out so that I could sort through some of Daniel's more personal belongings that I hadn't yet faced.

Daniel was the only one who used our en-suite bathroom. I braved it with a black bag and robotically swept all his toiletries, toothbrush and shaving things into it. Once it was done I shut the door of the bathroom and never went in there again.

As I began to sort his things in our bedroom I pressed play on our stereo. Unbeknown to me an album Daniel loved, by India Arie, was in there and it started to play at the beginning of a track called A Good Man. I will never know if he left it for me to find, as he hadn't left a suicide note, or if it was one of many uncanny coincidences that occurred after Daniel died. Either way it felt like a message from him and listening to the unutterably poignant lyrics broke my heart.

If the sun comes up and I'm not home,
Be strong.
If I'm not beside you, do your best to carry on.
Tell the kids about me when they're old enough to understand
Tell them that they're daddy was a good man.

I forced myself to go through all his clothes and personal things, tackling it like a mission and not allowing myself to feel anything. All his photos and memorabilia from before we met went into a box for his mum. Adam said he didn't want anything, but I put some photos aside for his dad and I had boxes of keepsakes for me and for each of the four children.

At the end I looked at the big pile of his clothes I'd put in a heap for the charity shop and thought, is it too soon? Should I have waited? That night I wrote;

'I feel guilty that I'm wiping out all traces of you. I just can't bear these things around me Daniel. I need them gone. I hope you understand. Your wardrobe is now empty and I can't bear that either. I have shut the door; I don't want to ever open it again.'

I started on the paperwork next. Daniel refused to throw anything away, he was a hoarder. I'm the opposite; I can't bear junk or clutter. He hated me throwing things out so I would compromise, tidying things away in various places around the house. He called me his little squirrel. It made me smile to remember his hilarious impression of a squirrel rummaging around the house, storing things away. It was an on-going joke that we shared. He used to infuriate me with his messiness and his disorganisation, but he could always make me laugh.

Over the next few days I threw out a whole forest. There were endless documents; ancient bank statements, letters and bills. I found a couple of life insurance documents but didn't know if any of them were current or if he'd kept up the payments during his unemployment. We never discussed these things; I just left them up to him. If only the pressures on Daniel hadn't been so huge. House, bills, kids. Why did we take on such a stupidly big mortgage? What did a house matter, in the end?

As I trawled through the paperwork that Daniel had stashed away I found some correspondence relating to a job that he'd left just before we met. When we talked about it he had seemed bitter and regretful, but he never really told me why he'd left. Reading the letters I discovered that he was paid off due to 'personality clashes' with other team members. I began to see a pattern in Daniel's employment history. He was very aware and insightful about his clumsy interpersonal skills at work and we had often talked about interactions at work that he felt regretful about. We both knew that his strong opinions and fierce expression of them got him into trouble sometimes. Daniel had a lot of self-awareness. He would openly acknowledge his weaknesses and was insightful in linking them to adverse childhood experiences. He was aware that he had issues with authority figures. These difficulties kept coming up for him and reading through the paperwork I could see that it had caused him to lose work before. He put on a brave face and his brilliance in other areas usually meant that he managed to find another job straight away. But I also know that he felt rejected and deeply hurt over and over again.

In the many days and weeks I had to think about Daniel and what had happened to him, I came to understand that his bipolar had been something he had lived with, unknowingly, for many years. It may have been triggered by the drug-induced psychotic episode he'd had when he was twenty. Daniel had told me that he'd been a rebellious teenager and had experimented with cocaine, LSD and cannabis in his late teens, and that he'd had a drug-induced psychotic episode when he was twenty that lasted about three weeks. It had frightened him and he had never touched drugs again. I wasn't unduly concerned at the time since I had worked in psychiatric hospitals and had seen many patients experiencing drug-induced mental health problems. For most of these patients, abstinence would be enough to prevent further mental health issues and so I trusted that Daniel had learned a harsh lesson in his youth and would never take drugs again. But recent research has revealed a correlation between all three of the drugs Daniel took and the onset of psychotic symptoms such as those found in schizophrenia and bipolar disorder. It is impossible to know if a genetic predisposition left Daniel vulnerable to an adverse reaction to the drugs or if the drugs left a permanent vulnerability to mental health problems later in life. What is clear from current research is that, for some people, taking these drugs can permanently damage their mental health.

Daniel had functioned very well for the twenty years between his drug induced breakdown and the one at the end of his life. No-one realised or picked up on the signs of his disorder; they were only there in hindsight. I thought about how much I had loved his larger-than-life exuberance, his crazy, take-it-to-the-limit enthusiasm. He took so many things to extremes; eating, drinking, socialising, kite surfing. It was as if he didn't have the capacity to moderate anything, didn't have a stop button. I wondered how I could have lived with him and not known.

Daniel was a survivor, he always had been. And his successful career had helped to keep him stable. When he lost it he tried so hard to ride out the setbacks, find another job and fix it for all of us. Nobody could have tried harder. But by that time the odds were stacked against him; a recession, two families to support, a stupidly big mortgage. I understood why he gave up; he had been beaten down by perpetual rejection and in the end he felt rejected by me too. If only he had understood how much I loved him. I just needed a break from his illness and to protect our sons.

I sat in bed every night writing to Daniel, telling him of my regrets, my fears, how much I missed him, how I wished, over and over again that I could wake and find everything restored to the way we were before, as though it had all been a bad dream. My sense of loss and regret was all-consuming.

I functioned for the boys and small steps were all I could take. I knew that the first was to sell the house and find somewhere to live. A friend contacted me, urging me to see her financial advisor and, reluctantly, I did. After what the first one had said I dreaded more bad news, but this one, Adrian, was far more sensitive and helpful. I gave him a handful of documents relating to the life insurance and various pensions that Daniel had paid into that I either hadn't found time to read or, in my fuzzy state of functioning, didn't understand. Adrian studied them, explained what they were and contacted them on my behalf. I discovered that Daniel had kept up the payments on his life insurance policies and he had set up separate policies for his girls and me and the boys. I was so thankful that my financially astute husband had made a will and set up the life insurance in a way that would prevent any squabbles over money. It was typical of Daniel to have planned it all so thoughtfully and thoroughly.

I was very, very worried about our finances. We sent in claims forms, but had no idea whether the life insurance companies would pay out. And in the meantime I was due to leave my job in a few weeks' time when my contract ended and that would mean the loss of my small income. I knew I would, at some point, need to look for another job but despite my money worries I was glad that my current contract would soon be over. I'd had two weeks off after Daniel's death, so my colleagues all knew what had happened and most of them didn't know what to say to me, which was awkward and uncomfortable. I was so sleep-deprived and worn out that it was a huge physical challenge for me just to get through the day. I was utterly spent and I needed a break, besides which, Mum's health problems meant that she couldn't continue looking after the boys. I still had a contract with another private health care company for one morning a week and I found a child minder so that I could keep that going and at least keep a toe-hold in my work.

In late April I turned 40. My birthday felt like one of the hardest days of my life. Theo went to nursery and my parents looked after Milo while I spent the morning crying. I just couldn't snap out of it, I kept thinking about my last birthday. The painting Daniel took so much trouble choosing for me, our day on the farm with the boys and watching him playing with them; a family together. I had been so full of hope.

This birthday I felt as if I had been crushed by a train. I thought back to Daniel's fortieth birthday, eighteen months earlier. Milo had only been a month old and I had felt so complete and content. Daniel had been offered the job in London and as the house and garden filled with our family and friends we were both full of relief and optimism.

The speed at which our world had imploded was hard to take in. I felt I was in someone else's life, looking desperately around for my own. It all felt unreal.

Daniel and I had always planned to be in Venice for my 40th birthday. I had told him I was happy to postpone it, I just wanted him to get well and for us to be a family again. I hadn't given up on that dream. I wish he could have held onto it too.

Mum and Dad left in the afternoon and I felt a little anxious. I had planned to take the boys to Dorset to stay with Tania and her family the next day, but I didn't feel confident that I could cope with a trip. I felt weak in every sense. My family had made sure they were with me every weekend since Daniel died; this would be my first without their support and I felt wobbly. I took the boys for a walk on the beach and then, on impulse, into the church Daniel used to go to. Being there made me feel closer to him. We said a prayer for him together and lit a candle and I felt a little better afterwards, as though I had been given enough strength to cope with what lay ahead.

The following day I piled the boys and our bags into the car and set off very early for Dorset. Without the crutch of my parents' presence I was painfully aware that we were now a family of three. The empty passenger seat beside me felt strange and so wrong. It should have been Daniel in the driving seat with me sitting beside him. I felt as if our family had been butchered. I had timed the journey well; it was the day of Prince William and Kate Middleton's wedding, so the roads were virtually empty. We stopped half-way at a Little Chef for tea and toast and the staff, with no other visitors, made a fuss of the boys, who behaved beautifully. I parked them in front of their DVD players in the back of the car for the rest of the journey. Daniel always sorted out anything technological and I considered myself clueless, but I had worked out how to install the DVD players and surprised myself with my own competence.

We found our way to Tania's by mid-morning. She wasn't in, she had sent me a text to say that she would be home soon and had left the key hidden for me. Theo and Milo were wild with excitement; there were loads of toys for them, a huge trampoline and an endless garden and when Tania arrived home she introduced them to the three horses, two dogs and flock of chickens.

Tania's three year-old twins, Luca and Malika were delighted to see us. Theo and Luca paired off and Malika dragged an uncomplaining Milo about as if he were her doll. In the afternoon we took the children for a walk and lost one of the dogs, which Tania was looking after for a friend. Eventually we had to give up looking and get the children home. That evening Tania and Marcus were due to go to a wedding reception while I babysat. We gave the children dinner and got all four of them in the bath and at that moment Tania received a call to say that the dog had been found.

She rushed out to collect him leaving me with four over-excited children squashed into a bathtub. I managed to get them all out and into their pyjamas and when Tania returned we began the monumental task of getting all of them to sleep. Milo was freaked out by the unfamiliar surroundings and Theo panicked as he realised that he would be sleeping in a room by himself. Meanwhile Luca was yelling and trying every trick in the book to stop his parents from going out. It was utter chaos but we did accomplish the mission and Tania and Marcus headed out while I settled down to watch the recording of the Royal wedding. I

couldn't help but think of my own wedding, three years earlier. We had such a magical day; full of love and hope and
the promise of a happy future.

My moment of reflection didn't last long; Theo woke
crying from a nightmare but couldn't tell me what it was
about. As I comforted him, Milo began to bawl. I got him
out of his cot and took him through to Theo so that I could
comfort them both together but as I sat down, Luca woke
and started screaming. I rushed in to find that he had wet
the bed, after winning the battle with his parents to go to
bed without a nappy. He was very cross to be greeted by me
rather than his mummy and cranked his volume up several
notches. Miraculously, Malika slept peacefully through the
competing wails of the three boys.

I explained to Theo that I needed to comfort Luca
because his mummy wasn't there. He accepted this and settled down. I took Milo with me and tried to comfort Luca
but he was furious and wouldn't let me near him. After
twenty minutes I decided to phone Tania as his furious
screams turned to trembling sobs. I felt bad about spoiling
her evening but she insisted she was happy to leave. After we
had got all three boys back to sleep, Tania turned to me and
said 'Did you feed the chickens?' 'Yes Tania,' I said, 'I really
am *bleeping* superwoman. I've had three toddlers kicking off
simultaneously, fed your whole *bleeping* farm and baked you
a cake. Would you like me to massage your feet now?' We
both giggled like teenagers and it felt good and weird to
laugh.

The weekend went well, but I was glad to get home on
the Sunday morning and grateful when Sam and Katie
decided to drive down for the day. Their warm presence
meant so much. I don't think I could have got through those

early weeks and months without the two of them, Tom and my parents. They all did their best to offer love and support and to ensure that we didn't spend our weekends alone.

Sam and Katie arrived at lunch time and took the boys off to see a circus, which gave me a chance to prepare for a meeting with the mental health team, arranged for later that week. When I had spoken to Dr Anton the day after Daniel's death he had offered to meet me and I'd decided to take him up on it because I had so many unanswered questions. I knew that the inquest might answer some of them, but I wanted to see the mental health teams face to face, to hear what they had to say.

Daniel would have told me to drop it. I could hear him saying that it was his choice to die and nobody else's fault. But he had not been in his right mind when he died and it had been their job to protect him. I had told them that he was suicidal and they had not responded. I wanted some answers. His suicide was certainly not out of the blue, there were so many warning signs and I felt that he had been badly let down. More than anything I wanted to know why they failed to act on the information that I was giving them and why they didn't section Daniel. They could have prevented his death.

Sam had offered to come with me to the meeting. I knew I would be nervous and emotional and didn't trust myself to speak, so he had agreed to read out what I'd written. He came down for the day and together we went to the local offices where Daniel had been so many times.

The meeting was chaired by a woman from a different mental health trust who would supposedly be unbiased. Dr Anton was there and so were Nathan and the manager of the crisis team. They were all very polite and patronisingly friendly and it became clear to me that they had met beforehand and had been briefed. I was asked by the chair-woman if I was going to be making a complaint against the service. I said no, that I just wanted my questions answered. I handed over to Sam to read what I had prepared. He got about halfway through before his voice started cracking and he was unable to go on. He said afterwards that reading it in black and white in that formal meeting brought home to him that Daniel had killed himself while under the care of two teams of professionals.

I was able to take over from Sam and finish reading it without faltering. I think I was fuelled by anger because I was acutely aware that those present had their guard up and were there to protect themselves rather than give me the information I so badly needed. I could see that Dr Anton was uncomfortable, his expression was pained and in his eyes I saw genuine regret. He and I both knew that I had been right in the phone calls that I'd made in the days before Daniel died, and that they should have resulted in some kind of urgent action in order to keep him safe.

Not a single one of my questions was answered. At the end of the meeting, the chairwoman suggested that, since I was clearly unhappy, I should make a formal complaint. And as I looked at them, their faces impassive, I decided that I had to.

Afterwards we met Mum with the boys in a little café nearby. It felt lovely to be with our two little cherubs whose only concern was which ice cream they were going to get. I ordered a strong coffee while Sam, still ashen, had a beer.

That night I wrote;

Daniel, I keep hearing you telling me that I'm wasting my time pursuing a complaint. In a way, I know that you're right. What have I got to gain from it? Nothing can bring you back. I hear you telling me not to waste my energy, it's past now and I must look forward and make a happy life for our boys. I know that's what you're urging me to do, but I feel so outraged and let down. Their judgement of you, of the risks your state of mind posed and of me, was so flawed. I need justice.

CHAPTER SEVENTEEN

For many months the world felt completely unsafe to me. I was constantly on high alert for the next tragedy and convinced that both my parents, who had health problems, were about to die. As for the boys, my mind went into overdrive as I imagined all kinds of gruesome scenarios, fearing that something awful was going to happen to them. I watched them like a hawk whenever we were out and didn't allow them to stay at my parents' home without me, even though Theo had been used to doing this all his life. I used the excuse that he was feeling insecure and needed me, which was true, but I was also feeling insecure and I needed the boys close to me. I couldn't bear the thought of losing one of them or them losing me so we had to stick together like glue.

Theo still wanted me to tell him that his daddy would be back. He insisted that Daniel would be back for his birthday despite me telling him gently that it couldn't happen. He had regular tummy aches and complained of feeling sick, storing his emotions in his guts. I tried to talk to him about how sadness can cause these symptoms and he seemed to understand, he was sometimes able to say that he had 'a sad sort of tummy ache'.

Most of the time, however, he was like a force of untamed energy; a loose cannon; hyperactive, chaotic, unable to settle down to anything at all and quite aggressive at times, especially with Milo and other young children. He was fine with adults but became hyper and overly boisterous with other children. He was an almost constant preoccupation for me – would he be alright, how would he cope with school, what could I do to help him? The play therapist, Ann, urged me to stop comparing Theo to other children of his age and to stop expecting him to behave as they did. She said that he'd had a very different life experience to most other children and it was unrealistic to expect him to not have issues. He was only four and he'd lived through a tremendous amount of stress, change, trauma and loss in his short life. Reminding myself of that helped me a great deal.

He had so many questions and such a vivid imagination about what had happened. He had drawn a picture of heaven as a magnificent castle perched on a cloud. Daniel was up there with Grandma's cat Muffin and God and Jesus. Daniel was standing and waving to us. Theo missed him so much.

He also became very faddy about food. This had started after Milo was born, when Theo was angry with me and communicated this by rejecting the meals I prepared for him. Mealtimes became an awful battle as he would really only eat a few favourites, fish fingers, spaghetti bolognese or tuna pasta, without a fuss. In hindsight, I can see that mealtimes gave Theo a sense of control and guaranteed him my full attention and concern. This intensified after Daniel died as he flatly refused to eat fruit and vegetables of any kind. I got quite clever at disguising them in various ways and was relieved just to get anything healthy inside him. Milo appeared to be happy and oblivious – although he was waking a lot at night. I knew there would come a time when he would understand what had happened and go through his own grief and I worried about both of them being permanently psychologically damaged. A bottomless well of fear for the boys kept me awake night after night. What was this loss doing to my sons and how could I possibly repair it all? I was indescribably exhausted, struggling to keep my eyes open to get through the day and then getting into bed at night only to lie awake for hours on end. Dr Shank increased my sleeping pills, while urging me not to take them every night.

Perhaps because I am very good at containing my emotions, I don't cry or get outwardly upset easily, they manifested as physical symptoms, and the extent of this surprised me. In addition to the faint and dizzy spells, I had strange sensations in my eyes; a flickering which didn't hurt but was uncomfortable. It made my eyes water, leaving me unable to see for a few minutes at a time. It also made me feel nauseous; it was like a migraine without the pain. If I was driving when it happened I had to pull over, and it was becoming more and more frequent. Dr Shank suggested I get my eyes tested, but I think we both knew it was caused by stress.

By May the prospect of the inquest loomed over me like a dark cloud. I had no idea what to expect from it, but I knew it would be harrowing. I had been told that I would have to read the statement I made and that I would be allowed to ask other witnesses questions. It all sounded very daunting, but I prepared my questions carefully, hoping that I might yet be able to get some answers.

Once again my family stepped in; Mum and Dad looked after the boys while stalwart Sam came with me. We arrived early to find most of the mental health professionals in the waiting room. I caught Dr Anton's eye and we mouthed 'hello'. It felt very civil and I imagined that he and Nathan felt as nervous as I did. I didn't feel malice towards them; I just wanted them to take some responsibility for what happened, in the hope that the same mistakes wouldn't be made in the future.

We were met by the coroner's assistant who told me I would be called first and who showed us the courtroom and the dock. My stomach was flipping over and over yet I also felt a steely determination. This was my chance to speak for Daniel, and I was not going to let him down.

Maggie, Adam and Imogen arrived together. They smiled hello and sat alongside me and Sam on the front bench, but there was a conspicuous gap between them and us. Daniel's father and his wife also arrived. The medical 'professionals' were seated behind us and behind them were the local press.

I could see that Adam was angry and I soon realised he had come with his own agenda for the day. He requested time to look at all the reports that the mental health teams and medical teams had submitted. The coroner adjourned for 45 minutes to give us the opportunity to read them but I was too nervous to read anything. I was putting all my resolve and energy into calming myself down before I was called to the dock, concentrating on breathing and counting in order to control my rising sense of panic. It did occur to me, in a moment of irony, that I was using the same techniques Daniel and I had used together when I was in labour.

When I was called I made my way to the witness box and read my statement flawlessly. I had expected to be stuttering, but I felt full of strength and determination. Perhaps Daniel was helping me. At the end, the Coroner, who was kind and considerate towards me, asked if I had anything else to add.

I said that this was a death that had felt inevitable; there had been so many warnings that Daniel was going to kill himself and that I had questions about the response of the professionals involved. The coroner asked me a few questions before telling me to return to my seat. I felt relieved to have got through it and amazed by my sudden burst of confidence.

Adam was the only other family member to be called as a witness. He had to describe how he found Daniel, alive and able to walk downstairs to the ambulance, and then watched him die a few hours later. The shock in the courtroom was palpable.

When the doctor who treated Daniel took the stand he described in clinical terms Daniel's last hours. As I discovered how much aspirin he had taken – more than three times the lethal dose – and what it did to his body, my strength drained away and I wept silent tears.

Adam fired a lot of questions at him. He clearly felt that Daniel could have been saved and wanted to prove that he died because of a medical blunder. They spent a long time talking about the fact that Daniel had walked to the ambulance when he was just hours from death. Had that worsened his condition? Why were we told that he would need some dialysis but would recover? Nobody seemed to think that he was at risk of death. This was clearly what had been haunting Adam and he spent the whole morning batting questions to the doctor.

I was quiet through most of this. I didn't share Adam's concerns about the care Daniel received in hospital. In my mind, it was too late to save him by then. I did ask if he would have had permanent health problems if he had survived and if he would have had a chance of surviving if he had been found sooner. I got a maybe to both questions.

The proceedings were stopped for lunch. It was strange to walk from the intensity of the court into a street full of people going about their lives. Sam and I headed for a small café nearby. It was a lovely, warm day and when I phoned home my parents were getting the boys ready to go to the beach. For a second, I contemplated making a run for it and spending an afternoon on the beach with them. My attendance wasn't compulsory, but I felt I had to be there, for Daniel and for my own peace of mind.

Sam and I sat in silence over our coffees in the café, each of us absorbing all that we had listened to in the morning. Hearing it was one thing but comprehending it and accepting it was quite another. Adam, Imogen and Maggie came in and sat at another table. They were friendly to us, but there was an unspoken distance. We were all reeling, spiralling in different directions as we tried to come to terms with our loss.

When I bumped into Adam outside the loos he told me that he'd seen Nathan vomiting in a cubicle. I had suspected, almost from the start, that Nathan was unwell, either physically or mentally or both. He'd had a lot of time off sick and he looked fragile and unhealthy and in my view was not up to the job. A number of times I had suggested to Daniel that he request another community psychiatric nurse but Daniel always stuck up for him. He agreed that Nathan was inefficient but he had a rapport with him. Perhaps, his inefficiency suited Daniel; it was easy for him to pull the wool over Nathan's eyes.

I felt sorry for Nathan; I didn't want him to feel responsible for, or haunted by Daniel's death and hearing that he'd been sick after the morning's events affected the way I asked my questions in the afternoon. I did feel that his actions were crucial; he dismissed the information I gave him about

Daniel's mental state in the last week of his life and missed a chance to prevent Daniel's death. But Nathan worked within a team who should all, collectively, have offered Daniel better care and I was acutely aware that that team was a cog in a much wider system of inadequate mental health treatment in Britain.

Dr Anton took the stand first in the afternoon and he gave a thorough and honest account of his treatment of Daniel. I did feel that he was suggesting there was a lack of communication from Nathan in the last week. I asked him a lot of questions and some were answered.

When Nathan took the stand I felt worried for him and the Coroner also seemed to be taking a gentler approach with him. Perhaps she had been informed of his frailty. I told him that I felt it was wrong to blame him individually and that I considered there were failures within the whole team. I did ask him, more than once, if he had passed on to Dr Anton the content of my telephone messages during Daniel's last few days. Initially he gave a vague answer and then he said, 'I can't remember'. A weak and inadequate answer but I let it drop. That said it all really. Nathan was weak and vulnerable and in no fit state to be working with other vulnerable people and making decisions that could save, or lose, lives. Seeing him that day gave me the answers I needed. Did I need him to admit his fault and take responsibility for his mistakes? Not really.

I think all the mental health professionals knew that they had made mistakes with Daniel's treatment but they weren't going to admit it. I could only hope that they would learn from them. I did lose my composure, briefly, when a nurse from the crisis team took the stand. She was the person who visited Daniel, in our home, on the evening that he took the overdose. She must have been the last person he spoke to and yet he successfully convinced her that he was alright, before consuming a vast, carefully stockpiled amount of aspirin. Her attitude made me angry. She said there was nothing in Daniel's presentation that suggested he was suicidal that night. I kept asking her why his recent history of suicide attempts coupled with my anxious phone calls telling Nathan that he was vulnerable didn't alert concern. Her answer was 'taking away a person's liberty and sectioning them is a very serious act, we can't lock people up forever'. I was livid but close to tears again, my voice was cracking and I was getting nowhere so I backed down. What I wish I'd replied was 'and allowing a vulnerable person in your care to kill himself in his family home, leaving four children to grow up without a father is a far more serious act. Nobody is suggesting that it's OK to lock people up forever, but sectioning Daniel under the Mental Health Act would probably have been for 28 days; long enough to keep him safe until his mood stabilized'. I so wish I'd said that.

To me, that nurse's attitude was; 'He killed himself. It happens, there's nothing we could have done about it. Get over it'. It made me so angry. My husband was a brilliant, loving family man who lost his way at the end of his life. They could have saved him and they failed to and all our lives will now be forever changed because of their incompetence. We will all have to live with this, and with the sorrow and loss, forever.

The verdict, after a nine hour inquest, was that Daniel intended to and successfully took his own life. The purpose of the inquest was to establish the facts around his death, not to hold anyone accountable, but I was reminded by the coroner that I had the right to complain about the treatment that he received. Her saying this, in court, meant a lot. It validated my sense of injustice and felt like powerful support. Days later the local paper reported Daniel's death under the heading 'Suicide Victim Failed by System'.

As we left at the end of the day I said goodbye to Daniel's family. It was clear that we all had a different experience and interpretation of his illness and death and we had all retreated to different corners to come to terms with his loss in our own ways. I have since understood that this is very common after suicide, the legacy of guilt and grief is so complex and destructive. It was heart-breaking that instead of being united in our loss of Daniel, it created separation. It was tough on my boys who not only lost their father but also some close bonds with family members. I remain hopeful that these relationships may rekindle as time softens the rawness of grief.

After the ordeal of the day I felt drained and empty. It was nice to get home, to help get the boys to bed and live in the moment, as they do, for a short time. Mum and Dad had to get home but Sam planned to stay for the weekend and I was so grateful that for the next few days I wouldn't be alone.

Once the boys were in bed, Sam went out for a walk and was gone for a couple of hours. I imagine he was trying to digest it all. I spaced out in front of the TV, too drained to think about the day's events. It had been harrowing and I felt as if I'd been beaten to a pulp.

I had hoped for a sense of peace from the inquest, or at least the feeling that I could now move on. But it achieved neither of those.

The next morning Sam and I dropped Theo off at nursery and took Milo with us to my gym. Milo went into the crèche for an hour while Sam and I did a circuit class. It was really therapeutic to have a hard workout and we got

home in time to have a quick shower before picking Theo
up from nursery. After my shower, I glanced out of the bedroom window and saw the council refuse lorry chugging
down the road. I'd forgotten to put the bins out so I threw
some clothes on and rushed out after it. I managed to catch
up with it and when I got home, I was greeted by Sam in
hysterics at the sight of me, half-dressed, running down the
road, dragging two wheelie bins. It felt good to laugh.

That weekend we went along to the Summer Fete at
the school where Theo would be starting in September. I
wanted him to become more familiar with the school and
it was nice to spend a few hours doing something easy and
normal. Theo went off with Sam to look at the stalls while
Milo came with me, dragging me enthusiastically towards
the cake stall.

We saw a few friends there but I found it very hard to
make small talk. I just couldn't manage casual interactions
when inside I felt so full of worry and fear. I felt like I was
living inside a hellish bubble, disconnected from the day to
day reality of other people.

Two weeks after the inquest I left my job in the secure
unit. It was a relief; I had lost any interest in my work. I
had always felt passionate about it, but it involved giving out
an awful lot of emotional energy and I just didn't have it.
I was spent. The truth was that my identity as a therapist
had taken a battering and I had lost a lot of confidence in
my professional competence. I felt embarrassed telling new
people what I did for a living, especially if they knew about
Daniel. I felt, and imagined that they thought, how could
I be helping others with their psychological issues when I
couldn't help my husband? I was used to being the one in
the role of the professional, but now I was on the other side
and that made me feel like a failure.

I was sad to say goodbye to some of my patients. One of them, a woman I was very fond of who ironically was suffering a mental breakdown following the suicides of both her father and brother, told me she had a goodbye present for me. In a very croaky and out of tune voice, she sang all of Amazing Grace; Daniel's favourite hymn. I felt very touched, I told her that it was a song that I loved and she said that 'the Lord' had asked her to sing it to me.

A few days later I was getting the boys ready to go out to the park when the post arrived. There were two letters. The first was a copy of the final, amended death certificate. I had been using an interim certificate which had the cause of death as 'unknown'. On the official death certificate, the cause of death is 'salicylate poisoning'. Reading it made me go cold; it all became very real when I saw it in black and white, in an official document. At least I would be able to show it to the many official bodies insisting they see the original. Some of the demands were so pathetic and insensitive. I was being hounded by Daniel's mobile phone company, with endless phone calls and letters demanding that he pay his bill. He owed them seven pounds. I had explained, several times, that he had died yet they still kept sending their relentless demands.

I put the certificate aside and moved on to the next official looking envelope. Inside this one was a cheque for a generous sum of money. There was no letter with it but I knew that it was from one of the life insurance companies. It wasn't the full amount that we were insured for but, I realised, when put together with the proceeds of the house sale, it would be enough to pay off our debts and enable me to buy somewhere to live.

At first I couldn't take it in. I took the boys to the park, met our friends and spent an hour or two there without thinking about it. It was only on the way home that it hit me – after all the weeks of desperate worry, we would, after all, be able to have a home.

As we walked back to the house, I felt Daniel. It was the strangest sensation, and the only time that I have really physically felt his presence. It was like a warm breeze embracing me with such love. I had goose bumps and I suddenly felt incredibly peaceful.

Everybody had been telling me that I hadn't a hope in hell of getting anything from the life insurance and yet this policy had paid some of it. I had a powerful sense that Daniel was behind me getting the money. If he had any kind of powers up there, looking after me and the boys financially would have been his first priority. I have visions of him pulling all the strings that he possibly could to get us the pay-out. I felt so grateful, and such a huge sense of relief. It would give us some security and that would bring me some comfort. It was Daniel's legacy to us.

In the weeks that followed, Daniel's daughters got a full pay-out. I discovered that the policy for me and the boys was not paying out in full on the grounds of non-disclosure. They had requested Daniel's medical records and argued that he had dishonestly answered the questions about his previous mental health issues. This wasn't entirely true, Daniel had not been diagnosed with a mental illness until June 2010, four and a half years after the policy was set up. At the time, I just felt relieved to have got anything at all and too exhausted to fight. However, it is frustrating and unjust that if my husband had died of cancer or a road traffic accident, my children and I would probably be living a lot more comfortably now.

A week after I received the cheque, I accepted an offer on the house. It was higher than the original one we lost when Daniel died and the new buyers were happy to wait until I had got through all the legal red tape and found a new place to live.

I threw myself straight into house-hunting. Some people urged me to wait and not to make any major decisions so soon after my bereavement. But apart from anything else, we couldn't afford to stay in the old house so I really had no other option.

I was keenly aware that ours was the only home that Theo and Milo had ever known and, of course, it was full of memories of Daniel. But we all needed somewhere we could settle without the shadow of financial fear and without heartbreak, regret and painful memories lurking in every corner. Finding us a new home, as soon as possible, felt like the right thing to do.

CHAPTER EIGHTEEN

One glorious summer morning a few days later, I walked into town with the boys and passed a house with a 'for sale' sign outside. I must have been past it hundreds of times, it was only five minutes from us, but I'd never noticed it before. It was smaller than our house, and set a couple of streets back from the seafront. The outside was shabby and dated, but I felt it was worth a look.

I went straight into the estate agents to arrange a viewing and Mum looked after the boys while I spent an hour looking at this house and three others. I was pleasantly surprised when I saw the inside; it was a lot more modern and well-kept than the exterior. I liked it, but it was close to a small park and I was worried that I might feel vulnerable living beside an open space. It wouldn't have crossed my mind if Daniel had been there, but on my own the world was no longer feeling safe, I felt unprotected and so responsible for the boys' safety.

That evening I wandered down to have another look at the shabby house. The park beside it was completely empty. No tramps, no teenagers, no suspicious looking figures. And for my high-octane boys a park would be a bonus. I decided to put in an offer.

The following morning, all thoughts of the house were put on hold when Tania phoned to invite us on holiday to

Corsica with her, Marcus and the children. Tania had told the boys she would take them on holiday, but I'd forgotten about it. Now she was keeping that promise. Sunshine and a change of scene did seem appealing, the boys needed some fun and so did I, but I was scared by the responsibility of taking the boys abroad on my own. How would I manage them both on the flight and in the swimming pool? What if they became ill? What if I did? As I packed our cases a week later, a myriad of dangerous scenarios whirled around in my head. The boys, of course, were delighted by the idea of flying in an aeroplane but I had to explain that it was not going to be possible for us to fly to heaven to see Daddy on the way. They ran around the house swinging their buckets and spades and asked endless questions about what the place we were going to would be like.

We spent the night before our early morning flight in a hotel near the airport. Over dinner in the restaurant that night Theo and Milo, over-excited and in unfamiliar surroundings, were a handful. Milo, uncharacteristically, was crying about everything and anything and Theo was chaotic and hyper and refusing to eat his food. We met another couple, friends of Marcus, who were going to be joining us with their four-year old daughter and baby, both of whom were impeccably behaved while their parents ate a civilised meal. My heart sank. Was I going to be able to cope with my two rapscallions?

The holiday resort was lovely and totally child-friendly, with kids' clubs and crèches in abundance. Theo, to my surprise, went happily to the kids' club and had a ball from the start, perhaps because there was a lot of stimulation and physical activity. He behaved well there, though occasionally he got over-excited around the pool and was a bit rough with some of the other children. Milo, on the other hand, was fretful and clingy in the absence of his familiar routine and surroundings. He didn't want to go to the crèche on the first morning, although he did eventually settle there.

With both the boys occupied I went running and then spent an hour reading or just reflecting. This time to myself was soothing to the soul and gave me a chance to process some of the madness of the previous few months and to think about our future.

I did feel a bit conspicuous being the only single person in a resort full of families, and I dreaded having to explain why I was on my own. I knew I wouldn't be able to bring myself to say that my husband was dead. I was with Marcus and Tania a lot of the time and I felt people were wondering which of us his partner was. Marcus cheekily started telling people who asked that Tania was his wife and I was his mistress, which made me smile. I could almost hear Daniel's raucous laughter.

I found all the socialising quite hard and most evenings I would have been happier spending the time quietly on my own, but I was very aware that everyone was there to enjoy themselves and I didn't want to spoil the atmosphere with my misery, so I made an effort to join in. On the first evening Theo was very keen to go along to the DVD club with Luca and his new friends, so I got Milo to sleep in his buggy before dropping them both off. I explained to the staff that they had recently lost their father and asked them to come and get me if Theo was not happy or behaving well.

When I went to collect the boys at about 9.30pm, I found Theo quietly sobbing in one of the camp beds. The staff assured me that most children are a bit tearful on the first night and that they hadn't felt it necessary to come and get me. I was cross because Theo's separation anxieties were far more acute than most children's. His world felt dreadfully unsafe; he was terrified that I would disappear and leaving him crying in a strange bed, with unknown staff and far away from home, was the last thing that he needed.

Despite this he wanted to go back, so after that first night I promised him that I would be there to collect him as soon as the film ended and this worked well for both of us. I was happy to eat a meal with the other adults but had no desire to stay longer and socialise afterwards. What I needed more than anything was sleep, so the three of us were all tucked up into one double bed by 9.30pm.

It was good for me to have a couple of hours each day away from the boys, although when the time came to fly home I was glad; home somehow provided a sense of peace and security for us all and despite my mixed feelings about the house, it was surprisingly comforting to get back there.

When we arrived I found a small, single white feather on the sofa. My parents had come to stay with us and Mum was convinced that it was a sign that Daniel had been there. I chose to believe that too, it was a very warming thought. Of course, I know that the feather probably just found its way out of the cushions on the sofa, but I liked the idea that Daniel had been in the home he loved so much, looking after it while we were away.

Dad came with me to have a look at the new house the next morning and he liked it, though it clearly needed a bit of work. My offer had been accepted and I'd managed to knock quite a lot off the asking price so there would be a little money left to spend on it. It gave me something to focus on and I threw myself into finding solicitors, arranging surveys and selling furniture, glad of yet more reasons to keep busy. I was afraid that if I wasn't preoccupied with things to do I would be engulfed by grief and become unable to function.

I decided I would sell all our furniture and start again. Most of it was too big for the new house anyway, but I also felt that I wanted to close some doors. There were so many dreadful memories that went with our home and I didn't want to hang onto them. Most of all I wanted to get rid of the bed in which Daniel had lain dying.

Sometimes I felt guilty that I was not an emotional wreck. A couple of years earlier if someone had looked into a crystal ball and told me that my husband was going to kill himself I would have believed that it would break me. But it hadn't and I was getting on with life, doing mundane things with the boys and coping. Falling apart just wasn't an option, I needed to create some security and stability for us all and getting us into a new home was the first step. I was reminded of the dream I had before Daniel died. Now I really was in that sink or swim situation and I was choosing to swim with all my might. I knew that when I reached a place of safety, I would have the space to mourn.

For a few weeks life seemed to be, if not exactly better, then at least heading towards a little pinprick of light at the end of a very dark tunnel. But just as I dared to feel hopeful, the world came crashing in on me again when my mother suffered a stroke.

Four months earlier, on the day that Daniel died, the specialist had told us she would need surgery on the aneurysm in her brain. In mid-July she went into hospital for a pre-surgical procedure in which a tiny camera was inserted through an artery and into her brain to establish the exact location of the aneurysm and to attempt to redirect the blood flow from it. Sam was at the hospital with her and I spoke to him before taking Theo to a party after his last day at nursery. Sam said he'd call in a couple of hours when the procedure was over.

Theo and Milo did a lot of singing and stuffed themselves with homemade cakes and when we left Theo asked
me if we could go to 'Daddy's church' which was nearby.
It meant an extra ten-minute walk in the rain, but Theo
was insistent. After twenty minutes in the church – during
which the boys raced around and were anything but peaceful – Theo seemed satisfied and we headed home. Sam
still hadn't called and I was beginning to feel edgy. As we
approached the house, he phoned. There had been complications during the procedure and Mum was not in a good
way. He thought she'd had a stroke but this hadn't yet been
confirmed.

I felt strangely calm. In my head, I heard Daniel telling me that Mum was going to be fine. I focused on that
and managed to get the boys home, make them dinner and
remain outwardly upbeat and normal. After I had bathed
them I took a moment to sit by our bedroom window and
looked out at the sea. The boys were bouncing on the bed,
but Theo stopped and came over to climb on my lap. He
gave me a cuddle and said 'I love you Mummy'. He knew
something was up.

Once the boys were in bed I spoke to Sam again. Mum
had suffered a stroke and initially her left side had been
paralysed, but they'd been able to treat her straight away,
this gave her a much better chance of recovery and a few
hours on she seemed to be making good progress.

After the call I sat and wrote to Daniel:

*I keep hearing you telling me that she will be alright. I am still
numb. I feel very powerless in this world at the moment; as if I have
no control over the things that happen.*

*I have decided not to go to visit Mum yet. There isn't much I
can do and I think it best that I stay here and keep things normal
for the boys. That last sentence has actually made me laugh out*

loud. What the hell is 'normal'? Nothing is normal anymore; I feel my life is spinning out of my control. I am on a roller-coaster that I can't get off. I can only hang on and hope that it will eventually stop.

It was a tough decision to stay at home, but Mum had Dad and my brothers and I needed to protect the boys from more tension and worry. Besides which, the last thing my poor worried dad would need was the boys running around causing havoc.

Thankfully, the news over the following days was good; as the medical response was immediate, a lot of the damage would not be permanent.

I kept thinking about the fact that the boys and I had been in a church while Mum was having the stroke. I'd never spent a Wednesday afternoon in church in my life, and yet somehow we had been there, in a calm and peaceful place. I felt that perhaps Daniel had guided us there, to his church, looking after us and looking after Mum as she fought for her life.

A week later Mum was discharged from hospital and sent home to rest. Dad drove her down to see us, in time for Milo's second birthday. She wasn't well enough to join us for his birthday picnic with his friends, but at least she was a part of Milo's day.

The picnic was at the same farm we'd been to the year before with Daniel. Throughout the party I had such a terrible underlying sadness, thinking of all Milo's birthdays to come, without his father. But he was a little bundle of happiness and I was so glad of that. We all needed a happy day. I made him a monkey cake while Katie made him a duck one – he was mad about ducks. He was scooting around on Theo's blue scooter before he could walk so I bought him a little yellow one.

It was good to see Mum doing physically better than any of us could have hoped, but I could see that she didn't seem at all well emotionally. She seemed vacant and I suspected that she was traumatised by what she'd been through and very frightened that she would have another stroke. There was quite a high risk of her suffering another stroke for a month after the first, so it was a tense wait.

When we talked, she described being conscious but unable to talk or communicate as the medics worked to save her. She really thought that she was about to die and she told me that her first thought had been of Theo and how he would survive another loss. The next day, after she had been stabilised, one of the consultants said to her; 'You had an angel looking after you yesterday'. Mum said she knew it was Daniel.

Over the next month she gradually got better and as time passed and there was no further stroke she seemed to regain her confidence. We all breathed a collective sigh of relief – she would be alright, although perhaps not quite her old self for a while.

With the boys on my hands every day over the summer I missed the structure and routine of nursery. It was impossible for me to get anything done until the evenings as the two of them were such a handful together. I couldn't leave them unsupervised because Theo was too rough towards Milo. And I felt I couldn't meet up with friends and their children for the same reason. Theo seemed to be able to play alongside other children but not with them. If I took the boys out to a park or play centre Theo would play alongside children that he didn't know. But if I met up with friends whose children he knew he would become rough and overly boisterous and it would end up with Theo and me both feeling bad.

This left me avoiding friends and feeling isolated. I could only hope that when Theo started school in a few weeks' time he would find things easier. He was wildly excited about it – he had been counting the sleeps until his first day since June. We got his uniform ready and after I sewed his name labels into every item he delighted in trying it all on so frequently that I had to wash the whole lot before his first day.

In early September I exchanged contracts on the house. I hadn't told the boys about it because I wanted to be certain. When I did tell them that we would be going to live in a new home Theo's behaviour deteriorated rapidly. I knew that he must be feeling scared and anxious. Starting school and moving house in the same month would unsettle any child, let alone one who had been through Theo's experiences.

As the move drew nearer I began to realise just how huge it was for all of us, practically and emotionally. Apart from all other considerations it was a financial necessity, there was no choice, so all I could do was get on with it and make the transition as smooth as possible.

I did spend many evenings thinking about how much the home we were leaving had meant to Daniel. He had put his heart and soul into it and he was still so present in all the work that he had lovingly done. He'd made the children's beds himself and built a wood shelter in the drive and there were quirky little signs of his handiwork everywhere, like the light switches made from driftwood. I couldn't bear to think of leaving him behind; I began to plead with his spirit to come with us and look after me and the boys in our new home.

When Theo's first day at school finally arrived he was ready in his uniform by six-thirty am, and had put his new 'Ben Ten' bag and water bottle in the porch ready to go. He was full of exuberance; his only disappointment was that he would be going for a half-day, rather than a whole one. It was a lovely sunny morning so I took some photos of him in the garden in his uniform before we left. As we drove to school, he said 'Mummy can you talk about Daddy in heaven please'. He had never asked this before. I started to reiterate the story of Daniel getting an illness in his brain that the doctors were unable to make better. Before I got to the next bit, Theo interrupted and said, 'Daddy is sad now'. I said, 'Yes, the illness in his brain made Daddy feel very sad', but Theo said, 'No Daddy is sad now. He is sad that he is not here when I am starting school. I know he is sad Mummy because he just told me that he is.' I was left wondering what he had meant. Did he really feel Daniel's presence; feel the regret that I, too, knew that Daniel would have felt at not being able to be with him on this important day? It was unusual for Theo to want to talk about Daniel and yet for some reason he urgently needed to communicate his sense of Daniel being there. And once he had he seemed to be quite satisfied and ready for his day.

That evening I wrote;

I hope he was right, Daniel, and you were with him this morning, although I hate the thought of you feeling sad and regretful. You suffered enough emotionally in this world, I want you to be free from all that now.

Daniel's birthday fell two days after Theo started school. I told the boys that it was Daddy's birthday and Theo sang 'Happy Birthday' and asked if we could get a birthday cake and some candles. He said that he would blow out the candles and wish for Daddy to come back. After school, we went to the beach with ten brightly coloured balloons. We bumped into our next door neighbour, Sean, on our way and Theo asked him to come and join us. He obliged but was totally choked with emotion and couldn't stop himself from crying.

Everyone misses you so much, you were so unforgettable. I sometimes wonder if you were always destined to burn out early. I feel that you are still with me. Please keep hanging around. I know you are guiding me and working hard up there to look after all your loved ones.

The following day I turned on the news and saw a bulletin about the tenth anniversary of 9/11. I watched it for five minutes and then crumbled. The grief engulfed me and I couldn't stop crying.

Hello Daniel, I am so tired. The weekends are really hard. I feel we are a disabled family, like a three-legged animal struggling to get by with a crucial limb missing. Theo has been really challenging for the past couple of weeks. He has been struggling since I told him that we will be moving house soon. It's such a mammoth thing for us all to do so soon after your death.

Milo has become obsessed with talking about you. Whenever he sees an aeroplane he thinks that it is flying to you in heaven.

I have been so lonely in the evenings, I keep fantasising that you have simply been away somewhere and that you will walk back into my life and we will all move into the new house to start afresh together. Magical thinking, I know!

The permanency of your loss is so hard for us all to accept.

CHAPTER NINETEEN

O ur move, which I had thought imminent, was delayed to the end of the month. We were in a chain of five and each day a new drama threatened the collapse of the chain. But eventually, on September 30, moving day arrived.

From the start I loved our new house. It took us a couple of weeks to settle, but with the house move behind us and Theo now in school, the manic busyness that had kept my emotions at bay eased. I felt that I had got the three of us to a place of safety from which I could now pause. The shock of Daniel's death was wearing off and giving way to grief and I felt constantly sad. I kept looking at men everywhere and thinking, they are alive, why isn't he? He was so young and full of life, his decline was so rapid. How could he be dead?

I kept a promise to myself that I had made in Corsica, to stop using sleeping tablets. It wasn't easy; I had become reliant on them. I did it by breaking them in half each night and then substituting herbal sleeping aids that I bought at the chemist. It wasn't the end of my insomnia but I felt more in control of my sleeping difficulties.

As I reflected on all that had happened I began to wonder what was in Daniel's medical notes to warrant the life insurance company's accusation of non- disclosure. I was both curious and annoyed that we had not been given the full amount. The insurance company had been granted access to his notes and had clearly made their decision to not pay in full after seeing them. So I went to visit Dr Shank to find out more about Daniel's previous breakdown and was shown the sections in Daniel's notes which related to his previous contact with psychiatric services, twenty years earlier.

It was clear that Daniel's breakdown at that time was longer and more serious than he had led me, and the insurance company, to believe. However, it had been labelled as 'drug-induced'. Daniel had not been given a diagnosis so hadn't knowingly 'non- disclosed' a mental illness as the insurance company claimed. I honestly don't believe that Daniel was deliberately covering up his past to me or anyone else. He didn't view himself as suffering from mental health problems and neither did anyone else. He had believed that his previous breakdown was simply a dreadful experience caused by adolescent, reckless drug taking and he chose to erase it from his memory. I read a few pages of the notes and had to stop because I felt too sad when I read how desperate and broken Daniel had appeared to professionals at that time. He had clearly been very unwell. The suffering and despair that he felt during those brief and infrequent low periods in his life were so incongruent with the gregarious, confident man that I fell in love with.

After reading the medical notes I wrote;

It feels as if there were two Daniel's; the strong, competent, loving, funny and reliable man and this other unknown person; a sick and very sad man. How can they be the same person? Today I realised that you had been in that terribly dark place before in your life. I feel so sad for you Daniel; you didn't deserve to suffer so much.

Until Daniel lost his job, ten months before he died, I had never seen him down. Throughout our relationship he was always so full of optimism, with a carefree attitude that

I envied. I am a worrier, but Daniel would put my concerns into perspective and make everything feel alright. He would say, 'the universe is unfolding as it should'.

When I left the doctor's surgery I felt relief that Daniel's suffering had ended. I could see that his illness had plunged him into a black pit. He had been there before in his life and had survived, but this time, although he tried so hard to pull himself out of it, he kept being knocked back down. In the end he felt that he had lost all that was important to him, including his pride, dignity and self-worth. He gave up, and I will never blame him; I understood it.

I had recurring dreams of him coming back, as if he had just been away somewhere and we were celebrating his homecoming. It was awful to wake from them to the realisation that he was gone. As my shock wore off, my pining for him intensified;

I'm missing your physical bulk. I've got your ashes in my bedroom. That's just weird. I can't get my head around it and have barely looked at them. I wish I could have that chance to see you one last time again. I see little 'mini you' bodies in our boys, they both have your broad physique and physical power and strength.

Theo was also struggling. He had recurring nightmares about 'scary things' like monsters or skeletons. Because of my profession I was acutely aware of the importance and healing power of dreams and of sleep, so when Theo cried in his sleep I had to fight my maternal instinct to wake him and comfort him. Dreams are the mind's way of processing life's events and experiences. I had trained in EMDR (Eye Movement Desensitizing and Reprocessing), a very well-researched and effective treatment for post-traumatic stress, and it had taught me that the right side of the brain is where traumatic and emotional events are experienced, and that in order to process and assimilate these experiences, the left side of the brain, responsible for more logical and rational thoughts, needs to be activated. REM sleep, in which the eyes move from one side to another, is a natural phenomenon which helps the mind to process difficult experiences healthily, by making use of the functions of both sides of the brain.

Theo didn't only have nightmares; he often dreamed that Daniel was at his school, either in the classroom or picking him up at the end of the day. He liked having these dreams, but he would become very upset when he woke to the reality that daddy would never go to his school.

One Saturday afternoon I took him to a school friend's party. A few of his friends arrived at the same time, all with their dads, and he asked, 'Where's my dad?' Of course he knew the answer, but he needed me to repeat it. It was hard for my boys to compare themselves with their peers, almost all of whom seemed to have two loving parents.

I lay awake worrying about my sons' genetic make-up. I knew only too well that mental illness runs in families. According to statistics my children had a 10–20% chance of inheriting bipolar. Some statistics placed the likelihood even higher, and when Theo was hyper, loud and very emotional, bordering at times on being completely out of control, I worried that he had inherited the bipolar gene. At times fear engulfed me. I just kept hoping and praying that his issues were a natural expression of the trauma that he'd had to endure, so that I could deal with them and help him to overcome them.

At school he was often chaotic and disruptive and he seemed unable to manage friendships. It was obvious that he was grappling on both an emotional and social level and I worried that, if he wasn't bipolar, he might be autistic or have Attention Deficit Hyperactivity Disorder (ADHD).

He was a very angry little boy and he had reason to be; his daddy was no longer here, I hadn't saved him, his brother had arrived and messed up his family and nothing felt right in his life.

The teachers at Theo's school were caring and supportive, he was offered counselling in school and so with heavy hearts we said goodbye to Ann who had been a huge support to us all. The school staff worked hard with me to help Theo through his first very difficult months there and the SENCO was especially sensitive to Theo's extra emotional needs and was generous in the time, kindness and support she offered me. However, I often felt judged by other parents. Almost from the start Theo had a reputation for being a 'naughty boy' and I knew that we were being gossiped about and that my parenting was being criticized by a small group of mothers who had been cold and distant with me. They avoided me and the boys and I could sense their disapproval and judgement.

As Theo's fifth birthday approached in November it felt important to give him a wonderful day. There was so much that I needed to compensate for. I knew he was anxious to have a party that wowed his peers and I wanted to give our new home some happy memories, so I invited twelve of his friends and a clown, who filled the house with laughter. It was lovely to see Theo so happy and untroubled, but the following day he looked at me and said 'Daddy didn't come home for my birthday'. That summed up what we were both grappling with; the reality and irreversibility of Daniel's death.

Had it only been a year earlier that Daniel had been discharged from hospital the day before Theo's fourth birthday; seemingly on the road to recovery? It felt incomprehensible.

In contrast to Theo's struggles, Milo didn't yet appear to associate Daniel's absence with pain. He would proudly say that his daddy was in the sky with the aeroplanes, it was as though he thought that Daniel just lived somewhere else. However, wherever we went, Milo would latch onto men. He grew attached to the workman who came to fit the windows, he would cuddle his swimming instructor and he would call any man with a shaved head Daddy. He had started talking and a very humorous character emerged. I often imagined how much Daniel would have laughed and enjoyed doing impressions of his funny little ways, like talking in a French accent and naming all of his teddies Pub. Milo was going to be a strong character, just like his brother and his father.

Ella and Hannah continued to stay with us on occasional weekends and seemed to be doing well. Like Theo, they didn't want to talk about Daniel; it was all too painful for them. I had to fight the urge to push them; I wanted them to get on with their grieving now, to get it out of the way so that they could move on with living. But I knew that was impossible, they would face their emotions when they were ready.

Christmas arrived and it felt so wrong and painful for it to be happening without Daniel. I kept thinking of the previous Christmas, it was unbearable to look back, knowing that it had been Daniel's last. New Year's Eve was awful too, Daniel had been so excited about the prospect of London hosting the Olympics in 2012 and now he wasn't going to be here to see it. It all just felt absurd. The only good thing, as the New Year dawned, was thinking that the worst year of my life was over.

As we limped into the next year I continued to have vivid dreams about Daniel returning or about his suffering and death and the fear and uncertainty that I had felt in the months before he died.

I was at our new house; Daniel had come back from hospital, that's where he had been all this time. Everyone thought he was better, but he had ripped out the new gas fire I'd had fitted and was scraping the paint off the newly-decorated porch. He was saying that he didn't like what I'd done to the house and wanted to decorate it his way. I protested and Daniel went to the kitchen and picked up a very heavy saucepan and came towards me in a rage. I was terrified and cowered, but just before hitting me with the pan Daniel stopped himself and said he didn't want to hurt me. I crept upstairs to the boys. I got Milo from his bed and carried him through to Theo's bedroom. I was pondering how I could get them out of the house; I couldn't carry them both at once and knew that if Daniel saw me escaping with them it would ignite him. Suddenly Daniel started bellowing, making loud frenzied sounds, like an animal out of control. He sounded crazy and possessed, and then he became conscious of making the sounds and wailed, knowing that he was losing his mind. I felt so sorry for him but was also terrified of him. I scrambled around looking for my phone, wondering if I should phone the police.

I woke from this dream full of fear and lay awake for hours. It summed up my whole experience of Daniel being ill. I was afraid, but I also desperately wanted to help him. I could feel his pain and his love for us and at the same time I was trying so hard to shield the boys from his illness. It was a terrible position to be in.

It still felt shocking and very difficult to tell anyone what had happened. I was fine talking about it to people who already knew, especially if they had known Daniel, but it was hard to tell new people that I met and to face their shock, horror and pity. They were genuinely upset if I told them what had happened, but many then avoided me. It was all so horrifying and out of the realms of most people's experience. My social skills deserted me too; I had lost my ability to socialise and to make small talk. I felt as though I was in a different world to other people, this dreadful experience had alienated me and disconnected me from my peers and I could no longer relate to them.

As we approached the first anniversary of Daniel's death, I became unwell. The boys and I all got a nasty flu virus. After a week the boys bounced back, but I struggled to regain my energy and picked up one virus after another.

Other people assume that after a year, the grief must be subsiding and you are over the worst, but for me, that was when the deep mourning started. I fell into a painful, impenetrable gloom.

This feels like the hardest time since you died. It's like going back to that agonising time a year ago without the natural anaesthetic of shock. In my mind, I am reliving the final week of your life, remembering every last detail. Thinking about our last meal together, our last hug, last conversation. Wondering if I could have done anything to change your mind. Why didn't I force you to come away with me that weekend? Or stay with you? Of course, this time last year, we were both in a living hell, there is no point in dressing it up, but at least you were still here and there was hope.

I feel weak and run down, tired of being strong and of coping. Both the boys have been having a bad time too. I've had reports that they've both been behaving badly at school and nursery. It is soul-destroying and very worrying for me. But I know that it would be odd if there were no signs of disturbance in them, of course they are feeling it. And as well as their own feelings of loss and grief, they are picking up on mine and I feel terribly sorrowful and hopeless at the moment.

I grappled with my indecision about how to mark the anniversary on March 19. What would he have liked? What would be best for the boys? What could I handle? Should it be very private or should I make it a big thing and give

Daniel's friends and family a chance to join us in our thoughts and love for him? I dreaded everything about it. I knew it would stir up all those emotions that were dangling there behind the daily humdrum.

In the end I opted for a short and simple service in our local church on March 17 (Saint Patrick's day, Daniel would have been pleased with a celebration on Saint Paddy's day). I had questioned my decision not to take the boys to the funeral and this seemed like an opportunity for them to take part in a tribute to their father, so I planned a very child-friendly service that included beautiful readings, poignant songs, a speech from me and a chance for all of Daniel's children to light candles and say goodbye.

In the end it went really well and was an uplifting and healing service, with our family and close friends all there. Some of my oldest friends travelled a long way to be there, while more local friends, like Clare and Helena, helped with the readings and making tea and coffee afterwards.

That morning I had opened the front door to find a beautiful bunch of flowers on the doorstep. It was from two friends, Elizabeth and Richard. I hadn't known them well when Daniel died but Richard and Daniel had been good friends; often kite surfing together and after Daniel's death they generously offered me any help they could. I hadn't asked often but if I needed help with childcare, for instance for appointments for Theo that I couldn't take Milo along to, Elizabeth was happy to help, despite having her hands full with four young children of her own. It was little acts of genuine kindness and thoughtfulness like theirs that really did make a difference.

I was proud of how well the boys coped with the service. Theo was excited, he knew it was a special occasion and was thrilled that his two best friends and Uncle Sam were there.

He was calm and well behaved all day. Milo had not fully recovered from a virus and so clung to me clutching his candle. He became more involved after the service when we released 41 coloured helium balloons on the beach, one for each year of Daniel's life.

Afterwards everyone gathered in the church hall. I'd had a cake made of a kite surfer and Ella and Hannah, wanting to contribute, had made chocolate brownies the night before. I could hear Daniel protesting about having tea and cake on Saint Patrick's Day. He'd have preferred a pint of Guinness or his favourite Jameson's Whisky and an Irish knees-up, but since we were in a church hall in the middle of the afternoon and surrounded by children, tea and cake had to suffice.

I had dreaded standing up in front of everyone to give a speech, but when the moment arrived, my nerves disappeared. I had written and re-written it many times, and in the end I kept it simple, recounting a couple of typically Daniel stories, including the one about the wood burning stove, after Theo's birth and the one about the white paint all over our garden after Milo arrived. I went on ...

There were so many facets to Daniel. He was sharply intelligent, witty and charming and endearingly warm, loving and generous. He was one of a kind and not someone who could ever be forgotten.

An unthinkable tragedy happened a year ago. My sense of outrage and anger towards the two mental health teams that were treating Daniel remains as acute now as it did a year ago. I don't think that it will ever be possible for me to forget how grossly inadequate the treatment that Daniel received was, or the total lack of protection or support for myself and my children during Daniel's illness.

It is hard to believe that a year has passed, or to reflect on the last year because none of it feels very real or comprehensible. In the first few days following Daniel's death, I felt that everything was going to crumble, that time would stop, how on earth would life possibly continue? But I quickly discovered that there really wasn't an alternative to gathering my strength, to keep on going.

Along with the support from my family and close friends, it has been the strength and courage of Daniel's four children that has inspired me and kept me going.

It is Ella, Hannah, Theo and Milo whose loss is the greatest and I have watched all of them courageously getting on with their lives in their own individual ways. Actually, Daniel would have referred to his four children in the following order; Theo, Hannah, Ella and Milo. This was because he liked the fact that in this order, their initials spelt THEM.

Daniel was a difficult man to buy presents for. He was brutally direct in telling me how much he disliked what I had chosen for him. Not long after we had Milo, I found a large, flat pebble on the beach and had the word THEM engraved on it. I hit the jackpot with this gift. He truly treasured it and took it everywhere with him.

It was heartening that people were able to think about Daniel with warmth and laughter. At the funeral, there had been so much shock, anger and blame in the air. The memorial was less painful; it was about Daniel and we were able to think about him and laugh and smile as well as cry.

My parents stayed on for the anniversary, two days later. It was a warm and sunny day, just as it was on the day he died. In many ways, the day was filled with the usual routines; getting the boys ready and taking Theo to school. The sunshine gave me a spring in my step as we walked to school. With the memorial service over I felt a weight had been lifted, it had been cathartic for me.

After dropping Theo off, I had a meeting with his teacher. I had thought about rescheduling it when I saw the date but then decided that I might actually be pleased to be focusing on something else. And I wanted to give his teacher some feedback on how Theo had coped with the memorial. It was a positive meeting and I was pleasantly surprised to hear that he seemed more settled at school. I came out of the meeting feeling relieved and thinking, he is actually going to come through this, he is going to be fine; he just needs time and love.

At lunch time I went to the church, lit a candle and sat quietly by myself, thinking about Daniel and reflecting on the service and how therapeutic it had been for the boys and for me. I dashed back from the church because I was expecting the delivery of a tree the boys and I had chosen to plant in our garden, for Daniel. A lovely, friendly gardener named Nick brought it in a pot. It was an Amelanchier; a small hardy tree that I'd been told could stand up to the harsh weather in our area. It looked like a frail collection of branches rather than a tree but soon after we got it, it came alive with the most beautiful white blossom.

Between five and six, the time of Daniel's death, I took advantage of my parents being there and went out to the beach. I hadn't really spent that much time at the beach since he died, even though it was on my doorstep, but when I did go, it still felt like Daniel's place. He spent so much time on the beach when he was well. It didn't matter what the weather was doing, what time of the year or day it was, he was always, 'just popping to the beach'. I would watch him from our bedroom window, kite surfing or sometimes just looking at the sea.

I had picked a good time to go and just caught the sun setting over the rocks. The sky was bright red and the sea my favourite turquoise. It wasn't calm and still as I like it, but choppy, textured and dynamic as he loved it. Truly beautiful and energising.

I thought about the many times we had gone to the beach together, often in the evening when Mum had been with us to look after the boys. We used to sit on the rocks and just watch the sea. Daniel never took for granted the beauty of the coast that was quite literally our front garden; he loved it with a passion. As I sat on the rocks that evening, I thought about how he observed and appreciated the beauty of nature. He was always getting me to watch a sunset, look at the moon, count the stars, smell the blossom, and walk barefoot in the sand in winter. I questioned how he could have tired of all the beauty in this world, and wondered if it was as beautiful where he was. Was heaven really blissful and free from pain? I hoped so. I knew that Daniel would want me to let go and move on with my life, and I wanted him to do the same. As I wrapped my cardigan around me and watched the sun set, I whispered, 'Rest and be peaceful Daniel'.

CHAPTER TWENTY

Weekends were the hardest. There seemed to be families everywhere, enjoying themselves together, while the boys and I struggled to get through endless hours of lonely time.

I felt so alienated from everyone around me. Not just because my husband was gone, but because I had a child with problems. I felt judged and excluded by some of the other parents. I knew that there were children in Theo's class having parties that he was not invited to, and I knew he was being taunted about it at school. Every time he got cross with me he would tell me angrily that I wasn't going to be invited to his party. His birthday wasn't for six months; this was clearly what he was hearing at school. We turned up for football one Saturday morning and none of his classmates were there because they were all at a party. Theo was so upset that he wouldn't play football, usually the highlight of his week. I felt as alienated as he did.

On the first day of the Easter holidays I felt utterly wretched. We were faced with an empty weekend, no plans and no company. In addition to the problems with some parents at school, losing Daniel had created a distance in many of my local friendships. Those friendships had been forged when we were all in similar circumstances, expecting our first babies. Our lives became so different that many of them now tip-toed around me, not knowing what to say.

I felt overwhelmed by the prospect of single-handedly raising these two, full-on boys. I was petrified of how the trauma would affect them in the long term. Searching for answers, I started re-reading John Bowlby's theories on attachment and loss, written in the 1950's. I had read them when I trained as a therapist, but now I re-read his work with Theo and Milo in mind. Bowlby said that human beings need healthy attachments to others in order to develop a secure and healthy inner view of themselves and the world. He wrote a lot about how experiencing separations from attachment figures in early life can have devastating effects on a child's psychological development, cognitive functioning and developing personality. Bowlby's studies of mourning, in both adults and children, were influential in the social acceptance of grief as a healthy rather than pathological process. Until Bowlby's work, children were thought to be unable to mourn an emotional loss as adults do. Today his theories underpin the work of contemporary child bereavement organisations. He outlined the stages of mourning as; numbness, yearning and searching, disorganisation and despair and reorganisation and said that children go through all the stages, apart from the numbness, just as adults do. Today, these stages have been adapted and simplified to; denial and isolation, anger, bargaining, depression and acceptance. I could identify with so much that he wrote, although I don't believe that the process of grief is as linear as these stages suggest. My worries for my boys eased, especially after reading that anger (commonly acted out through aggressive behaviour in children) and acute anxiety were natural reactions to the trauma they were experiencing.

In a book about John Bowlby's work, psychiatrist Dr Jeremy Holmes reflects on the impact of grief and loss on young children;

'The manner in which a child's carers respond to her or his reactions to loss, whether major or minor – to the anger and pining and demandingness – may crucially influence that child's subsequent development. The establishment of a secure internal base, a sense that conflict can be negotiated and resolved, the avoidance of the necessity of primitive defences – all this depends on parental handling of the interplay between attachment and loss that is the leitmotiv of the Bowlbian message.' ('John Bowlby and Attachment Theory', By Jeremy Holmes 1993).

I found this quote heartening and hopeful. It made me feel less helpless about the cards that Theo and Milo had been dealt. I could minimize some of the damage by the way that I loved them, raised them and helped them to grieve. In moving to our new house I felt I had re-established a secure base for them, I knew that they had a secure and healthy attachment to me, and in time I hoped they would begin to feel more secure within themselves. Tough as it was on my own, I loved them to bits. Milo was such a mummy's boy, always wanting a cuddle, he was a bundle of funniness, while Theo, outgoing and gregarious like his father, had started playing the clown, having discovered that it got him attention and made him feel popular.

Daniel died a month before Easter, so it felt like a difficult holiday for us, made worse by the story of the crucifixion. The boys were told the story at school and church, and I was left to explain how one man could die and come back, but their daddy could not. They were too young to comprehend it.

We spent the Easter weekend with my parents. Sam and Katie took the boys to Legoland on Good Friday and they came back buzzing. The following day Sam taught Theo to ride his bike without stabilizers. I was so pleased, but couldn't help feeling sad too, thinking about how much Daniel would have loved doing that and how proud and delighted he would have been. That evening the boys were bathed and in their pyjamas, bouncing around before bed, when I realised that Milo had wandered off. I found him sitting at the table with a whole Easter egg in his paws and chocolate all over his face. He looked up and said, 'me hungry Mummy!'

I was grateful for these humorous moments and for my family's support because I was having a miserable Easter. I'd spent a night with acute earache and was diagnosed with another ear infection. Soon afterwards my eardrum perforated, which brought some relief, but I was unwell all through Easter and over the next couple of weeks I continued to have one illness after another. I was in and out of the doctor's surgery with infections in my chest, throat, sinuses and ears. On one visit I told Dr Shank that I was aware that all my ailments were psychosomatic and caused by grief. He offered me anti- depressants but I wasn't depressed and I didn't want to mask my grief, I wanted to face it head on and be done with it. I felt strongly that this was the only way to heal. I thought about what all these infections were expressing. Anger, guilt, rage? People assumed that I must be angry with Daniel for leaving me and the children in the way that he did, but I hadn't ever really felt anger, just a deep, unrelenting sadness, firstly for Daniel, and then for all four of his children, and then for myself and his family.

What did make me angry was the response I got to my complaint about the way Daniel was treated by the mental health services. I had persevered for a year with the complaints procedure but I was getting nowhere. The tone of their letters was condescending and they gave endless excuses and justifications for their decisions. They clearly wanted to cover their backs and their attitude left me full of fury and frustration. I kept hearing Daniel telling me to drop it and move on. But we had lost him and my family was now disabled and defined by his loss. Surely I was entitled to some answers?

In one letter they wrote;

'We are confident that all the risks were carefully considered and that the appropriate interventions were offered at the right times.'

I wanted to scream at them. These 'appropriate interventions' failed to save Daniel's life.

Referring to their last meeting with Daniel the night before his death they wrote;

'We may never know whether your husband had any intent or plan on 18th March 2011 to take an overdose or whether something triggered this act in the hours that followed.'

This last comment made my blood boil. It was an attempt to absolve themselves of any responsibility by suggesting that Daniel wasn't suicidal when they saw him at 6pm but something may have happened in the few hours afterwards that made him decide to kill himself. It was laughable, especially as he would have had to visit at least eight chemists to get the amount of aspirin he took. How had he managed that on a Friday night?

After a year of such correspondence, I could see that I was getting nowhere and it was dragging me backwards. Evidently their judgement of Daniel's mental state was grossly inaccurate. I wanted them to acknowledge that. I thought that if they had the grace to admit that mistakes were made, it might help others in the future. I'm sure they were afraid I would sue them if they admitted any kind of mistake, but that was never my intent. I didn't want money,

I wanted honesty. But it was futile and I knew it. I had to let it go and focus on my boys and our future.

My anger also extended towards a few 'good' friends who didn't stay in contact. After Daniel died so many people had said, 'If there's anything I can do...' but after the first couple of weeks these offers dried up and often I didn't hear from the person again.

When a friend introduced me to a woman whose husband had committed suicide at Beachy Head soon after Daniel's death, it was comforting to meet someone else in the same situation. She had been eight months pregnant with their first child at the time. I felt so sorry for her and identified with her obvious pain. She was young, intelligent and had a beautiful child and I could see a future for her where she couldn't see it for herself. I realised that was probably how others saw me but it was hard to feel it myself.

Daniel had asked for his ashes to be scattered in Ireland, and I had long planned to take them there in May, just after our wedding anniversary. I wasn't going to take the boys with me, until a conversation with Theo at breakfast one morning. It was 6.20am and I was barely awake when he asked angrily, 'What's God done with my daddy's body?'

His question threw me. I had told him that when people die it is just their soul that goes to heaven and that their body stops working and is not needed anymore. I couldn't possibly explain cremation to him; he associated fire with danger and pain. Fumbling for an explanation I said that when you die, your body turns to dust and the people who love you take the dust to a special place that you have chosen. I told him that I would be taking daddy's dust to a beautiful place in Ireland where he went on holiday when he was a boy.

Theo said, 'Can I go to Ireland with you Mummy?' I looked at his earnest little face and knew he needed to come, so I spent the next week rearranging the trip to include the boys. Sam was coming and would help me with them and it felt right, I liked the idea of showing them their father's Irish heritage. I invited Ella and Hannah to come with us, but they chose not to. They were old enough to understand so much more than the boys, and for them it would have been more painful and complicated.

Our wedding anniversary arrived and, much like my birthday a couple of weeks earlier, it was a little less painful a year on. I did feel terribly sad, thinking about how wonderful our wedding day had been. Daniel used to say that meeting me was like coming home and I felt so safe and settled with him. I didn't do anything to mark the anniversary, I went outside and looked at Daniel's tree, but that was all.

Two days later we flew to Ireland. When Sam arrived the evening before, he told me he had checked the security rules for taking ashes on the flight. They needed to be transferred to a plastic container with a screw top and I had to take the death and cremation certificates along. The box that came from the crematorium was sealed and I had never opened it to look at the ashes, I hadn't dared to really. But now it was a necessity and I was surprised that I managed to get on with the task quite clinically, in the kitchen, after the boys were in bed. I had envisaged the ashes being fine and powdery, but they were actually coarser than that. I felt very anxious about spilling any, it seemed so important that none was lost. Before we put them in the plastic container, I took a little out and put it aside. Theo had been quite upset that Daniel's 'special place' was in Ireland. He was feeling hurt and confused that his daddy hadn't chosen for them to be here at home, with us. Daniel made his will before the boys came along and I thought he probably would now want to keep some of his remains closer to his children. So I decided to keep a little of his ashes to scatter at home.

A few well-intentioned people said to me, 'Hopefully, scattering his ashes will give you some closure,' which I found terribly annoying. Daniel's absence would always be a gaping void; it could never be closed for us. I had to keep his memory alive for the sake of Theo and Milo. But scattering his ashes did feel like a milestone and I knew it would be a relief to cross it.

I think I'm going to stop writing to you after your ashes are scattered. I don't think it's healthy that I spend so much time telling you every detail of our lives. I think it's time to let you go. I can't hang onto you anymore. I know you would want me to move on with my life so I'm going to try to do that. I'm not ready for another relationship, I need to find some happiness for myself first and get to the point where we have adjusted to being a family unit of three. At the moment, I still feel that our family is disabled without you.

We arrived in Shannon at about midnight and checked into our hotel, where the four of us slept in one room, which was comfortable and cosy. The next morning the boys slept in until 7.30am, which was blissful. Milo woke up and announced, 'this is not my house!' But he soon got into the excitement of staying in a hotel. Theo was delighted that he got co-co pops and chocolate spread for breakfast. While I sorted the boys out Sam went off to collect the hire car and we were on the road to Galway by nine.

Looking out of the window at the lush green country-side it dawned on me that we were in Ireland; Daniel's home and heritage. He was so proud to be an Irish man and so passionate about the country. It felt absolutely right that this was where his remains should return.

We found Daniel's cousin Annette's house with ease. The last time I saw her we had both just married. She was warm and hospitable and her house soon filled up with more cousins, aunts and uncles, and of course his mum. It all felt surreal, everybody chatting, making polite conversation and being jolly.

We drove in convoy out to Lettergesh Beach in Connemara. The boys sat in the back watching Puss in Boots over and over again for the two hour journey. The last time I had been there, with Daniel, it had been raining, but now it was clear and beautiful.

Lettergesh is a vast, sandy beach; rugged and stunning. As we made our way down to the sea Theo and Milo took off their shoes and socks, despite the cold. I was so grateful that the sun shone down between the clouds but the wind was nippy. Daniel's family stood around in little groups, all of us with no clear idea of what we were going to do. Theo and Milo began to get impatient and asked if they could have some of Daddy's dust now so I just let them take the lead. They each had a little yoghurt pot that they scooped ashes into, before running excitedly down to the sea. They paddled in and scattered the ashes before bouncing back for more. We all followed them down to the water's edge and I watched our two little boys innocently scattering their daddy's remains into the sea. It was beautiful and heart-breaking. I had been unaware of the tears rolling down my cheeks until I felt Sam's arm around my shoulder. My tears were not for Daniel in that moment, they were for these two little boys who were so oblivious to the significance of their happy game.

The boys' fearlessness and lack of morbidity, the way that they embraced the occasion with joy was infectious. After a few minutes of watching them, I gathered some dust in my hands and waded into the water in my designer boots (that I discovered were not watertight) and sprinkled the ashes into the sea.

I asked Daniel's relatives if they wanted to join in but they politely declined and stood back to watch the boys and me scatter his ashes in the sea that he loved so much. His mum took a pot full and scattered them in the sand dunes. She wanted to do it in her own private way. Afterwards she told me that he and Adam used to spend hours playing in those sand dunes when they were little boys.

After the ashes were scattered we all let off some helium balloons, in what was by now a tradition for the boys. We spent some time just hanging around on the beach watching the children play and I sat in the sand dunes with Milo who referred to them as his 'den'. It was lovely to shelter from the wind and we found one of those little plants that you blow on to make a wish. We blew it together and I wished for happiness for the boys. I looked up at the sky and, just for a few seconds, I felt Daniel's presence.

We travelled home the next day and I arrived feeling exhausted and drained. So much travelling in just three days had taken its toll and Theo had been whingey and tearful all day.

Sam had to leave as soon as we arrived home and after we waved him off I felt empty and bereft. I knew I had to get the boys bathed and settled for the night and prepare Theo's school uniform, but it felt like a colossal task and I felt an unbearable sadness welling up in my stomach. It remained there like a lump, no matter what I did, a sensation I had been through many times since Daniel's death.

I managed to get the boys to bed, unpack, sort out the washing, iron Theo's school uniform and polish his shoes before collapsing in front of the television, hoping to escape my feelings. But the emotional lump in my stomach was still there. I needed it to go, I wanted to be able to get on with life now that we had got through the trip. After a few minutes I began to sob, violently and urgently. It felt as though I was vomiting, purging out the pain. It brought me some relief but left me feeling totally drained. I fell into bed and slept deeply.

A couple of days later the boys and I took the remaining ashes to the beach in front of our old house. There was a memorial bench opposite the house in remembrance of somebody who died young doing the sports that he loved. Daniel often paid his respects to the unknown young man who had died. The boys always loved to play on it; in their imaginations it became a pirate ship, a space rocket, a fire engine and a camper van. So when they scampered onto the beach with Daniel's ashes the first place that they ran to scatter them was the memorial bench. They poured some of the ashes onto the seat and then ran off to scatter more in the sea. I looked at the ashes, sitting there, on display in such a public place and felt a little uneasy. But I decided to leave them, they were where Theo and Milo wanted them to be and I reasoned that nature would scatter them further for us; it was a pretty windy day.

I followed the boys down to the water's edge to find Theo, in his school uniform and new school shoes, paddling in the sea. I was touched to see that he was placing his ashes on top of the groins. He loved the groins when he was tiny, Daniel used to take him down to the beach and help him 'steppy-stone' along them.

As we stood on the beach Milo began collecting stones 'for Daddy' and Theo soon joined in. They filled their pockets and my handbag with pebbles for him. I suggested that we take them home and put them under Daniel's tree. We saved some of the ashes for our garden too. The boys lovingly sprinkled them in the soil beneath the tree and placed the stones randomly in the earth. They seemed to know they were doing something important for their daddy.

That evening I remembered a conversation Daniel and I had about euthanasia and the reasons why people might choose to end their lives. He felt strongly that we should all have the right to do that, whatever the circumstances. I mentioned people with mental health issues whose feelings may be strong but temporary. We batted this topic around a bit between us before Daniel said, 'life is like a party and if a guest chooses to leave early, for whatever reason, then they should be freely allowed to. If that disappoints the other guests or leaves them feeling uncomfortable, it is for them to deal with'.

His views were always so black and white, with no grey areas. He never was a conformist or a people pleaser. Thinking back on this conversation gave me some comfort. Daniel felt so strongly and he was well when he expressed these fierce views.

I was beginning to rationalise and make sense of all that had happened, and to see that it was not my fault. Daniel's life was separate from mine and had its own trajectory. I began to absolve myself from feeling guilty and responsible for his death and in the days that followed I felt a huge sense of release and my health steadily improved. And I kept my promise to stop writing to Daniel.

I vowed to stop writing to you after the ashes were scattered and now I am procrastinating about saying goodbye to you. My head tells me that I must let you go now, accept that you are gone and move on, but my heart wants to cling on to you.

I loved you totally, you were everything to me and you gave me so much. I know that you truly loved me too and were devoted to your four children. I know that you would want me to remember you as the capable and strong man that I fell in love with, not the very sick man that you became at the end. I will do that Daniel and I will pass on those memories to our boys and your girls when they are older.

With you, I experienced the most joyous and the most sorrowful moments of my life. Thank you for our two lovely boys and for enabling me to become a mother. Thank you for the happy times that we had together and for giving me love and security. Thank you for helping me to open up my heart and life to you. I will always miss you. You will be in my heart and mind forever. Goodbye Daniel x x x x x x x x x x x

Chapter Twenty-One

Two weeks after I stopped writing to Daniel I still felt like an addict in withdrawal, frequently talking to him in my head and curbing the impulse to write while consciously trying to move on and crawl out of the dark hole I'd been in since his death.

I had felt for so long that the boys and I were simply surviving, detached from all those people around us who were getting on with their 'normal' lives. I felt that I was faking it; going through the motions of living on the outside, appearing to be fine while feeling totally alienated and lost in my grief and worry.

I was beginning to be aware of how isolated I had become, especially amongst my local friends and community. Totally consumed by looking after Theo and Milo and by the practicalities of running a home, earning money and raising two young children alone, I had no energy or time for anything else. But it wasn't just a matter of time and energy, the truth was I still found it hard to relate to anyone outside my small circle of close family and friends. Suicide is such a taboo, it evokes disquiet and awkwardness and although I felt comfortable in talking about Daniel's death, I was very aware that others did not. It was easier not to mention how Daniel died, but that felt like denying a huge part of my life. How could I form new friendships without talking about it?

Soon after we scattered Daniel's ashes I made a determined effort to socialise, inviting some friends around for an evening and forcing myself to go to the wedding reception of our old neighbours. I managed to go through the motions but that was all it was. I felt like a spare part, worried that the people I talked to felt stuck with me and very conscious that I had become known locally as the tragic widow of the very popular and sociable Daniel. I hated the word widow, I never used it, and I hated feeling pitied. It hurt to see others all around me living the life I'd had ripped away from me; I didn't fit into that world any more, but nor could I go back to the single life I had before I met Daniel. I was now a very stretched and exhausted single mother and I didn't know where I belonged. I had lost my identity and had yet to shape a new one.

Father's Day, in early June, was a very tough day for our little family of three. Without Daniel's vibrancy and energy, we were limping along and, on a day meant for celebrating fatherhood, I felt deeply aware of it. We went to a family fun day, which should have been blissful for a five year-old, but Theo was stressed and unhappy for most of the afternoon. He couldn't wait in the queues for the rides, his ice cream wasn't right and he spent most of the time whining and teasing his brother. I wondered if this was how he felt without Daniel – that nothing could be right, because nothing could fill the gaping hole inside him.

In the evening, I talked about Father's Day and tried to voice the sadness for him. He asked to look at the photo album of him as a baby with his daddy and he looked at Milo's too. He seemed to find it a comfort; he slept with both albums in his bed for the next few nights. My poor little boy; how I longed to repair him and make his world safe and secure once more.

At that time, Milo was such a happy and contented little boy despite being surrounded by stress and heartache all his life. I did worry about what he must have absorbed, but I knew that he had been shielded from a lot of it because he was, quite literally, still attached to my breast during the early stages of Daniel's decline. Milo had really only ever had me as his caregiver and that had been a constant while Theo had a loving relationship with two parents and then gradually and brutally lost one of them. His life changed totally and his sense of security was shattered. When I was at my wits end with worry, Milo's sunny disposition was an antidote to all the stress, though I was aware that he would go through his own grief as his comprehension grew. He was already beginning to test the permanence of Daniel's absence. He would say, 'my daddy's in that boat' or 'my daddy will get me a superman outfit for my birthday'. He had no concept of death, so why shouldn't he hope that his father would come back one day? One afternoon he was in the garden throwing a ball in the air, insisting that he was throwing it up to heaven for Daddy to catch. Then he began saving bits of his favourite food; biscuits and cakes, to send to Daddy in heaven. I followed the advice of bereavement specialists and consistently reiterated that daddy had died and could never come back but Milo was too young to grasp this.

For Theo it was all so much more painful. His self-esteem had been crushed during the year of Daniel's illness and as he struggled to comprehend why Daniel would leave us he asked, 'did I make Daddy ill because I was naughty?' At school things were tough for him too. He became friendly with a popular boy in his class, who came to play twice at our house. When Theo went to play at his house I told the boy's mother that my husband had died the previous year and that Theo had some behavioural issues. She seemed sensitive to this and the play dates went well. But a couple of weeks later, the other boy took his party invitations into school and handed them out very publicly in the classroom. Theo had not been invited and when he asked why, the boy told him that his mummy didn't want him there because Theo had pushed the boy off his scooter and thrown his hat over a wall at school. These were typical examples of the behaviours that Theo struggled to control, not malicious but impulsive and overly boisterous. Theo was upset for the whole weekend following this and when he saw a psychologist a few weeks later he told him that this was the saddest day of his life. It was a rejection that resonated deeply with his father's death. The psychologist was excellent and was a huge support to both Theo and me. His view was that Theo's difficulties were the result of trauma and grief and his opinion reassured me that I was doing as much as I could to help Theo. He did some trauma work with Theo, who responded well to it. He was able to express a lot of his anger towards Daniel for 'making a mistake' in taking too much medicine and towards me for 'letting it happen'.

As his reception year drew to a close everything started to feel a little easier. His report said that he needed extra support with some of the emotional and social aspects of school but that he was improving and I felt proud of him. He'd had so much on his small shoulders and yet he had managed to keep up with his peers as best he could.

As spring gave way to summer, my health improved and I began to feel lighter. Not happy, but as if the grief and despair had eased. People commented that I was looking better and I began gradually to be more comfortable with being sociable, meeting friends for coffee and managing small talk. It was as though I had been in a thick cloud of smog which, while it hadn't yet lifted, was thinning. An interesting analogy when I thought about how my asthma flared up when I was stressed and grieving, leaving me feeling unable to breathe.

Milo's third birthday arrived in late July and he asked for a superman party. As I rushed around making last-minute preparations I was hit by a wave of missing Daniel. Each time I got in the car between errands the tears flowed. The Olympics were on and I couldn't believe that he wasn't around for them. On the day of the party, I had 16 little superheroes running around the garden and a very nice man dressed as superman who kept them entertained for an hour. I had spent three evenings making Milo a superman cake and his glowing face when he saw it more than justified the effort. It was lovely to see him so happy, but I couldn't help thinking of what Daniel was missing. He barely had time to get to know Milo. Daniel would have been very amused by his quirky little ways. In addition to naming his teddies Pub, he had acquired an imaginary friend, also called Pub, who was responsible for all the naughty antics in our house. I had never really got used to laying the table for three, so when Milo started setting out extra cutlery for 'Pub' I didn't mind in the least; I knew that it would have tickled Daniel.

In August we went on holiday to Wales with my parents. The boys loved the pool, with its water slides, and the indoor adventure centre, but for the adults a week of those activities was a bit much. After two afternoons whizzing down the water flumes, I felt as if I had been on a fast spin in the washing machine. It was especially hard for me because the void in our family somehow felt so much more obvious on holiday, where we were surrounded by families. It would have been a completely different holiday with Daniel, who would happily have thrown himself into the activities with the children. Everything felt like such a struggle without him.

When the boys went to a kids club one morning, I spent a couple of hours in the spa. It should have been a chance to relax, but as I sat in the sauna I felt another wave of shock. How could Daniel be dead? How did our life together just crumble away so quickly? How did my own life become such a muddle? It was as though I had only then, sixteen months after his death, felt the full force of the ghastly, shocking reality of what happened to Daniel and to our family.

At the end of the summer holidays we went to visit Maggie in Dorset for a night. It was the first time we had stayed at her house since his death and she had gone to a lot of effort to buy food that we would all like and to rearrange her bedroom to accommodate us. But as soon as we arrived at her house, Theo became disturbed and angry. He was upset by a collage of photographs of Daniel that hung over the fireplace. He was fine on an outing to the forest in the afternoon, but as soon as we got back to the house he became angry again. Maggie responded to his behaviour in a very loving and non-judgemental way but it was difficult for me to see him so distressed, especially since his behaviour had been steadily improving. I also felt unexpectedly grief stricken. I'm not sure if it was the photos or the memories of being there with Daniel, lighting a fire and sitting in the garden, but I felt drained, and had a lump the size of a boulder in my throat. In the evening, Maggie showed me a DVD made by one of Daniel's old school friends. There were photographs of Daniel as some very beautiful classical music played in the background. At the end there was a film of a kite surfer flying through the clouds towards a bright, white light, followed by a touching tribute to Daniel. It was beautiful and I watched it through streaming tears.

As we drove home the following day, Theo, unprompted, said sorry for being naughty, but he remained extremely angry. He said that his daddy was stupid for dying; that Maggie and I were stupid to feel sad about him and that he wanted to forget about daddy and wanted me to as well. When we got home, he demanded that I take down all the photos of Daniel and he remained very angry and had trouble sleeping for about a week. I felt totally worn out by him and utterly helpless. It was so much for him to understand and process.

Thankfully by the time he went back to school in September he had calmed down and seemed to feel happier. Being back in his usual routine and getting plenty of stimulation at school helped. All the staff were supportive and Theo was blessed with an exceptionally wonderful teacher who took him under her wing. Her approach was to focus on his strengths and play down his weaknesses; she lavished him with praise and rewarded him generously for all his good qualities. He often came home proudly displaying stickers or little certificates, concrete affirmations of his goodness and worth which helped to repair his self-esteem. She contributed hugely to changing the way Theo felt about himself and I was extremely grateful to her.

As Theo started to feel better about himself, his behaviour gradually improved. At home he began spending hours in the kitchen drawing. It was a blessing, as he'd never been able to focus on anything before for more than a few minutes. Now he began churning out hundreds of very expressive drawings. I didn't need to be an art therapist to see that his drawings were a raw and powerful expression of his anger; black with sharp, furious deep lines etched into the paper. There was the occasional splattering of red as if he were literally bleeding onto the page, a very literal representation of his inner pain. The stories that he elaborated about his characters were always about 'badness' and 'evil' and terrible things happening. There was never an option for resolution or reparation, it was all very bleak. I knew that it was healthy that he was expressing himself and getting this stuff out so I listened to him and, mindful not to intervene or try to become his therapist, I simply encouraged him to keep drawing.

As Theo moved into year one, Milo started pre-school for two full days and two mornings each week. He settled in well, but he also began to realise that it wasn't the norm to have a daddy who had died. He began to question me, going through the names of his new friends at pre-school, asking me if their daddies were in heaven too. He so desperately wanted to hear that another child's daddy had died too, it was heart-breaking. He started telling all sorts of people, including random strangers, that his daddy had died and that God was looking after him in heaven. He told the poor shop assistant who was measuring his feet in a shoe shop and then asked her if she was going to die soon too.

With some time to myself, I increased my running, extended my work hours and began to see a little more of friends. I was beginning to feel like myself again, but it was never a linear process. There would be good days and bad, steps forward and steps backward, days when I felt more a part of the world and days when I wanted to shut myself away.

One awful setback came a week into the autumn term, when I took Theo to his beloved Saturday morning football. Although most new people that I'd met had been sensitive and supportive, I had been aware that some parents at his school were making snide comments, suggesting that the boys were unruly because I didn't know how to discipline them and that their father's death was just an excuse for bad behaviour. That Saturday it all came to a head when Milo roughly squeezed the face of another small boy, whose father then shouted at Milo and told me, harshly and loudly, that I had no control over my badly behaved children and should do something about it. I felt tearful and shaken; it was the comment that I 'should do something about it' that hurt the most. He had no idea that I was spending every minute of my life trying to help my children and doing the best that I could in very difficult circumstances.

Incidents like this reminded me how different our lives were without Daniel. Without him I felt unprotected. That father would not have dared to behave that way towards Milo and me if Daniel had been by my side. I felt so conscious that I could never compensate the boys for what they were missing from him; his fun, his knowledge, his musical and theatrical talents, his love of the sea and water sports. There was so much that he would have given them that I couldn't.

One night I read a story to the boys called Up in Heaven. It was about a dog who had died and the sadness of the little boy to whom the dog belonged. The dog could not fully experience the joys of heaven because he knew that the little boy whom he loved so much was so full of sorrow and unhappy without him. The dog sent the little boy dreams assuring him that he was now happy. Guided by the dog in heaven, the little boy was able to move on and asked his parents for a new puppy. He found joy again in the new puppy and the dog in heaven was able to enjoy the lushness of heaven without worrying about the little boy. They never forgot each other or stopped loving each other but they both had to accept that they were now separated. It was a sweet and comforting story and at the end Theo said, 'maybe Daddy sent the book to us from heaven because he wants us to feel better'.

By Theo's birthday we had been a family of three for 20 months and I felt we were all adjusting to our new normality. Theo, excited about his first wobbly tooth and the prospect of turning six, was in great spirits. As usual I had gone over the top with his party, and he and his friends enjoyed two hours of raucous mayhem. And unlike the previous year, he didn't mention Daniel once. Mum. Dad, Tom, Sam and Katie all came to stay for the party and I was so grateful to them. Not just because they shared the workload, but because with them around I felt we were a proper family, they helped to ease the void Daniel left and gave me comfort and support beyond measure.

That autumn the leaves on the memorial tree we had planted in our garden for Daniel unexpectedly turned vibrant red, Daniel's favourite colour. It was a lovely surprise. That little tree in our back garden had become special to us all. Since we didn't have a headstone it was important for all of us to have a tangible object to focus our memories on.

In mid-December Ella and Hannah came to stay with us for an early Christmas as we weren't going to see them over the holiday. We had a lovely time, the dynamics between all the children seemed to have become smoother and less fractious and I knew Daniel would love to have seen his four children enjoying each other so much. At just fifteen, Ella astounded me with her insight, maturity and wisdom in our discussions about Daniel's death, his illness and how others reacted to it, while Hannah seemed to find comfort in remembering the good times. The three of us would huddle on the sofa after the boys were tucked up and reminisce about the unique and often hilariously funny man that their father was. He brought so much laughter to the house and we all missed that terribly. There would always be jokes around the dinner table, silly impressions and lots of affectionate teasing. He liked to start the weekend early on Saturday mornings by putting music on the stereo, cranking the volume up to full pelt and getting the whole family dancing in the living room. The children all loved it and secretly I did too. I missed the carefree mischief that Daniel created, his light-heartedness. It was not what I was good at. Of course, left to Daniel, our home would have been utter dysfunctional chaos, but between us we created a healthy balance.

For the first time, I left Ella to babysit while I went out for a Christmas meal with friends. Daniel would have loved the idea of his eldest daughter looking after the little ones. I wanted to keep them babies, but Daniel was always looking forward to the next stage and he would have been so proud of how much they had all grown up since he left.

The Sunday before Christmas I left the boys in Sunday school and enjoyed a quiet hour in church. At the end of the service, they came bounding in with all the other children, eager to show me the angel Christmas cards they had made. Milo had used traditional yellow to colour the angel's wings and halo and he had given her a red smiling mouth and had sprinkled silver glitter over his card. Theo's was, of course, a black angel and looking at it instantly brought a lump to my throat. The whole card had been etched with the jagged black lines that I was used to seeing in his artwork. But the face of the angel was different. Instead of the gnashing teeth and angry, menacing expression of a monster, it had a desperately sad upside down, black mouth. The black

pen had smudged leaving what looked like tears streaming down the angels face. This was the first time that I had
seen a glimmer of real sadness in Theo's artwork. I said that
it looked like a very sad angel. He shrugged and said 'it's
a dead angel'. It broke my heart to look at the desperate
sadness in his angel but it marked a turning point. In the
months that followed, his anger subsided and he began to
express his sorrow.

As Theo did his Christmas shopping (buying almost
everyone chocolate in hope that they might share) he said
that he wanted to buy a present for Daddy and suggested
sending him some balloons on Christmas day. We were staying with my parents and we went to a friendly and very busy
little gift shop in a Cotswold village near their house and
bought twelve helium balloons. As the boys squabbled over
the colours the shopkeeper asked if we were having a party.
Milo matter-of-factly replied that they were to send up to his
daddy in heaven on Christmas morning. Silence fell and the
whole atmosphere in the shop changed. The boys seemed
oblivious and were excited and pleased with their balloons
but I felt painfully conscious of people's pity and sadness for
my little boys, whose loss had become their norm.

CHAPTER TWENTY-TWO

I started 2013 determined to make it a better year. We had come so far, my boys and I, and been through so much. Now I wanted to move beyond simply coping and existing, I wanted to find some real happiness for the boys' sake as much as for my own.

In mid-January snow fell, a glorious blanket five inches thick. The last time it had snowed Daniel had taken Theo out sledging. He recorded them both whizzing down the beach on the sledge and squealing with delight. This time Theo had a flu virus and he felt too rotten to take any interest in the snow. He became very tearful, crying over every little thing. Amidst the tears spilled for minor things, he said, 'I want daddy to come back,' and 'I miss my daddy'. After his anger and defensiveness over the previous months this felt like a breakthrough. Even after he recovered and went back to school, Theo continued to open up about his sense of loss. He told me several times that he missed his daddy and one evening in late January he got cross with me because I didn't play football with him enough and then he wailed, 'I want my daddy'. My heart broke for him but I was so pleased that he was beginning to put his grief into words.

He continued to do well at school. I went to a meeting with his teachers and was so relieved and pleased to hear that there were now no major concerns about his behaviour.

He took part in a class assembly and I was overwhelmed with pride to see him, bursting with enthusiasm and no different from the other children.

At home he seemed happier and more secure too. He was sleeping better and his food and separation anxieties had also calmed down. For the first time in many months I no longer felt engulfed by my worries over him. For almost a year after Daniel died Theo was absolutely terrified that I would suddenly die too, he hated me being out of his sight. But that had now improved; he was finding his feet in the world and beginning to manage situations without me.

Just as Theo seemed to be emerging from the worst of his grief, Milo began to piece together what had happened and to embark on his own struggle. I felt I had just got Theo through the worst of it but was back to the beginning of the process with Milo and that was hard. Milo grew into his grief. It had not been immediate because he had been too young to feel Daniel's loss in the acute way that Theo did, and when it did come it was grief for what he knew he was missing rather than what he remembered having. Starting pre-school had been the trigger, he had begun to understand that our family was not the norm. He became aware that his classmates had daddies around and realised that he was missing something huge and he started asking me lots of questions, demanding to know where heaven was, where his daddy was and why couldn't he see him. He went through a similar process to Theo in wanting to go up and see Daniel. He told me that he was going to grow a beanstalk in the garden so that he could climb up it and see Daddy in heaven. He wanted to feel the same as the other children and I often overheard him making up stories to them about his daddy, telling them that his daddy was an astronaut and was on the moon or was a cowboy in

America or simply that his daddy was at home hiding in a cupboard.

He became almost obsessed with death, asking what happened to your body when you died. It was difficult to answer his questions, I tried to be as straightforward and factual as I could without alarming him, but he was a confused little boy.

One evening when I was putting him to bed he asked to look at the photo of Daniel that sat on his windowsill. He gave the photo a kiss and then lay on his front and buried his head in his pillow. I asked him if he was alright and he said, 'I'm sad'. I asked, 'are you sad because Daddy has died?' and he answered, 'yes, I want Daddy to come back now and live in my house with Mummy and Milo and Theo'. After that he would kiss and cuddle the photo of Daniel every night. One evening he dropped it down the side of his bed and became really distressed. I had to get him up, pull the bed out and retrieve it. It wasn't broken so I put it back on his window sill but Milo was still upset, worried that Daddy might have bumped his head.

As he realised his loss he went through troubled times at pre-school, being a bit rough and defiant, while at home he became more clingy and testing. I could see that he was grappling to make sense of it all and was going through many of the things Theo had suffered eighteen months earlier and while I understood that it was a necessary process, it was hard to find myself worrying about a second child after the enormous worry I had gone through over Theo.

In late February my grandfather died. He was 92 and died very peacefully at home just as he'd wanted and I found his funeral unexpectedly therapeutic. The service was simple but touching and it all felt natural and right. I had flashbacks to Daniel's funeral, when the atmosphere was polluted with pain, shock and anger. I hadn't been able to stop shaking and I had felt as if I was sleepwalking in a horrific nightmare. In contrast my granddad's friends and relatives had gathered to acknowledge their fondness and respect for him and to say goodbye and I felt pleased that he had such a lovely send-off. It was how death should be.

The second anniversary of Daniel's death fell only two weeks later. March, once a month that Daniel and I loved so much, will now always be difficult for me. Although that second year I didn't feel as emotionally engulfed as I had on the first anniversary, once again I became ill. This time it was an unusual eye condition for which I had to take steroids. Both my eyes were very sore and I had a constant headache for two weeks. Ironically, I was told that part of my eye problem was chronically dry eyes and I was given eye drops that were like fake tears. Clearly I needed to be crying more.

The anniversary fell on a Wednesday, so we held a day of remembrance on the Saturday before. I wanted to make it a day of fun in remembrance of Daniel's fun-loving spirit and as the weather was atrocious we went to the Sea Life Centre in Brighton, which was a huge hit with the boys. They were fascinated and in awe of all the sea creatures, especially the 'real live sharks'. All I heard from both of them all day was, 'awesome'! They really did have a lovely day, and I did too. When we got home, we battled the ferocious wind and rain to head down to the beach with our helium balloons. I had never seen balloons disappear into the sky so fast.

In the evening, the boys snuggled up on either side of me on the sofa and laughed out loud as we watched You've Been Framed, and I felt very, very lucky to have them. I had a sense of us being a stronger unit. We had been forced to adapt and live with a terrible gaping hole at the heart of our family, yet despite the daily squabbles and friction, we had become a very tight, loving and strong little unit and in that moment I felt that we were OK. After what had seemed such a long time in turmoil, trying to survive the storm that had engulfed us, we were beginning to travel in calmer waters.

The day before the second anniversary, Mum went into hospital to have further brain surgery for her aneurysm. She had made such a good recovery in the intervening twenty months since her stroke, but of course we were all fearful that she might have another. Thankfully the surgery went well this time, she had eleven tiny metal coils inserted into the aneurysm to prevent it from rupturing and we were all relieved and hopeful that this would prolong her life. She was home within a few days, but it did take her a few months to fully recover from it.

On the actual anniversary I got on with my day as normal but I felt drained and tearful. I kept imagining how it would be for us if Daniel had got the help he needed. We would be looking back on a terrible few years, closer and stronger as a family. Daniel had lived the vast majority of his life as a happy, successful man. Surely he could have got back to that? Theo had exactly the same thought when he asked me, 'what would have happened if I had stopped Daddy from taking too many tablets and chucked them all in the bin?' It is so hard to live with 'if only'. I don't think that the pain will ever lessen. It will always be with me, and with the boys, I think it is just a case of learning to live with it as best we can.

By April, with the anniversary past, my eyes cleared up and I began to feel better. We went to my parents' for Easter and as I had to go back to Sussex to work for two days in the middle of the week, I booked Theo into a football holiday club for both days. I'd been sure that he would love it, but when the time came to drop him off I felt very uneasy and protective. It was clear that he was the youngest child there and all the other boys knew each other. But while I felt daunted, Theo didn't, he was excited and just sat himself down amongst the bigger boys and waved me off. He was always naturally a very gutsy, sociable and outgoing little boy but those qualities had been crushed by his experiences. Now he was getting back to who he really was.

Life was becoming more enjoyable rather than a constant struggle, for both Theo and me. On my birthday, for the first time since Daniel died, I had a really good day. My parents and Sam and Katie came to stay and the boys went off with Dad and Sam while Mum, Katie and I enjoyed a day out in Brighton. It was lovely. We ambled around the shops and chatted over a lazy lunch. It was Mum's first outing since her operation and we all felt that we had turned a corner.

A few weeks later I went to meet my friend Clare for a coffee. She was late so I sat in a busy café which was buzzing and full of life. I felt in awe of all the people around me, just getting on with their lives. I wanted to be like them, to feel I was living and enjoying life again. I had never been carefree; I am a worrier and always have been. But before Daniel's illness I had felt young, alive and hopeful. Sitting in the café made me realise that I had been merely surviving, just getting through the days and I didn't want that any longer.

I was beginning to accept that Daniel was dead and that it was not my fault. I loved him and tried very hard to help him, but I couldn't save him from the illness that was bigger than both of us. Gradually I was beginning to free myself from guilt.

In June I joined a peer support group run by Rethink Mental Illness for people bereaved by suicide. I wished I had known about it a year or so earlier, but I had never been given any information about possible support. It was a work colleague who, unaware of my situation, told me that she worked for this service. The group consisted of a very eclectic mix of people and I probably had very little in common with any of them, but it helped to meet others who had experienced a similar bereavement and who understood the taboo surrounding it. Unexpectedly, despite our shared sorrow, we found humour. We spent one session doing impressions of the 'pity face' that we had all experienced from others and it was good to laugh.

Ella and Hannah still came regularly to stay with us. The boys adored their sisters and I was touched by what lovely young women they were growing to be. At 16 Ella was studying admirably hard for her GCSE's and hoping to be a doctor while 13 year-old Hannah, with her enviable long limbs and striking looks, had her mind set on modelling. I knew we would always feel the gaping hole of Daniel's absence, he was such a strong patriarch and still bound us together, but we were rebuilding ourselves as a family unit who could, just sometimes, be happy without him.

For Milo's birthday in July I bought both the boys second-hand bikes. Milo had a little one with stabilizers which he loved and Theo got a mountain bike for getting a good school report. Daniel would have been so proud of how well he was doing; bombing about effortlessly on his new bike. I thought of the bike with the little blue seat which Daniel used to pop Theo into when they went out. He would have loved going out with Theo now, side by side, on their bikes.

In September, Theo moved up to year two and Milo started school. He was excited, but I didn't feel ready for him to go. He was only four and one month and it seemed too soon. My sweet and smiley little companion who had kept me going through the tough times was suddenly no longer a toddler. He did have a bumpy first term, but he settled after that.

With Milo in school, I had a bit more time on my hands. I increased my work hours and took on more private clients, though I avoided any work that involved acute mental health or bereavement. Gradually my confidence as a therapist returned and I started to enjoy it again. I went to an art therapy conference in London and met three other art therapists that I already knew. It was good to see them and to feel that I was doing something other than being a mum.

I also ran a half marathon with Clare, the first I'd run since Daniel became ill. We ran it in London, on what would have been Daniel's 44th birthday and I thought of him with every step.

During that October half-term, the weather was stormy and gale force winds wreaked carnage in the back garden. The back fence came down and the boys' wooden play house keeled over and landed directly on Daniel's tree, completely flattening it. I was terribly upset that something else was now dead; it felt like a bad omen. I wanted to replace it, but the gardener I had bought it from told me to give it time because the roots may not have been damaged. Dad helped me strap it to a supportive structure and repair the broken branches. It looked better after some TLC but was still a sorry sight. We would have to wait to see if it would survive.

A few weeks later Theo turned seven and he spent a happy afternoon at Brighton and Hove football stadium with fourteen of his friends. He was managing friendships so much better, and he was also being more affectionate and loving towards me. He had been so angry about all that had happened in our family and I had been the target of that anger for a long time, but his anger had subsided and we had regained our close bond.

However, shortly after his birthday he seemed to relapse into anxiety. He had several nightmares in which I died or disappeared during the night and it made him afraid to go to sleep. He would lie awake for hours, frightened that I wouldn't be there when he woke in the morning. He became anxious about separating from me in the day time too if we did anything that was out of our normal routine. There was no obvious trigger, so I read everything I could about children's grief and their emotional development and learned that seven is roughly the age when children are more able to understand what death means and how permanent it is. It made sense to me that, as Theo understood more, his anxieties about it increased. All I could do was reassure him that I was young and healthy and that daddy's death was unusual, most people die when they are old.

I contacted the child bereavement charity, Winston's Wish. I had been in touch with them shortly after Daniel died and they had offered me helpful advice over the phone but at the time, the boys had been too young for their services. The time now felt right for both the boys to see a bereavement specialist and we were put on a waiting list for a home visit.

CHAPTER TWENTY-THREE

I felt as if I had been in survival mode for a long time, and at last I was beginning to live again. I wanted to do things, to see people, to participate in life. It was as if I had been living in black and white and at last colour was seeping back into my line of vision. I no longer felt that Daniel's death defined me. It was something that happened and would always be a part of me, but it was not who I was. This was a big change for me. But just as I was beginning to feel more like my old self, Theo seemed to have relapsed and was once again a very troubled and frightened little boy. His terror that I would disappear became so overwhelming that if I was in another room at home it could lead to panic. When I put him in the car, in the few seconds it took me to walk round to the driver's door he would become so anxious that twice he climbed out of the window to find me. The realisation that his problems were still so present was hard to bear.

Theo's school had organised a trip to see Brighton Albion play and initially he had been full of excitement, but as the date drew near he told me one evening that he didn't want to go. When I questioned him about this change of heart, it was clear that he felt upset because most of his classmates would be going with their dads. Then, out of the blue he said, 'did Daddy die on purpose?' I felt winded. I had been anticipating this question, I knew it would come someday, but I still felt knocked sideways by it. I told him that Daddy's mind was very ill and this meant that his thoughts and feelings were all mixed up. I said that he had become very sad and muddled and for a short moment he thought that dying was the only way he could get away from all the horrible feelings in his head. I tried to stress that he would never have felt like that if he wasn't so ill, he would have wanted to stay with us. Theo asked me what he was so sad about. I told him that he was sad that he was ill and didn't feel like his usual self and that he couldn't get a job. I explained that Daddy liked to look after us all and provide us with all the money that we needed and he was sad because his illness stopped him from doing those things. I said that he was also sad because we were going to lose our house and he didn't know where we would be living in the future. It was a scary time. Theo said, 'I feel so sorry for Daddy'.

As we sat around the breakfast table the following morning, Theo's sadness poured out. He whinged and cried about every little thing. His porridge was too stodgy, the honey tasted different, I'd not poured his drink into the right cup, he didn't want to get ready for school, Milo was annoying him and I was the worst mummy in the world. We were running late and I needed to get to work, so I was getting irritated and didn't immediately make the connection between this difficult behaviour and the previous night's conversation. As I nagged him to get dressed for school with one eye on the clock, he asked, 'did Daddy want to die because I was naughty?' Poor Theo, I should have realised that he would feel guilty and responsible, as I had. I think most people who have lost a loved one in this hideous way do, at some stage. I reassured him as much as I could that it was not his fault, that Daddy loved him and that we were all just very unlucky that this happened in our family.

As family life began to feel more 'normal', the boys were both more able to talk about their daddy and how they felt about his death. One day, after a walk by the river close to my parents' house, Milo announced that he would like to die today. It caught my breath when I heard the boys talk like that, it just felt so wrong. He continued, 'yes, I want to die so that I can go up to heaven and give Daddy a big cuddle'. It was all so innocent and heartbreakingly matter-of-fact to him. Theo joined in and said that he wanted to die too so that he could see Daddy again. Then, as suddenly as this conversation had started, it ended, with Milo changing the subject and announcing he was going to become a superhero and fight all the baddies.

As the third anniversary of Daniel's death loomed, in March 2014, I wasn't sure whether to mention it to the boys, thinking that I might be unnecessarily unsettling them by flagging it up each year. But Theo knew and brought the subject up himself when he saw Easter eggs in the shops. I asked the boys how they would like to think about Daddy and Milo said that he wanted to go to Legoland, while Theo thought a quick trip to Australia would suffice. I'm sure Daniel would have approved of us remembering him in such fun and adventurous ways, but in the end we settled for releasing balloons on the beach followed by ice cream in the park. It was a really lovely, sunny weekend, warm with clear blue sky, just as it was on the day that Daniel died. After going to a birthday party on the Saturday morning, Milo came with me to buy the helium balloons while Theo was at football. Milo chose the red one as his personal balloon, but when we got home this caused a major conflict as Theo's current favourite colour was also red and there was only one red balloon. I couldn't help thinking that Daniel's favourite colour was red and wondered whether, on some level, they remembered. After much negotiation Theo was persuaded to have the blue and purple balloons.

The following morning, both boys remembered that it was 'Daddy's memorial day' as Theo put it. They were eager to go down to the beach early and were excited about the whole thing. It soon became a fierce competition, they were both desperate for their balloon to take the lead and disappear first. Aptly, the very popular red balloon stood out from the others and led the way into the sky. It was a really pretty sight, the vibrant colours floating up into a crystal clear blue sky.

As we walked home, Theo was uncharacteristically subdued. He was so much more aware of the significance of the day this time; I could tell that he was feeling as sad and bereft as I was when we let go of the balloons. But the grief was not as overwhelming or as all-encompassing as it had been the previous year, or as painfully raw as the first year. It was still there and it probably always will be but I had a sense of it becoming assimilated into our lives rather than engulfing us. We had a busy weekend, with parties, discos and school projects to get on with, and that was good. My boys were living their lives fully, both throwing themselves into all the fun and excitement that the world offered.

On the actual anniversary of Daniel's death, three days later, I did feel awful. I slept badly and then woke feeling achy all over and fatigued. After dropping the boys off at school I walked to church to look at the tribute for Daniel that I'd had inserted into the book of remembrance and to light a candle and spent a few minutes thinking about him. On the way home, I stopped at the memorial bench on the beach outside our old house and then walked down to the sea. It was windy and cold and I stood, braced against the elements, and looked out to sea, sensing that Daniel was out there somewhere. I felt glad that there was no grave-stone in a churchyard or cemetery. That would have felt too conventional and constricting for Daniel, he would want to be wild and free and the sea was the best reminder that I had of him, along with the Amelanchier tree which had, against all odds, survived. It was not yet the thriving tree we'd planted, but it had come through a brutal battering by a ferocious storm, just as we all had. Like the tree, we were not the same, but we had survived, and we were healing.

Once the anniversary was behind us I started to feel better, and in April we had our first session with Winston's Wish. An enthusiastic young man, Ross, and a kind and wise woman, Mary, came to our house and very skilfully estab-lished a rapport with both the boys, as Ross made drawing a family tree fun and interesting for them. Ross and Mary told me they would visit us five more times in order to assess how the boys were doing. After two sessions it was clear that both the boys found it too difficult to talk directly about Daniel and how they felt, so Ross decided simply to play with them and observe them in that way. He quickly became a paternal figure to both of them and that meant that as well as wanting fun and affection from him, he became the recipient of some very powerful feelings of anger that both boys felt in relation to Daniel. Ross did an amazing job of engaging them in a very playful way whilst also holding and accepting the anger and roughness that was projected onto him. Although on the surface these visits didn't amount to much more than a game of football in the garden or sitting round the kitchen table drawing, I was aware that all kinds of emotions were surfacing for both the boys.

As part of the family bereavement work, I had lengthy chats with Mary about how the boys were coping. She seemed to think that Theo was old enough to want and need more information about Daniel's death and to develop his own narrative that he could use when facing questions about his daddy. I sensed that she thought I had been quite soft in the language that I used and she suggested that I be more explicit. Thinking about it afterwards I felt uncomfortable, my approach had always been to give information as gently as possible when they asked for it, trying to protect the boys from the pain of it all.

Theo was so tuned in to me that I sometimes felt as though he could read my thoughts. A couple of evenings later he blurted out, 'why did my daddy kill himself?' Milo was in earshot and stood there looking confused and bewildered before asking the same question. I had never used such graphic language and hearing them say it cut right through me. I did my best to answer honestly, but later I began to question whether the bereavement work was helping. The therapists at Winston's Wish felt that it was best to be as open and forthrightly honest at all times and in theory I understood that, but it was hard to put it into practice. Like all parents, I was biologically wired to protect my boys on all levels.

For a few days Theo was very angry with Daniel, but a week or so later his anger subsided and he wanted to talk more about Daniel's illness. He expressed fears that I would get the same illness or that he would when he grew up. I reassured him that my mind was healthy and that Daddy was just really unlucky that his wasn't. He wanted to know what would happen to him if I died young too. I couldn't give him guarantees that I wouldn't die too but I reassured him that if it did happen, he would be looked after by Sam and Katie who loved him very much. Talking about it all so frankly was almost as hard as having to tell Theo when he was just four that his daddy had died. But in retrospect

I could see that these brutally honest conversations were necessary and that Ross and Mary had been right in nudging me to have them. Gradually, in the weeks that followed, Theo's acute separation anxieties eased and as summer approached everything remained calm and stable. The boys were both doing well in school and there were days when I felt happy. The feeling was often tinged with guilt. It was hard to feel that I could take pleasure from life when Daniel was gone. But our life had to go on, and I felt encouraged by the boys' sheer joy in living.

One sunny day in June I packed a picnic and we went to the beach with another mum from Theo's class and her three children. All the children played happily together; frolicking in the sea, climbing the rocks, finding crabs and collecting shells. Theo and Milo were just two very normal, healthy boys and I was able to relax and chat with the other mum. It was a wonderful feeling.

We were all doing better and I felt lighter and more comfortable with myself and with being a single parent. I still didn't think of myself as a widow, the word just felt too fuddy-duddy and negative. The truth was I still felt married, just to a man who was no longer here.

I joined an organisation called WAY (Widowed and Young), which offered activities and outings for families in which a parent had died. I felt it would be good for all three of us to spend time with other families in the same situation.

When I went to my first WAY social event it was daunting to turn up at a restaurant and meet a dozen strangers. I didn't know what to expect and dreaded telling them that my husband had died by suicide, as if that somehow made me less eligible to be a member of the group or less worthy of sympathy. I assumed that their spouses had all fought hard to live while mine had chosen to die. But everybody that I met that night in the restaurant had a tragic story and in many ways my story was not that different from theirs; a happy life interrupted by a cruel illness which, after a battle, killed their partners. We were now all in the same position of having to live with our own loss whilst raising our bereaved children alone; a really tough job and not one that any of us signed up for. I recognised in the other bereaved parents an absolute determination and commitment to be the best parent possible, we were all grappling with trying to compensate for all that our children had lost. I admired all the people I met and, despite the weight of our collective experiences, the atmosphere at our table was fun and the evening was full of laughter and banter.

I took the boys along to some WAY family events and they made friends with other children who had lost a parent. It helped them enormously to realise that they weren't the only ones without a parent. Theo was able to articulate how 'special' these friends were and amazed me with how calm and content he clearly was in their company. They had learned that terribly sad things happen in other families too and that they are nobody's fault. Life just isn't always fair.

As term drew to an end I felt quite emotional, reflecting on another milestone passed without Daniel. Milo, still not yet five, was heading for year one and would no longer be the baby of the school. And Theo had settled happily and achieved well in every area.

The following Saturday, at the last football training session of the season, there was a small presentation and the coach called on some of the children to come up and be awarded a medal. Theo didn't get one and I felt gutted as I knew he would take it badly. Then the coach reached into his bag and pulled out a gold trophy which he said was for one boy who was 'player of the year'. He said that the trophy was for a boy who not only played excellent football but who also listened, behaved admirably on the pitch and was a good team player. When his name was announced, Theo's face lit up. And my pride was immense because nobody at that football club, none of the coaches or the other parents, knew that Theo had lost his father. I had never told anyone, simply because there had been no reason to and sometimes it was refreshing not to have it hanging over us.

A week later, on August the 1st, Sam and Katie married. They had been such stalwart, loving supports to us throughout the past few years and we couldn't wait to celebrate with them. Ella and Hannah came too and we all stayed at my parents' house the night before.

Theo and Milo were pageboys. Bursting with pride in their grown up suits with purple ties and matching braces, they both spent an age in front of the mirror styling their hair, while Ella and Hannah looked radiant in floral vintage frocks.

The wedding ceremony was simple and beautiful and Theo and Milo, along with their big cousin Oscar, did a grand job of leading the bride down the aisle. Miraculously, the boys were a delight all day. I lost count of how many wedding guests commented on how well behaved they were. Ella, Hannah, Theo and Milo stuck together like glue, so I was able to mingle a bit knowing that Ella would keep an eye on the boys.

The sit down meal took three and a half hours and I was impressed that the boys managed to sit still and quietly through it all, with the aid of the huge box of loom bands that Sam had thoughtfully placed on my chair. Theo made one for each of the wedding party and all the guests on our table, while Milo stood behind me practising his dance moves ready for the disco.

Ella and Hannah barely knew anyone except my immediate family but they seemed confident and relaxed and I think they enjoyed being a part of Sam and Katie's big day. Ella was mature, sociable and charming, while Hannah was constantly tickled by Milo's cheeky antics; the two of them had a very strong and touching bond.

After the meal, as we all mingled on the patio, Mum came to let me know that Ella was upset. I found her crying and took her up to our hotel room. She felt embarrassed by her tears and couldn't talk, but she didn't need to say what it was about, I just said, 'he should be here,' and she nodded. All happy occasions are now bitter-sweet for us.

Ella re-applied her mascara and we went downstairs to see the first dance. As we stood and watched Sam and Katie, Theo, who had been clinging to me rather tightly, asked me why Ella had been crying. I told him that she was feeling sad because Daddy wasn't with us, and tears rolled down his cheeks. I held him and just let him cry on my shoulder.

When the band got going, Milo was desperate to hit the dance floor and show off his cool disco moves so we all joined him. I hadn't danced since Daniel died and it felt lovely to be dancing as a family. The boy's favourite song of the summer was 'Happy' by Pharrell Williams, and as I danced alongside Daniel's four lovely children, I did feel truly happy and proud that we were all there together, getting on with living without him as best we could.

By ten that night the children were exhausted. We retired to our room and all four of them crashed out in their beds. Unusually, I was the first to wake the following morning. I looked at Daniel's four children in a deep slumber and thought how happy this would make him. He was always at his happiest when he had all his children together with him under one roof. They looked so peaceful and it was warming to see how close their bond had become. They had all leaned on one another in different ways at the wedding and that had given me a great deal of comfort. I hoped they would be able to do that throughout their lives. They were bonded, not just by their shared genes, but through their shared experience of loss.

I was reminded of something Ann, the play therapist, had said to me during a session with Theo and Milo. Sensing my worry and despair about how all the trauma and grief would impact on them she said, 'remember Louise, they are not made of glass. If you drop glass, it shatters. Instead think of your children as crystals. If you drop a crystal, it doesn't shatter. It may be cracked, marked or dented but, over time, these soften and become a part of the crystal, adding depth and beauty and making it unique.' This was a perfect description of how losing Daniel affected us all. The marks that it had left on us would never go away but would become a part of who we are, and add to our strength.

At Daniel's memorial service my friend Helena had read the section on joy and sorrow from Kahlil Gibran's The Prophet. At the time it was hard for me to comprehend how such polarised emotions could be linked, I could only relate to the sorrow. Now I can see that one enhances the other just as life and death, and love and grief, are intrinsically linked. Daniel's death has given my life a different meaning, I have emerged stronger, wiser and with a greater appreciation of the fragility and joy of life. I have discovered depths of resilience, perseverance and determination that were unknown before. I no longer take anything for granted and I am clearly focused on what is really important in this short time that we have on earth.

When I drove the boy's home from a swimming lesson recently, we were confronted with a beautiful orange and pink sky. I pulled into a lay-by and got my two excited boys out of the car to stop and drink in the sight, just as Daniel would have done. He lives on in us.

Daniel had a favourite saying that I think of often. 'The universe is unfolding as it should'.

We will be alright.

AFTERWORD

One of the hardest aspects of my own grief has been coming to terms with the fact that losing Daniel was so preventable. Suicide is utterly devastating but the mood disorders that underlie the majority of suicides are treatable. Daniel was let down badly by the two mental health teams that were treating him; as were all the people who loved him. Ours is a very sad story and what makes it even more tragic is that it is a very common one.

Writing my story gave me an outlet for my grief and helped me make sense of what felt utterly incomprehensible. Writing has given me a voice and while I cannot bring Daniel back, I can do my bit to bring the subject of suicide into the open and help prevent other tragic deaths. Suicide is horrific and uncomfortable to think about but it needs to be confronted and addressed and I hope that sharing my story will help to chip away the social stigma and shame that adds to the pain of anyone grieving after losing a loved one to suicide.

Current suicide statistics are extremely alarming and cannot be ignored. It is estimated that somebody dies by suicide every two hours in England. Suicide is now the biggest killer of men under the age of fifty in the UK and the latest available figures, for 2014, show that the highest risk group is men aged between 40-54.

The World Health Organisation (WHO) estimates that the annual number of suicides worldwide is about one million. That equates to one suicide in the world every forty seconds; more than the number of deaths by war and homicide combined. And the true figure is likely to be higher as suicide is often under-reported for reasons of stigma, religion and social attitudes.

Daniel's story shows that suicide can happen to anyone. We were a very ordinary family. It is widely recognised that suicide is the result of a confluence of factors but researchers have concluded that mental illness is the single most common and dangerous trigger. The suicidal act is a symptom of such an illness rather than a choice made by a rational, reasonable and healthy mind. It is estimated that mood disorders such as bipolar and depression are an underlying factor in ninety per cent of suicides and when combined with basic life stressors or other factors such as substance misuse, impulsive personality, social isolation or childhood trauma, the chance of suicide is greatly increased.

The more that is understood about mental illness, the better chance we have of preventing so many deaths. Nobody is immune to it. There is no class, race, intelligence or educational protection from it. Mental health organisations now say that one in four of us have a mental illness each year and it is thought that 1–2% of the adult population has bipolar. Of those diagnosed with bipolar 25–30% will make one suicide attempt and 10–20% will succeed.

There is so much that society could do to prevent many of these deaths. It's shocking that in the last four years there has been a reduction of 1,500 mental health beds and 3,300 specialist nurses despite the number of patients requiring care increasing by thirty per cent. The huge pressure on the NHS to make financial cuts, too often leads to cuts being made in mental health services. Mental illness is the largest cause of disability and currently accounts for 23% of the 'disease burden' in the NHS, yet only 11% of the NHS budget is spent on treating it. There was an 8% cut to mental health services over the course of the 2010–2015 government, at a time when referrals to community mental health teams like the one treating Daniel rose by almost 20%. Equality between physical and mental illnesses needs to become embedded into the minds of all health professionals as well as the politicians who manage the health budget. I am hopeful that the tide is now turning; it was announced in the March 2015 budget that £1.25 billion would be allocated to mental health services in the UK.

In 2012, The Government published 'Preventing Suicide in England-A cross government outcomes strategy to save lives'. It is a 58 page document that outlines strategies aimed at reducing suicide rates and offering better support to those bereaved by such deaths. It outlines that national suicide prevention needs the support and commitment from Government, Health, Education, Justice and the Home Office in addition to involvement from voluntary and statutory sectors, academic institutions and schools, businesses and the media. It makes clear that mental and physical health have to be of equal importance and priority in our country and recommends continued monitoring of the internet industry so that any content that actively promotes suicide and suicide methods is removed. The Government is also now backing the current national anti-stigma and discrimination programme called 'A time to change' which recognises that the stigma associated with mental health problems acts as a barrier to people seeking and accessing the help that they need. The care and support that is recommended for people who are struggling from mental ill health that is outlined in these proposals, for their families and for families in the aftermath of a suicide, is a million miles away from the treatment and support that Daniel and our family received. There is no doubt in my mind that if the recommendations outlined in this document were active in 2011, just a year before it was published, Daniel would still be with us. I can only hope that they will be implemented to prevent future deaths.

Although my story highlights some deficiencies in our mental health services and what I believe was incompetence in some of the professionals treating Daniel, I know that, having worked in such services myself, there are many brilliant, dedicated and compassionate mental health professionals out there doing an amazing job in difficult circumstances.

And they deserve more support. I would like to see mandatory specialised training for all health professionals on how to deal with people who self-harm, who are expressing suicidal thoughts or who have a history of suicide attempts. I also believe that it is essential that all health workers receive regular supervision and support. It was always clear to me that Nathan was fragile and perhaps could have been more effective in his job if he worked in an environment in which the emotional and mental health needs of its employees were met.

Daniel should have received a comprehensive psychological assessment as soon as he was under psychiatric care, so that the right type of therapy could be offered. He was really only offered drug treatment and a monitoring service until, after six months of us requesting psychological help, he was finally offered counselling. However, supportive talking therapy was not the right psychological intervention for him. It's not 'one size fits all'. In the six weeks that he was in hospital he received Cognitive Behavioural Therapy, which helped him enormously, but it stopped when he was discharged. I believe that psychological services should be widely available within all mental health services and also within GP surgeries and within our education system. Government investment in state registered psychologists, psychotherapists, counsellors and arts therapists in our public services could prevent many mental health issues reaching crisis point.

Appropriate residential treatment for people in crisis is crucial. Financial investment in more specialised units for different mental health conditions such as eating disorders, substance abuse, post-natal illnesses or depression as an alternative to lumping everyone with any type of mental illness in one large, daunting psychiatric hospital in their most vulnerable hour could make a difference. It would provide a middle ground between coping at home and the harshness of a psychiatric hospital and might mean that individuals would be willing to get help voluntarily rather than being sectioned. May Tree in North London is a registered charity, the only one of its kind in the UK, which fills a gap in services between the medical support of the NHS and the helplines of the voluntary services. Founded 20 years ago by two former Samaritans, it provides a refuge for people in extreme distress and despair. Almost all of its guests report fewer suicidal thoughts and attempts after their stay. Undoubtedly more units like May Tree in the UK would save lives.

There also needs to be an integrative, multi-agency support system for families bereaved by suicide. It is known that experiencing such bereavement leaves people vulnerable to emotional and mental health issues and that suicide often runs in families. I was not offered any information on relevant support by my GP, the mental health teams, the police or the coroner, all of whom had contact with my family in the immediate aftermath.

Although, it is widely thought that many risk factors for suicide are psychological and social, further understanding of the genetic and biological factors involved in mental illnesses and suicidality is crucial to developing preventative strategies. Scientists and researchers are working hard to learn more about illnesses that impact upon the brain and destroy lives, and although this research is still in its infancy, we already know that the brain is an organ just like the heart or lungs and can similarly become diseased or impaired, and that there are measurable chemical changes and imbalances in the brain chemistry of people who attempt, or carry out, suicide. Serotonin is known to have a calming influence on the mind. Anti-depressant drugs work by binding serotonin transporters allowing them to transmit its soothing effect. More than two decades of research have linked serotonin impairment to depression, aggressive behaviour and impulsivity. Studies on the brains of people who have died by suicide or on those who have exhibited suicidal behaviour, highlight malfunctions in the chain of chemical events in the brain that transmit serotonin. It has also been discovered that people who have died by suicide and those who have made very serious suicide attempts, have a bigger abnormality in the serotonin system than those who make less serious suicide attempts. Some researchers have suggested a link between extremely adverse early life experiences or drug taking in adolescence and impairment in brain chemistry. This suggests that early responses to stress or chemical changes in the brain due to drug misuse may leave an imprint or chemical malfunction that leads to vulnerability in later life. Some research suggests that mental health problems in adult life may partly originate from environmental trauma that has been encoded in the brains chemical receptors and transmitters. This can be compared to the 'kindling' phenomena in epilepsy in which the sensitivity in brain cells becomes progressively worse with each seizure, so what starts as a response to an environmental stimulus eventually becomes an intrinsic feature of the brain.

After mental illness, gender is the second biggest factor in suicide risk. I have my vulnerable young sons in mindwhen I read that of the 6,122 registered suicides in the UK in 2014, 76% were male and many of them, like Daniel, ended their lives whilst in contact with mental health services. The enormity of this problem needs to be addressed with accessible gender specific preventative services and as a society we need to reflect on the messages we are giving our boys. We need to evaluate and adjust the expectations and stereotypes that weigh heavily on boys and men in our culture. Studies have proved that there are no differences in the emotional needs or responses between young boys and girls, yet culturally males and females are taught very different ways in which they should express, respond to and feel about their emotions. Generally men are conditioned to repress all emotions other than anger and taught that they must be 'strong' and that seeking comfort, help or support is a weakness. Men have been taught to suffer in silence which results in a detrimental effect on their mental health. If our societal view of masculinity shifted so that both males and females could appreciate empathy, vulnerability and emotional expressiveness, the male suicide rates in the western world would, undoubtedly, fall.

The link between the use of recreational drugs and mental health problems needs to be more explicitly defined within our education system and media. Daniel used LSD and cocaine, both class A drugs. LSD is a powerful hallucinogenic which disrupts the interaction of nerve cells in the brain and interferes with serotonin. Cocaine can also lead users into mania, often followed by depression and/ or psychotic symptoms. Some users may experience the effects of these drugs beyond withdrawal, leaving them with permanent psychological effects. Daniel also told me that he used cannabis during his late teens. Cannabis is often thought of as a soft drug and it's classification as a class B drug reinforces this message, yet it is the most commonly abused drug amongst people diagnosed with bipolar disorder. Although cannabis is technically illegal in this country, laws against its possession are lightly enforced, giving the wrong message to young people. There is now growing evidence from scientists and mental health experts that links the most widely available form of high strength cannabis (known as skunk) with psychotic episodes. Skunk, used by over 80% of cannabis users in the UK, has much higher levels of a chemical called THC than low strength cannabis (known as hash) which was more commonly used during the sixties and seventies when it was widely thought of as harmless. THC interferes with brain receptors and leaves many users with high levels of paranoia, anxiety and mania. In a 2015 study carried out by researchers at The Institute of Psychiatry at Kings College in London, it stated that a quarter of new cases of psychotic mental illness are caused by cannabis use. They conclude that '*there is an urgent need to inform young people of the risks of high potency cannabis*'. These recent findings will add substance to a 2012 report by the schizophrenia commission which recommended the need for 'warnings about the risk of cannabis to mental health'. In a world where the trend has been to relax the laws on cannabis and in light of crime survey figures in England and Wales suggesting that over a million youngsters aged 16–24 smoke cannabis in the UK, there needs to be more explicit warnings about its damaging effects. It is time now to have a thorough inquiry into the dangers of mind altering drugs, both legal and illegal. I feel that we are currently on the brink of a huge medical revelation about the effect these drugs have on mental health.

I have not published this story without deep thought and consideration. It has felt like something that I have been guided to do (perhaps by Daniel, who always told me that I should write a book) and that has been stronger than my many reservations about it.

When I think about Daniel, amidst the many precious memories I have, I remember his big, kind and giving heart. Throughout his life, he took on the role of helping, rescuing and looking after people. It was a part of his identity and when he could no longer sustain that role it contributed to his disintegration. If publishing this story helps other individuals and families who are dealing with similar struggles, then it will be a wonderful legacy to a unique and amazing man.

Part of the profits from the sale of this book will be donated to CALM (Campaign Against Living Miserably), a registered charity that exists to prevent male suicide in the UK.

For further information visit www.thecalmzone.net.

Contacts

I have listed below some organisations that offer help for many of the issues raised in this book. Some of them have helped my boys and me along this journey.

Mental Health/Suicide prevention.

CALM (Campaign Against Living Miserably)
T: 0808 802 5858
E: info@thecalmzone.net

The May Tree - A sanctuary for the suicidal.
T: 0333 252 1796
E: maytree@maytree.org.uk

MIND
T: 0208 519 2122
E: contact@mind.org.uk

Rethink Mental Illness
T: 0121 522 7007
E: info@rethink.org

Samaritans
T: 08457 90 90 90
E: jo@smaritans.org

SANE (Mental Health)

T: 0207 7375 1002

E: info@sane.org.uk

Bereavement

Child Bereavement UK

T: 0800 02 888 40

E: enquiries@childbereavementuk.org

Cruse

T: 0844 477 9400

E: helpline@cruse.org.uk

Grief Encounter (Child Bereavement)

T: 0208 371 8455

E: contact@greifencounter.org.uk

SOBS (Survivors of Bereavement by Suicide)

T: 0300 111 5065

E: sobs.admin@care4free.net

WAY (Widowed and Young)

T: 0870 011 3450

W: wayfoundation.org.uk

Winston's Wish (Charity for Bereaved Children)

T: 08452 03 04 05

E: info@winstonswish.org.uk

ACKNOWLEDGEMENTS

Many thanks to my agent, Andrew Lownie for your support and encouragement.

Also, a huge thank you to Caro Handley, for your unwavering belief in this book and for your expertise in helping me to create it.

Thanks in abundance to my parents and brothers. You are always there, in good times and bad. Thank you for being my crutch and enabling me to be the best mum I can possibly be. Without you this would have been a very different story.

An extra thank you to Sam and Katie for providing the 'fun factor' on the darkest of days and for shielding the boys from so much of the horror and pain in the initial aftermath. Your continuous love and commitment to your nephews is invaluable and helps to fill the massive void in their lives. You have given them many happy memories and I am so grateful for that.

My warmest thanks also to others who have been part of our journey;

To Tania and Marcus, in troubled times your friendship went above and beyond. Marcus, your generosity is outstanding and you couldn't have done more to try and help Daniel get back on track.

To my good friends, Sarah and Clare. This journey has taught me the true meaning of friendship. Thanks for just always being there.

To Ann Walker, you threw me a lifeline when I was drowning in worry. You helped the boys and me enormously in times of crisis.

To Roger Squier, simply for listening.

To the staff at Theo and Milo's school who have been consistently supportive and understanding.

To everyone who loved Daniel, I sincerely wish you peace and healing.

To the many other people out there who have lost a loved one to suicide and to those who are struggling with mental health problems, I hope that sharing my story offers you some hope and comfort.

Finally, to Daniel, thank you for the brief happiness that we shared, for our two awesome sons and for enriching my life with your lovely daughters. I miss you.

22330012R00166

Printed in Great Britain
by Amazon